Minister's Daughter

# Minister's Daughter

## One Life, Many Lives

Charlotte Zietlow with Michael G. Glab

Michael G. Glab

GlabWorks

# CONTENTS ▌

CONTENTS

For Paul, my husband, the love of my life.

For my children Rebecca and Paul and their families: Rebecca's husband David and their children Alice and Zoe; and Nathan's wife Sarah and their daughter Nina. In memory of Nathan and Sarah's son Henry.

For my parents Gilbert and Margaret Ernst Theile. For my sister Harriet, my constant support, and her daughters Lisa and Martha. Through my brother Mark I learned much about mental illness.

For the Bloomington and Monroe County communities--they are my family as well.

For Marilyn Schultz, my business partner and dear friend, and Kathy Aiken, who saved my life.

With gratitude to Michael Glab

*Charlotte Zietlow*

# Introduction

The year was 2009. My wife and I had just arrived in Bloomington that fall and I'd found a part-time job at the Book Corner, an independent bookseller. One gray late morning in November, an aging woman wearing a wide brimmed hat burst into the store, accompanied by a gust of autumn air and radiating an energy that would make a person half her age envious.

The store's proprietor, Margaret Taylor, pulled me aside, nodded toward the woman, and said, "She's someone you have to meet. She's an institution."

So, Margaret introduced me to Charlotte Zeitlow. Charlotte wasn't unfriendly but she wasted no words. "Hello," she said, shaking my hand and looking me straight in the eye. "Has my book come in?" That told me much about her. She was pleasant but terse, an insatiable reader, and forever in a rush. She would fly into and out of the store on a regular basis, taking short, staccato steps, the hangings around her neck—a dangling watch, necklaces and beads, a pendant or two depending, I suppose, upon her mood that day—jingling and jangling as she flitted about. When she left the store that first day, she leaned into the breeze, reaching up to hold on to the brim of her hat. Somehow I knew she'd remember my name the next time we'd meet.

That's the mark of a good politician—someone who remembers every name and every face. It's a gift. I'd learn later Charlotte had a magnificent recall, reciting names and events on demand, throwing in compelling details and tangential anecdotes. It was as if her entire life, everything she'd ever seen or heard or read about, was part of a single, continuous tale, the relating of which was ongoing and never dull. That tale could be described, simply and fully, as the story of her life.

From the day I met her she was stooped over, her hair was white, her voice already creaky. She'd seen a lot and exuded a certainty that she'd see a hell of a lot more in her time left on this planet. Most people coming up to their 80s tend to take it easy. Not Charlotte. There was plenty to do and, damn it, she was going to do it all.

Charlotte became a public figure in South Central Indiana at a time when most women still identified themselves by their husbands' names. Christmas cards coming to my boyhood home were still addressed to Mr. & Mrs. Joseph Glab in the year 1971. But a new era was dawning. I was part of the new generation; at 15 years old, I was puzzled that women, as a rule, had no identity other than as wives. Charlotte that year was already 37. She'd grown up in another era, an era that was somehow both swiftly and glacially coming to an end.

When Charlotte first ran for public office that year, she was referred to in the newspapers as "the PhD housewife," as if it were cute that a good little homemaker should do something as silly as earn her doctorate. Charlotte, though, lived in a way that could be best described by the adage, *Facta non verba*—Deeds, not words. And, surely, she'd have been able to translate that from the Latin. Words were her passion—her PhD was in Linguistics, earned at one of the nation's premier bastions of that discipline, the University of Michigan. She loves language and she loves languages.

Yet words, speech, talk, have never been enough for her. "You have to do something to make a difference," she told me once when I asked her what drove her. "I have a need to do something."

Charlotte Theile got married to a gentle, brilliant, aspiring English Literature professor named Paul Zeitlow in 1957. At the time, she recalls, her parents —her mother especially—seemed to want to convey a caveat to their future son-in-law. "They never said anything directly to him," Charlotte remembers. "But the implication was, 'Charlotte's going to be a lot of work for you. She's a handful. She's very independent.'"

So independent, in fact, that she strode, however blindly, however briskly, into adult life without ever having so much as a role model. "I had no mentors," she confesses. "Nobody, except for Paul, gave me the benefit of the doubt."

To this day she counsels and supports people running for office or hoping to do some kind of public good, especially women. "There never was anybody like that for me," she says, without bitterness or regret. Her lonely path to adulthood simply *was*.

Years before, her mother had counseled her: "You're very smart. Don't let anybody know it." That independent young woman, perhaps from that day forward, made it her business to let the world know she was smart, preferably through her deeds rather than her words. *Facta non verba.*

Now, after nearly half a century in politics, in public service, in the community, doing things her way, the *right* way, there's still so much more to do, more than any single human being can do in a lifetime. "I feel the importance of time," she says. "I have to get as much done as I can."

After getting to know her a bit, I started suggesting to Charlotte that she write a memoir, recounting her time in a changing world, in a changing Bloomington. "Do you think so?" she'd ask, skeptical. I assured her I did. Eventually, I offered to help her do it. Then, in the winter of 2014, I had her on my then-new WFHB radio interview program, Big Talk, as one of my first guests. At the time, not only was Hillary Clinton the frontrunner for the Democratic nomination in 2016, she was the only true contender for it. And the Republican field was populated by a gaggle of ho-hum politicians. A certain flamboyant billionaire with a dicey reputation had not even thrown his hat into the ring yet.

Toward the end of the interview, I said, "It looks as though we'll have a woman president in a couple of years. How will you feel," I asked, "when Hillary Clinton takes the oath of office in January, 2017?"

And just like that, the no-nonsense, forceful, direct, too-busy-for-small-talk Bloomington institution began to cry. It would be, Charlotte said, the realization of a lifelong dream.

I spun that interview off into a profile of her in the *Ryder* magazine. After the article appeared, she came into the book store and said, "My children have read the piece. They both think you've captured me perfectly. They said it sounded like me."

The next time she came in, Charlotte asked, "Are you serious about doing a book with me?" I certainly was, I said. With that, we embarked on a years-long journey, an archeological dig, an investigation, a search for some kind of holy grail. We talked into a digital recorder countless times. Other times, I typed as fast as I could, trying to keep up with her as anecdote after anecdote spilled out of her. We delved through banker's boxes in her basement, leafing through old newspaper clippings, meeting minutes, memos, notes, campaign flyers, letters both complimentary and critical, and the innumerable treasures and detritus of a life lived in the public eye.

Our own lives continued apace. Charlotte lost her husband in 2015. I underwent treatment for cancer in 2016. Then, in 2019, the world seemed to want to crash down upon Charlotte. Her grandson Henry, whom she adored, was killed in a head-on collision on an icy two-lane road in northern Wisconsin. She suffered a stroke a month later. After spending weeks in a rehab facility, Charlotte, back home, to the surprise of no one, started going about town— perhaps a step or two more slowly than before— until, in the spring, she almost lost her life in a choking incident in Chef Michael Cassady's Uptown Cafe.

I sense a panic coming over Charlotte these days, born of an awareness brought on by the passing of loved ones and the breakdown of her own body. "There's only so much time," she says, as near to an admission of defeat as one will ever hear issuing from her lips.

This is her story, her life. It comes from her own memory, in her own words. I've done my best to verify her stories through public records, contemporary news reports, and primary and secondary sources. Like anyone—like everyone— Charlotte remembers through a haze of interpretation, perception and misperception, vanity, and the wish to knead the nuggets of the past into something heroic, or at least favorable to her. That doesn't mean she lies or even stretches the truth, the way you and I might. She is as devoted to truth as she was to her beloved husband of 58 years and to democracy itself, something she came to cherish all the more after she spent a year in communist, repressive Czechoslovakia. It's just that truth, when filtered through memory and ego, tends to become, shall we say, *elastic.*

"Memoir," the author and Syracuse University professor Mary Karr has said, "is not an act of history but an act of memory, which is innately corrupt." Once, in an interview about her 1995 book, *The Liars Club,* a bestseller about her upbringing in a hardscrabble Texas oil town that jump-started the memoir market, Karr admitted, "No doubt I've gotten a million things wrong."

Charlotte got far fewer than a million things wrong but, being human and all, it's a certainty that Charlotte missed on at least a few things. We did our best to minimize as many of those errors and those that remain are in no way meant to harm or unduly disparage anyone alive or dead.

If, by the way, Charlotte's memory is corrupt, it's the only such venality she's ever indulged in.

In keeping with her kids' assessment of that magazine profile I'd done on Charlotte, I've kept her words as close as possible to those she herself originally uttered, save for a usage or number or sentence construction tweak here and there. Suffice it to say I've altered her words so sparingly that, at times, it might appear this text hasn't even been edited. It has, by a talented stickler named Emily Esola, a recent PhD in English Literature and a visiting lecturer in the English Department at Indiana University. I implored Emily to preserve the essential language of Charlotte, even if it might go against her grain or violate this or that grammatical precept. Charlotte, by the way, is a magician with languages so at times she might use a German construction, say, for an

English line, the result of which sounds somehow simultaneously elegant and clunky. Emily and I strove to preserve that. The goal has always been for this text to sound like a conversation between Charlotte and me.

As plain-spoken as Charlotte is, she occasionally rips a character or two in no uncertain terms. She's made countless friends and a few enemies. I attempted to steer her out of trouble now and again as she recounted this or that conflict or disagreement. Once or twice she even agreed with my effort to calm the waters. "Maybe you're right," she'd say, "Maybe we shouldn't say that."

Make no mistake, though, this is no soft-soap job. Charlotte calls them as she sees them.

She's had a lot of practice doing just that since she was a little girl, which seems to me to be the perfect place for us to begin her story.

*Michael G. Glab*

# 2

## Prologue

When did I first realize that I had power? That I could decide what I wanted to do? That I was in charge of my own life?

Margaret Clements, a graduate student of my husband, Paul Zietlow, reminded me of a story I'd told her years ago. Paul was a literature professor at Indiana University. Margaret and I became friends. I was wondering aloud about those questions one day not long ago. "Think of your birthday party," she said.

I'd never had a birthday party as a little girl. When I was in third grade I thought, "Wait a minute. Everybody else has a birthday party. I'm going to have a birthday party!"

That day at school I announced to my friends, four or five of them, "I'm going to have a birthday party after school and you're all coming home with me."

I made a map so we could go to all their houses as quickly as possible. We trotted from house to house so they could pick up things that could pass as birthday presents.

I went home with this string of people and told my mother, "We're having a birthday party."

It was news to my mother but she rose to the occasion. She baked a Lazy Daisy cake, a vanilla cake made with hot milk and covered with coconut shreds. And I had a birthday party.

It wasn't the best birthday party in the world. We didn't pass out prizes. It was kind of strange because I'd made it up just that day.

But I'd taken charge of my life and had my birthday party. That was one of my earliest put-my-foot down moments. It was a telling moment in my life because I decided what I needed and what I wanted and I was going to make it happen.

I've continued to do that ever since. That's how I started being an activist. People came along with me and they've done it, time and again, ever since.

I've continued to come up with ideas that would make things better—or what I would consider better. In that case what I did was for me, but later, down the line, I'd pull people together and say, "Let's do this." It was for all of us.

Three years after that birthday party when I was in sixth grade, I realized there was no library in my little parochial school. So I gathered together all the books I could find in the school—we had random books lying around here and there—and made a library. I set it up, alphabetized all the books, indexed them, and made stamps for them.

We had a library! I did it because we needed one.

That was another forerunner of what would become the pattern of my life. It came from inside me. I just knew that's what I could do, so I did it. To this day my problem—and maybe it's a virtue—is I'm bothered by things that aren't happening.

I'm bothered when I see people not thinking, not listening, not paying attention. It was my commitment to doing all those things that spurred me to run for Bloomington city council in 1970 and '71 with a motley crew that overturned city hall. I'm one of the last survivors from that group of people. I still have the same drive to make things happen that I had 49 years ago.

I found then that a lot of people didn't have that same kind of commitment. A lot of people today don't have that commitment, the commitment to work at something until it works!

Not all ideas work but some are worth working toward. It's a commitment to getting an idea, cleaning it up, turning it into a doable thing, and then doing it. And getting people to go along with it.

It's hard work and it's a commitment to knowing what's a good idea, why we want to do it, and why it should work. It's a contribution to the world. It's the intention to improve and share with others.

It's the idea of a village. I love the idea of a village. The village saved my life. At the Uptown Cafe in May, 2019, I choked on a piece of meat and wasn't able to breathe or talk. At which point people tried to save me, five other diners plus the barkeep and a waitress. Taking turns, they either performed the Heimlich Maneuver or did CPR. None of it worked. Then a gentleman came over and using his phone flashlight and a spoon as a tongue depressor located the piece of meat. Another jolt from the Heimlich dislodged it and then I was rolled out on a gurney and taken to the hospital. Or so I understand because I was unconscious. The upshot was I had broken ribs and a broken sternum. But I'm alive.

It took this village to save my life.

Bloomington is a village. That village exists because of the people who made it, who encouraged it, and who nourished it. When the motley crew I was part of was elected in 1971 and took office in January, 1972, we nourished it with ideas, ideas that we codified, ideas that became ordinances.

The neighborhoods of Bloomington were created by the neighbors. That sounds simple and elementary but it's not always the way. The ideas that define our Bloomington neighborhoods today were created by the neighbors within them when the motley crew and I took office. We listened to those people.

The people were involved, they decided what they wanted to see in their own neighborhoods. That's the essence of democracy, people making sure their neighborhoods are what they want.

Community is a big idea. It's a word used a lot. It's a word not to be used lightly. It's a commitment. We have to work at it. It's not easy and it doesn't happen accidentally.

A community can be a powerful thing. It requires commitment and openness and the acceptance of other people's ideas. It's a commitment to use our common resources in ways that aren't selfish. But the fact of the matter is people end up serving their own well-being while considering others' well-being.

People want to live in Bloomington because they see the possibility of a community. They see it as something they can be part of, they can participate in and they can shape. They see it as a neighborhood they can love.

*Charlotte Zietlow*

# 3

## Minister's Daughter

**A note: The italicized blocks of texts in the ensuing chapters are the words of co-writer Michael Glab. They serve as explanations, transitions, caveats, and at times, perhaps, pleas for understanding. The text in Roman style is all Charlotte, save for some bits of elbow grease applied to make the words shine, grammatically and editorially.**

*The town of Bristol, Wisconsin sits next to Interstate 94, the busy main route between Milwaukee and Chicago. Today, Bristol is surrounded by a thriving cluster of outlet malls and shopping centers horseshoed around vast parking lots. In 1934, the year Charlotte Theille was born, Bristol was barely a dot on the map, a hamlet in the midst of cornfields and cow pastures.*

*Each of Charlotte's parents came from a line of Lutheran ministers. Each descended from German immigrants who'd come to America in the 19th Century. Charlotte was the first-born child of Margaret (Ernst) and Gilbert Theile, Bristol's Lutheran minister. Even though he carried on his family's cleric tradition, Gilbert had a touch of the rebel in him. He passed that strand of rebel DNA down to his eldest child.*

*While Charlotte may have been born a small-town girl, she grew up, mostly, in big cities. As Gilbert advanced in the Wisconsin Evangelical Lutheran Synod—an extremely conservative branch of the Protestant denomination — he would tend to successively larger congregations in Milwaukee, St. Paul, and finally, St. Louis. Through her teens and into young adulthood, Charlotte would visit—and, at times, live in—some of the historic and cultural centers of Europe.*

As an adult, she'd see more of the world and she dreamed of living, one day, in some cosmopolitan capital but it was Bloomington, Indiana where she'd move and settle at the age of 29. Landing there changed her life, as well as the lives of Bloomington and Indiana people then and now.

*But her story begins some 300 miles north of Bloomington, in the extreme southeast corner of Wisconsin.*

\*\*\*

We lived in a very small town in Wisconsin. Bristol, just west of Kenosha. My father had a church there. I remember the house. I remember the neighbors. I had long curly hair and we had a neighbor, Mrs. Moser, who would braid my hair. She pulled it in tight ringlets. It hurt.

I remember being aware that we didn't have any money. This was in the middle of the Depression. The people of the congregation didn't have cash to pay my father his salary. So they brought food. People brought food all the time. My mother canned and otherwise preserved lots of that food—tomatoes and peaches and cucumbers for pickles and cabbage for sauerkraut. They also brought things like cantaloupe and corn, things we had to eat right off. My mother was deathly afraid of botulism so she only canned things with high acid content. If green beans came, we had to eat them right then and there.

The house was cold and drafty but it was a real house, not an apartment or a trailer. Because it was the Depression, people came and knocked on the door and asked for food. There was this story—people said it and believed it—that certain houses were "marked" somehow, indicating it was okay for people to come to the door and ask for food. I don't think we ever turned anyone away. That's my memory. I don't remember my parents saying, 'Oh, these people....' My mother wasn't very welcoming to strangers but she wasn't ungenerous. They didn't get past the front door but we did give them something to eat.

When I was a young girl, I was very shy. My father was a very gregarious person. He was a minister. He was larger than life—everybody would have said that—and really kind of overwhelming.

We would travel to different congregations for mission festivals and to strange churches and there would be strange people. I just wanted to stand way back and not be there, but he dragged us along—usually me, never my sister Harriet and seldom my brother Mark. My father made a lot of sick calls; I went with him so I knew all the hospitals and all the nursing homes around our homes in the cities we lived in. My mother didn't come with; she was not interested. She didn't like being a minister's wife.

\*\*\*

*In 1937, Gilbert and Margaret had a second child, Mark. The next year the family moved to Milwaukee, just 40 miles north, but a world away from Bristol. Gilbert had been called by the Synod to lead a startup Lutheran mission in the middle of a city that, at the time, boasted a population of more than half a million people. Charlotte's parents had a third child, Harriet, in 1940.*

*By 1940, six-year-old Charlotte was becoming aware of the larger world. She first read of and heard about Eleanor Roosevelt, the independent and socially progressive wife of the president. As the years went by, Charlotte would learn more and more about Eleanor's works and the obstacles she faced as a woman. But even as a kid, Charlotte knew enough about the activist First Lady to admire her.*

\*\*\*

We moved to Milwaukee when I was four. My father got a church there, Parkside Lutheran, on Sherman Boulevard and North Avenue. The Lutheran congregation had bought the church from some other denomination. It was a very big building but we didn't have a very big congregation.

At first, we lived in an apartment near Washington Park, where the Milwaukee County Zoo was. It was a couple of blocks from the church. Then, in 1940, just before the war began, we rented a home on Sherman Boulevard two blocks from the church.

A dentist and his family lived next door. He had a son who was in the Navy. He came home for Christmas on a furlough and he bought me a doll. It was really touching because I knew he was going off to war.

The house was a four-square brick structure with a big glassed-in front porch and a big playroom in the back that was always messy. You had to go through the porch to get to the front door and just inside there was a staircase with one of those railings you could slide down—and I did! I don't remember ever being yelled at for it.

We lived there for a several years and then the congregation bought a smaller house on Grant Boulevard for us.

During this time, I went to First Central Lutheran School, which was part of the Missouri Synod, not my father's Wisconsin Synod.

The Wisconsin Synod at the time was a small denomination. It also was becoming very, very conservative. But my father was not very, very conservative. He traded pulpits, for example, with ministers of other denominations, which was frowned on by the Synod. He had an ecumenical streak. I really think he wanted to be a Catholic priest because he loved all the ceremony that goes with the Catholic ritual, the pomp and circumstance. He liked the show. He used to take me to vespers at a convent on the south side of town. We would take the bus. The female choir was beautiful, chanting, and there was lots of color all around.

I assume my father was a strong Democrat. I did not know that for a fact. We didn't talk politics, at all, in my house. I do know the day Roosevelt died, my father and I were in the car. He was driving me to piano lessons. We heard about it on the radio. My father pulled over to the curb to kind of pull himself together. And I remember the day after Harry Truman won in 1948, my father was ebullient. He was very happy.

The people in our church were not Democrats. They felt about Franklin Roosevelt the way people later talked about Barack Obama—only worse! There were people you couldn't be in the same room with and say the word "Roosevelt."

My father wouldn't speak about political things from the pulpit. Absolutely not. In public we were very apolitical. I just picked things up along the way.

Then the war came. I think my father would have gone as a chaplain but he had three children and he had a job that was considered "essential." He became an air raid warden for the neighborhood, with the helmet and the flashlight.

As the war dragged on, there weren't men available to be counselors at the YMCA camps so, during the summers, he did that. Each year he'd go up to Camp Manito-Wish, nearly 300 miles north of us, near the upper peninsula of Michigan. He'd come back home on weekends to perform his ministerial duties.

Today I have a big picture of Eleanor Roosevelt in my dining room. And I've read the biography of Frances Perkins, who was the first female cabinet secretary in American history. I didn't know anything about her at the time. Frances Perkins pushed President Roosevelt to enact a lot of the New Deal programs.

***

*Charlotte's maternal grandparents Augustus and Emma Ernst had come from the Saxony and Weimar region of what would eventually become the modern nation of Germany. At the time of the US Civil War, Otto von Bismarck of Prussia organized a block of Germanic regions, including Saxony and Weimar, to fight France in the Franco-Prussian War. Augustus's grandmother, Emma—Charlotte's great-great grandmother, also a minister's wife—feared her seven sons would be conscripted into the Prussian army. "She did not want them to fight with Bismarck," Charlotte explains. "She hated the Prussians."*

*So Emma sent the seven boys off to the United States. "She would never see them again," Charlotte says.*

*In America, several of Emma's sons became Lutheran ministers, the traditional Ernst calling. One of their sons, Augustus, married Emma von Rohr, who'd come from a semi-noble German family in Austria. Augustus and Emma eventually settled in St. Paul, Minnesota. Augustus became pastor of the Twin Cities' Emanuel Lutheran Church. One of their children was Margaret, Charlotte's mother.*

*In the 1940s, during the war and after, Charlotte spent a lot of time with some wealthy Ernst relatives in the eastern United States. Being thrust into the world of luxury had a profound effect on Charlotte.*

*Augustus's niece, Louise—known to all as Louie—was extremely wealthy. She'd come from money—her father, Augustus's brother, had helped develop a mass production process for the artificial fiber Rayon. Louie married and she and her husband Arthur, a wealthy stockbroker, lived in a luxurious home in Montclair, New Jersey. The Great Depression cost Louie's husband a great deal of his wealth and he hanged himself. Augustus's daughter—Charlotte's Aunt Agnes—was recruited to move in with Louie to help her cousin through her grief and take care of the widow's two children.*

***

We had this interesting relationship with my mother's younger sister, Agnes. We called her *Tante* Aggie (the German word for aunt) but she hated that because she said it made her feel old. She just wanted to be Aggie.

Aggie, like my mother, had attended the University of Wisconsin, then had been a social worker for the welfare department in St. Paul, Minnesota. When I was five or six, she had a complicated back surgery and recuperated at my Uncle Charles' house on Philadelphia's Main Line, where the upper crust lived. While she was there, Louie's husband committed suicide.

Louie had two children and no practical life experience. She had servants: a cook, a maid, a gardener, some fancy cars and a chauffeur. She had a three-story house on four acres—but she did not know how to balance a checkbook. Aggie ended up recuperating and taking care of Louie at the same time. Louie needed somebody with her.

Aggie was very assertive. She took over the business part and she helped bring up Louie's children, Michael and Rosemary. Aggie never left. They were together, the two of them, for well over fifty years. They became companions.

It brought that family very close to my family in very complicated ways.

Of course, coming from the Midwest and near-poverty, I was impressed and intimidated. I started developing some strong feelings about wealth during my first visit to Louie's home because I felt certain they looked down on me.

Most of those people were not very nice. They were arrogant. They were dismissive. I didn't have the right clothes. I didn't speak the right language. I was like Cinderella. And I came from nowhere!

***

*Aggie and Louie would take long summer trips without Louie's children Michael and Rosemary each year, visiting places like Jackson Hole, Wyoming. As wartime travel restrictions increased, the cousins had to spend their summers closer to home so they rented a summer cottage on Nantucket Island. Later, they'd buy a 17th-century home with two acres of land there. Charlotte would spend summers with some or all of Louie's family throughout the 1940s.*

***

Michael was two years older than I was. During the war, he came out to Wisconsin to go to the YMCA camp. My father would spend summers with him there. They developed almost a father-son relationship.

Rosemary was a little bit younger than I. They had to do something with her so they sent her to my grandparents' house in St. Paul. My parents sent me to St. Paul to be her companion.

When I would go to my grandparent's house in St. Paul in the summertime to be with Rosemary, she would bring a whole box of new toys but I didn't have any. She wouldn't let me play with hers.

My Grandmother Emma had aristocratic notions, too. She indicated that a person's value had something to do with money. She had me doing the menial work around the house.

My mother had some of her mother in her, a kind of superiority complex. She didn't think highly of my father's parents. I think there were some doctrinal differences. My father's grandfather ran a seminary in Wauwatosa, Wisconsin. My mother's grandfather ran a seminary in Watertown. These Lutherans, they can find anything to disagree on.

You see, I've had a lot of experience in Lutheran theological and ecclesiastical politics, which is not pretty and is not full of love and kindness. It certainly colored my view of the whole world.

I went to parochial school, First Central Lutheran, in Milwaukee. It was a Missouri Synod school. I was in the minority there because I was Wisconsin Synod. The girls in my class were Girl Scouts. I could not be a Girl Scout because the Wisconsin Synod did not approve of the Girl Scouts. It just seemed strange to me that I couldn't be a Girl Scout. Everybody else was!

There was a library a block away. The Riverview branch of the St. Paul Public Library. That was a good thing. I ran to the library and read. Rosemary taunted me because I was a bookworm. I just read and read and read. The librarian, Miss Room, took me under her wing.

The '30s produced a spate of really good children's books, like *Mary Poppins* and *The Yearling* by Marjorie Rawlins—I got a Scribner's edition of that one for Christmas. *Alice in Wonderland* and *Through the Looking Glass* weren't written in the '30s but I found them full of useful thoughts. Alice wasn't supposed to jump down the rabbit hole, but she did. She was always observing. She was always wandering from one group of curious people to another. She tried things. And she was always sticking her foot in her mouth.

There were a whole bunch of books. The librarian would give me books about girls growing up and I would just read them and read them and read them. Mainly fiction. That really helped me live, I think. For me, books were a haven. That's why I'm a reader.

***

*In 1945, when Charlotte was in fifth grade, the Theiles moved to St. Paul, Minnesota where her father became associate pastor of the Emanuel Lutheran congregation with his father-in-law, Augustus. Sum-*

*mer visits with her wealthy extended family continued to shape Charlotte's childhood.*

***

I spent some summers in Nantucket which was quite an experience. It was pretty pristine at the time. I learned to swim in the ocean. I had been terrified of water, even though I lived in Wisconsin by Lake Michigan. I was scared of it. But my Aunt Aggie, a great athlete, just took me out to the surf and taught me how to swim. I loved it. I loved the surf.

We had bicycles and we rode all over the island and went crabbing and clamming and blueberry picking. We went out and foraged for all sorts of strange things. I did horseback riding.

But I was always the poor cousin. Louie's sister and her husband had a house in an elegant little town, Bernardsville, New Jersey. They owned a lot of horses. He was a chemist at a major pharmaceutical firm. They all had lots of money. Louie's younger brother, whom they called "Boy," was a stockbroker. They all didn't work. They all lived by their stocks and bonds. They were all snobbish. They all kind of disregarded me as the poor cousin from the Midwest. I didn't matter at all. I got to not liking them very much.

I wondered, "Why would that be? It has only to do with money? That just doesn't seem right. How can I possibly have the right clothes—I don't have any money. It's not a matter of taste or anything." I certainly did get the sense that that made me inferior and I resisted it.

I was smarter. I knew that. I always had that. I could figure things out better. I learned faster. I had this strong sense of unfairness. That wasn't fair, what they were doing. I didn't accept it.

I had a streak of feistiness. My mother used to say, in a scolding voice, "You're so independent!" She said that until she died.

I remember once having a dress. I'm sure it was a beautiful dress. It was red. It had smocking on it. I'm sure it was expensive. It came from Switzerland or someplace like that. I hated it. I was five or six. I have no idea why I hated that dress. My mother made me wear it and I would be unpleasantly resistant to it. Ultimately, once we'd gone down the line of unpleasant scenes, I didn't have to wear the dress anymore. I was adamant that that dress was not going to be on me!

I don't know where that came from but that's a big part of me and it's developed over time. I find myself on more than one occasion disagreeing with a room full of people—that's really not comfortable—and yet I've stuck to it.

***

*Perhaps Charlotte's feistiness came from her father. By the 1960s, he would be brought up on charges of heresy by the Missouri Synod, which ran his seminary. By that time, he'd received his doctorate in theology and had become a professor at Concordia Seminary outside St. Louis.*

*Gilbert Theile preached that the true main doctrine of Christianity was the resurrection of all humanity's corporal bodies on Judgement Day. Martin Luther, the man behind the Protestant Reformation, had argued the same thing in the 16th Century. The idea was, when people died, their souls remained in repose with their bodies until they reawakened at the end of the world and either went to heaven or hell.*

*The men who headed the Missouri Synod insisted, rather, Christianity was embodied in the immortality of the soul. It was always alive and with God, an idea that originated with the ancient Greeks.*

*Gilbert never burdened his family with information about his ordeal. They wouldn't find out much about it until many years later, after he'd died.*

***

He didn't share it with us. But he certainly was under sort of an inquisition—sort of like what the Communists did in Czechoslovakia after the Prague Spring—for heresy, for several years.

It was so innocent! It was a theological difference and, from what I know about historical theology, he was absolutely right. It was clear as mud on anybody's faces!

But the ones who had the power in the seminary didn't want to believe it, so that was that. The interrogation—that puts it back into the Communist setting—was whether or not resurrection of the body or immortality of the soul was *the* Christian doctrine. My father was absolutely accurate but it was unacceptable. It seems so strange.

The Synod leaders believed their dear mothers were looking down at them from Heaven! Luther—and my father—said they were doing no such thing.

When my father died, we went through his papers and I began to understand the length of time he was involved in this inquisition.

Then my mother burned all his papers.

I didn't realize she was going to do that. She never wanted to be a minister's wife. She didn't like the whole thing: "Get that stuff out of here; I don't want to see it ever, ever, ever again."

\*\*\*

*Living in St. Paul, Minnesota, Charlotte attended University High School, a lab school affiliated with the University of Minnesota that adhered to the pedagogical philosophies of the innovative psychologist and education reformer John Dewey. He advocated for schools that stressed interactive participation by students in their learning and that the school was the breeding ground for social reform.*

*Some of the higher values imparted to Charlotte and her peers at University High reflected an idealism not existent in the world she and they would eventually become part of.*

\*\*\*

I went to a fancy high school, a lab school that constantly gave standardized tests to us as control groups. I was told anybody can do anything. I had the highest scores in the class and I could be anything I wanted to be or do anything I wanted to do.

That wasn't true at all!

I studied French. I liked French but I thought it was too easy. We learned a lot of basic sentences, which is useful but you have to support that with grammar, otherwise you're re-living a child's life and I didn't have time for that. We learned a lot of songs. I can sing "Stardust" in French to this day—and "Deep Purple" and "La Marsellaise." We went to French restaurants. Edith Piaf, we knew well. That was their approach to language teaching. They just weren't very good teachers. That's just not an efficient way to teach a language.

Russian was supposed to be hard. At that time, University High bragged it was one of two high schools in the country teaching Russian. I thought I'd rather do something that's going to be really challenging and few people have this opportunity. So I took Russian. It was a very small class, maybe eight students, because nobody wanted to bother with the Cyrillic alphabet.

We did a lot of sentences from the US Army's *Manual of Spoken Russian*. It was the 1945 War Department Technical Manual they used at Army bases as a basic primer.

I developed a pretty good Russian accent. I loved the language; it felt good in my mouth. There was a sentence I especially loved: "I'm going to the station to meet my wife and children." Years later, in Vienna, I actually had a use for a variation on that line!

Miss Birkmaier wasn't a very good teacher. We memorized things and she was gone a lot because she was so "important." Emma Birkmaier—she was kind of a martinet. We danced and we sang and we ate borscht. And we spoke Russian sentences that were never going to be used again. And I was bored.

I said: "Can I do some extra credit?"

"Well, yes. Here are some little books. See what you can do with them."

I took them home. One of them was Pushkin, poems and short stories, and there was Turgenev and Lermoncov. There was a glossary and there were notes at the bottom of each page. If you put that all together you could figure it out. I puzzled over them and worked on them.

In languages, you have to make leaps when translating. And you have to guess. You're making leaps all the time. You just can't translate verbatim. So I made those guesses, just intuitively.

One day, may parents said: "Charlotte, we have to go to U. High to meet with Miss Birkmaier and Dr. Stout."

Dr. Stout was the principal, later fired from his position as president at the University of Nevada-Las Vegas, by the way. Anyway, they said," Well, Miss Birkmaier believes you have been plagiarizing."

"What? Plagiarizing? I don't even know what that is!"

"You turned in some poems by Pushkin that you couldn't possibly have translated so well."

I said, "But I did! I just guessed at it. I used the glossary. I did that. It was me."

They said, "We believe you."

My father was so good at languages. He'd gone down to Latin America to preach in Spanish and he didn't really know Spanish but he did it; he spoke English and German and used Latin to speak Spanish and Italian. He probably knew that what I'd done was possible and that I wasn't stupid and that I was capable of doing that.

In any case, we all went to see these guys and they said they accepted my plea that I hadn't cheated but I don't think they believed it.

That was a terrible experience. This was a so-called progressive school. They didn't trust me; they had no respect for me as a student. They hadn't even talked to me ahead of time.

They taught badly. Geometry: We were asked what we wanted to learn? Come on! I found out later from my future husband Paul, geometry was a system of logic. I said *No!* Shocked. We had no idea. I was good in math. I got A-pluses in all my math classes.

It was a very Dewey school. It was super-Dewey. But it was a distortion. Dewey would not have endorsed this. It was a perversion of Dewey. It was so un-progressive. It was so ugly, so mean. It was a waste of time.

For example, I don't know exactly whether Dewey believed in history but they said, "We will not teach history. History is finished. That's the past. We look to the future."

For me, that was particularly ironic because I left the school totally ignorant of history—except for little bits and snatches I got from books I read—and went to Switzerland which is hundreds of years of history! It was really a shock. To this day, I'm resentful. I felt unprepared.

Some time later, when I was a senior, I was the copy editor of the yearbook. We did a very unusual yearbook that year.

We couldn't do just any old yearbook. We worked really hard on it. I stayed after school every day for months, working on it. One day I was in the hallway and said something to my yearbook friends that made us all laugh. Dr. Stout came out of his office and said, "Charlotte Theile! You are a silly girl. You will never get anywhere. You won't get any honors; I'll see to it that you don't!"

It turned out at the senior honors assembly I got inducted into the thespian and the journalists and the future homemakers of America honorary societies—but not the National Honors Society. There were three of us who were the best students in class—pretty much agreed on—who did not get into the National Honor Society. We were bad characters.

After that assembly, the social studies teacher, the English teacher, and the theater teacher—they were the best teachers—took us aside and said, "There was a huge fight about this. You should know. That was no unanimous decision; Dr. Stout forced it on us and we're quitting." They left!

At that point, I knew I was going to Europe for a couple of years so I kind of let it go. But I took a competitive exam for a college scholarship from a Lutheran insurance company and I won the scholarship.

At the same time, Smith College wrote to me and said *Please apply*, based on my college boards. But my focus was not there. We would be in Europe. When the time came to focus, I came back to Valparaiso.

*** 

*Charlotte's mother was right all along—she was independent. When the time came for her to take a summer job while she was in high school, she struck out on her own.*

***

I got my first job between my junior and senior years in high school. Three of my friends from school and I decided that we would go and can corn.

Watertown, Minnesota was a small town about 30 miles west of Minneapolis. It's in the middle of farmland that produces sweet corn. The town was home to a big Jolly Green Giant canning factory. When the corn was ready to harvest in August, temporary workers would come in from all over the area. Two of us stayed with one family and the other two stayed with another family. Both homes were within a block or two of the factory. The townspeople were used to making arrangements like that.

We had to be instantly available every time a truckload of corn came in. There'd be an alarm, a whistle, that you could hear all over town. We had ten minutes to get to the factory.

The goal was to get the corn in the can and sealed within several hours of it being picked. It was a 24/7 operation. We worked eight-hour shifts. Sometimes we worked two shifts a day. We were just getting the corn out as fast as we could.

We wore hairnets and aprons. They dumped the corn from the truck directly into a chute. My job was to take each cob and lay it in a little slot as fast as I could, with the tassel away from me. A blade cut off the bottom of the cob and then a machine tumbled the cob and got rid of the husk and the silk. The clean cobs went into another line where the kernels were cut off. The kernels were immediately put into cans and the cans were filled with some sort of solution and sealed. And then the corn was cooked in the can, very very fast, because corn sugar turns into starch quickly. The timing was important.

The person who hired us said, "Girls, this'll be hard work. You won't find it very exciting. But you'll never forget that you have worked in a factory. It will stay with you all your life; you will know what it's like in a factory."

It was his way of telling us to go to college.

We were 17 and we felt free in this small town. We were earning money and had irregular hours and we were out on the streets in the middle of the night sometimes, and reading books in the cemetery, and sliding down this coiled tube fire escape hooked on to the third floor of the elementary school. We had a good time. And we learned a little bit about life in a very small town.

We learned about the people. Some of the boys who worked at the factory invited us to go to a wedding in the next town. One of the boys had a car and so we all packed into it and went. It turned out these small town weddings were moneymakers. These young couples getting married would earn fifty or sixty dollars from strangers.

They would have a polka band and you could pay a dollar or two and dance! You could drink beer and have something to eat—we paid for that too.

It was terrific. The boys danced with great gusto, very athletically. We got around the floor very fast. It was lots of fun. It was a different way of doing things.

The best pot roast sandwich I ever had in my life was in Watertown. There was a bakery and they made bread and they made pot roast. The bread was warm and the pot roast was hot. The sandwiches cost a dollar, very expensive. And they were so good! That was our indulgence.

The next summer, after I graduated from high school, I found a job at Cut-Rite. It was a chain of supermarkets in St. Paul. I got to work in the downtown store, the flagship store, although it was the oldest one and not as nice as the rest of the stores. It was on the streetcar line so it was easy for me to get to.

The downtown Cut-Rite served many senior citizens who obviously had very little money. In those days, a lot of older people lived downtown in cities. The housing was cheap because it was falling apart.

The first day, the union steward came up to me and said, "Before you start work, Charlotte, you have to join the union." I said, "Really?

I get to join the union?" I paid my dues very happily. It was very exciting.

I sorted produce. I took out all the rotting produce and put it aside so these senior citizens could come and pick the best of the rotting produce and get it for just a few cents. That was a real eye-opener for me. People were so restricted in their income that they couldn't eat decent food.

The people who ran the store were humane and thoughtful and understood what was going on with these elderly people: they had to buy this flawed food to survive.

My parents never had much money but we had farmers in our congregation so we always had fresh food. Seeing these elderly people rummage through the celery and the tomatoes and the fruits going bad was particularly disturbing to me.

I worked my way up to cashier. We had no barcodes at that time so I had to remember the price of everything. It became an obsession: I'd sit down at the dinner table and say, "Ah, peas. Yes. Twenty seven cents. A potato, twelve cents a pound."

It was a very good job. The manager wanted me to stay on. He thought I had the makings of a manager. But I said, "Actually, I'm going to Europe for two years." He said, "Well, you should do that and then you should go college."

Two jobs in a row and they both told me it would be better for me not to work there.

\*\*\*

*Charlotte continued to witness hypocrisies and experience unmet aspirations both at school and in her father's church.*

*The Mississippi River flooded in April, 1952. Officials ordered the evacuation of more than 2600 families, most of them poor residents of the river flats.*

\*\*\*

We had this big church in St. Paul. The American Red Cross came to our church with its large basement and multiple bathrooms and a big kitchen and said, "This is a perfect place for a shelter. We would like to put a hundred people in your basement."

My father called the church board. They said, "Absolutely not. We don't want those people in our church. They're dirty and they're just going to mess it up. We can't do that."

My father hit the ceiling. They had a meeting in our house. He had a study and they were in the study. I was outside the study, overhearing. There was a big fight. It ended up we did open it up as a shelter. But my father had to really fight for it.

When I was confirmation age, we memorized the small catechism—"Do Unto Others as You Would Have Them Do Unto You" and "Love Thy Neighbor as Thyself." I was paying attention. I was learning my catechism and memorizing my Bible verses, and they all went one way. The congregation was going a different way. That just didn't seem right.

It seemed there was a disconnect. I couldn't understand why there was an argument when it was so clearly the right thing to do. You can clean the basement up when they leave! Come on! It's all washable. That was an *aha* moment for me about the church.

Hypocrisy just rubs me the wrong way. It is not comfortable to disagree with people; you want them to like you. It's not fun. I wanted to be liked. I've always wanted to be liked. I didn't think anybody liked me. It was a struggle.

But there's something more important than if they don't like me. I've certainly got more comfortable with that over the years.

# 4

# Hey, That's Not Fair!

*From the Fall of 1952 through the late summer of 1954, the Theiles lived in Switzerland as Gilbert worked on his advanced degree in theology at the University of Basel. Charlotte was enrolled in the Mädchen Gymnasium, a secondary college preparatory school for girls. She was placed in the seventh of the Gymnasium's eight levels. Harriet, 13, was slotted in the first level. Mark attended the Real Gymnasium for boys, where he learned classical languages—Latin and Greek—and math as opposed to poetry.*

***

The reason we went to Switzerland was my father was getting his doctor's degree. The University of Basel was one of the two leading Christian theological facilities in the world at that time. And he spoke German. I was seventeen when we left. Wow, what an experience! That was amazing.

My rich relatives, Aggie and Louie, paid for it. Louie underwrote the whole trip. It was not to be known among the rest of the family but we'd done a lot for her. Our lives were very intertwined.

We really supported them. My cousin Michael had trouble getting through middle and high schools for acting up. He'd come to live with us in St. Paul. He finished eighth grade at Emanuel Lutheran, went back home, and because he was thrown out of Choate prep school, he finished high school while living with us once again. He eventually got into Harvard and then graduate school at New York University.

My father was a father-figure for him. My grandfather, too. So we were there for Aggie and Louie. They really appreciated it. Michael studied biochemistry and worked with steroids and irradiated materials. He died at 28 of leukemia.

Paying for my father's education was something they could do; they had money so they did it. It was a very generous gift. They paid for everything: we had a car, furniture, we lived in nice circumstances, we traveled, we ate well. It was all truly appreciated.

By then I saw life turning into a very interesting place. There was always something new to learn.

We sailed in November, 1952, on the SS Maasdam. We sailed from Hoboken to Cork, from Cork to South Hampton, and then we were headed from Southampton to Le Havre and finally to Rotterdam. It was the ship's maiden voyage. We learned about Dwight Eisenhower's election while on board.

The English Channel, of course, is about as wide as my kitchen, and there was a terrible storm, one of the worst storms in years. A Panamanian freighter was shipwrecked right at the mouth of the Rotterdam harbor, blocking it. So we were forced to stay on the boat for seven whole days. They had to throw out much of the food so there was very little to eat. And everybody was getting seasick so the crew had to rinse and mop, rinse and mop. They used a disinfectant that for years, whenever I caught a hint of the odor of it, it would make me sick.

But there were 200 Dutch air force men who'd been training in Texas on board with us. And I was seventeen years old so there was lots of dancing. I spent the seven days doing a lot of dancing, in between bouts of seasickness.

\*\*\*

*Charlotte had taken a correspondence course in the German language in the summer before the Theiles left for Switzerland. Both her parents spoke fluent German. Gilbert held a service in German every Sunday in addition to regular English service. Still, she was unfamiliar enough with the language so that she felt lost wandering around the Gymnasium those first weeks.*

***

I went to school at the Gymnasium in Basel knowing a smattering of German. I had some understanding of it; at least I'd heard it throughout my life.

There was geography class—I could tell because there were maps. Chemistry class, we were in a lab. Math, I could figure out what that class was.

Then we went to a room and a very austere looking woman walked in. She marched to the front of the room and sat down and started talking. It was a week before I realized it was History class. The word for History in German is Geschichte [pronounced: geh-SHEESH-ta] but geschichte is also a word for stories. So I wasn't clear whether she was telling us a story or it was history. I sat there dumbly and eventually began to understand it.

Here I am, 17 going on 18 years old, going to school with kids who've spoken the Swiss sort of German for their whole lives. I couldn't possibly be speaking German as well as they did. So I made mistakes. I mean I'd had two months of German. Being Swiss, they laughed at me. The Swiss are known as extremely judgmental.

My reaction was: Hey, that's not fair! I can't possibly know as much as you do. So laugh at me; I don't care. I'll learn some more tomorrow and I'll learn some more the next day and I'll get there eventually. But you don't have the right to laugh at me.

***

*As the school year progressed, Charlotte found it challenging to keep up with students speaking a foreign language. She considered quitting Gymnasium and anguished over the decision and what to tell her parents.*

***

It was daunting. It was really a lot of work. I was exhausted. By about April I really felt as if I was being stretched too far. I was in the seventh class and I was supposed to stay in Gymnasium until the eighth class. At the end of the eighth year you take the Matura so I was in line to do that.

I sat down with myself and began to think about it: "Does this make sense? You don't have to do this. It's driving you crazy. You're wearing yourself out. When you get back to the United States you don't have to have a Matura. Meanwhile, there are a lot of things you aren't doing in Europe because you're learning seventh-year French—in the German language! Is that really worth it all?"

I worked it out. I went to my parents and said, "I think I want not to do this anymore."

\*\*\*

*Charlotte used this tortured construction because she wanted to soften the message, afraid her parents might be averse to her plan.*

\*\*\*

I wanted to go someplace where I could think. There was a mountain called Niederhorn, in Interlaken. My parents arranged for me to stay in a chalet, way up, for three or four days. It took a ski lift to get there. It was the spring. I took some poems with me, these orange Penguin books. I think I had T.S. Eliot. I was by myself and I walked around—hiked around—working it over in my mind, weighing the concept of quitting versus feeling freed. I came back and said, "I'm not going to do it anymore."

They agreed with my decision! They were quite willing to accept it.

\*\*\*

*Charlotte came up with a plan to continue taking certain classes at the Gymnasium as well as some others at the University of Basel. The Gymnasium teachers gave Charlotte a special latitude because she wasn't a native.*

\*\*\*

I continued to take chemistry and math and geography at the Gymnasium. The chemistry and trigonometry teachers were really happy to have me because I was obviously interested in those subjects. Switzerland is not a flexible country but they sort of let me create my own path.

I took courses in English literature at the University. I felt free to think and travel and so forth.

And I played basketball. There was a girls basketball team at the Gymnasium and they didn't know how to play. So I was the leader although I didn't know how to play either, but I knew more than they did because I'd seen basketball being played when I was in high school.

I'm curious to this day to figure out how I had the nerve to do what I did there. It was the right thing to do.

***

*Meanwhile, Charlotte's mother, Margaret, had met another American woman named Lydia Shinnamon. Lydia's husband, Charles, was a major in the US Air Force. The Shinnamons were soon to be transferred near Heidelberg, Germany. The University of Heidelberg had a program, the Dolmetscher Institut, that was a breeding ground for many United Nations interpreters, a place for non-German students to learn German.*

***

My mother became acquainted with this Shinnamon woman. She was staying in Basel while her husband looked for quarters in Heidelberg. They had two small children. She and my mother came to an agreement that it would be nice for the Shinnamons to have a live-in babysitter.

I thought: "Why don't I go to the University of Heidelberg? They had a Dolmetscher Institut. I could do that. So I went to Heidelberg.

***

*Heidelberg opened Charlotte's eyes to the wonders of history. It was one of the very few German cities left relatively unscathed by Allied bombing in World War II. The University of Heidelberg is Germany's oldest such school. The city had been described by Mark Twain, who visited numerous times, as "the perfect city." It was also the setting for the Sigmund*

*Romberg operetta, "The Student Prince," featuring the famous song cho-*
*rus, "Drink, drink, drink!"*

*Freedom suited Charlotte, even as her mother continued to label her*
*"independent."*

***

I spent a semester there. It was during Fasching. Fasching starts on
November 11th, at 11 minutes after 11pm. You start dancing. There
were lots and lots of parties. I had a lot of people invite me to balls at
fraternities whose members had slashed cheeks. That's where the
stereotype of the Prussian with the scar on his cheek comes from. They
did duels and the scar was a badge of honor. So I learned to know the
Germans. They were wonderful dancers.

I was independent. And the question was, How did that happen?
The fact is my parents had encouraged it to a certain extent. They took
me off to University High instead of Humboldt High School in St.
Paul. That was the public high school two blocks from our house. Instead, I went to U. High, an hour and fifteen minutes away on the campus of the University of Minnesota. They'd taken me out of the
Lutheran milieu and put me in the big world with students from all
over the Twin Cities.

My best friends from U. High were very close. There were about 64
people in the class. We all learned to know each other well. We were serious in a lot of ways. We talked about the world and what it's all
about. Philosophy? They didn't teach us that so we had to figure it out
ourselves.

We had a class reunion lunch recently. There were seventeen of us
and a mixed bag, too. It was about twenty below that day but we all
managed to get there.

***

*After nearly two years in Basel, Gilbert Theile finished his studies*
*and began to write his dissertation for his ThD. Margaret decided to*
*take the three kids and move to Vienna, Austria, while Gilbert remained*
*in Switzerland to work on his paper.*

\*\*\*

In the spring of '54, my father was well into his dissertation and the rest of us didn't have to be there in Basel anymore. We thought, "Let's go someplace else. He can use the apartment to get his dissertation done. Where will we go?"

We thought about it and thought about and thought about it. We ended up going to Vienna. Austria was occupied by the Russians at the time but Vienna was a four-power city.

We piled in the car and went to Vienna and found an apartment. It was owned by a woman who had been very well off before the war but couldn't afford to keep her place by herself by the time we arrived. A common story in Vienna.

We lived in this nice apartment and we didn't have any responsibilities at all. We had plenty of money and we just went to concerts and operas and plays and museums and ate wienerschnitzel and sausages.

It was the three of us and my mother. She had a good time. She was happy in Europe anyway. She'd taken organ lessons in Basel and she felt relieved she was away from the Church. She could do what she wanted. She wanted to be independent but she never really felt she was.

\*\*\*

*Margaret and the kids stayed in Vienna for three months. They returned to Basel and Gilbert drove the kids to Holland, where they sailed for Dover, England. Margaret returned to Basel with Gilbert until he finished his dissertation.*

*The kids took a bicycle trip through England and then came back to America in time for the new school year. The two younger kids stayed with their grandparents, Augustus and Emma, in St. Paul. Charlotte moved to northern Indiana, starting her college career at Valparaiso University. In the meantime, Gilbert was called by the Synod to teach at Concordia Seminary outside St. Louis, Missouri. The Theile family—minus Charlotte for the time being—would move to St. Louis after Gilbert and Margaret came back home around Christmastime, 1954.*

\*\*\*

There I was unclassified, at Valparaiso. They couldn't figure out what to do with me. They said, surely there are credits in all this stuff you've done in Europe. Meanwhile, I took every class I could think of to get out of Valparaiso as quickly as I could.

I had that Lutheran insurance company scholarship to pay for my tuition at Valparaiso. Smith College had invited me to apply and would have given me a scholarship but my parents didn't pay any attention to that. I think I probably would have gone to Smith but my parents didn't care one way or the other. I didn't know enough to understand Smith would probably have been a better option.

So I went to Valparaiso. It was inertia that got me there.

So there I was. I became one of the handful of foreign language majors by default, almost because it was the easiest way out. The fun part was I created my own curriculum.

I had good teachers at Valparaiso. Many were defrocked ministers—or they were no longer practicing. Many of them were no longer the conservatives they had started out being. Many of my professors had gotten their doctor's degrees at Indiana University. They talked about it a lot. They said, "Bloomington, Indiana is the end of the world. You can't even get there from here. It's nowhere-ville, just nothing going on down there."

I actually had fun putting my studies together. I did an 18th Century semester; I took German and French literature and English literature and history. Then I took an "ancient" semester. I took Greek philosophy and ancient Greek history. Then there was a year where I took biology, chemistry, and physics, plus a number of other things, thinking, possibly, of becoming a pre-med student.

I learned that biology was chemistry. Chemistry was physics. And physics was mathematics. I did very well; I got Highest Honors.

That's another thing I learned: I knew how to learn.

*** 

*Spring, 1955. Charlotte had been back in the United States for nearly eight months but still was having trouble re-acclimating herself. She*

*thought of a boy with whom she'd become close back in high school, now a*
*Yale student, named Paul Zietlow.*

*His family, like the Theiles, originally had come from a small town*
*in Wisconsin. When Paul was a teenager, he'd spent a couple of years in*
*Frankfurt, Germany immediately after World War II when his father*
*served there with an organization of ecumenical ministers doing reconcil-*
*iation work on a continent that had just experienced the Holocaust.*
*When he returned to America, Paul also had experienced the re-entry*
*problem—making new friends, rekindling old ties, re-learning how to act*
*and speak in public so as to fit in with his new/old culture.*

***

Paul's father had left the Evangelical United Brethren, a kind of
German Methodist church, during the '30s because of fascism. They
heard Fr. Coughlin on the radio. Paul's father strongly believed in social justice; that was his religion. He heard this fascist demagogue spew-
ing his anti-semitism and he couldn't abide by it. He said, "There's
something more I have to do." He joined what was then called the National Conference of Christians and Jews and became the Twin Cities
executive director. But he and his family went to Germany soon after
the war was over.

Paul and I saw the world very similarly, but he had the support of
his family and I was in conflict with my background.

In high school, a burden for me was I almost always had the highest
marks. That was really hard for me. I'm smart. I learn quickly. Now I
know that's an asset. To this day I just gobble everything up, to the extent that it's almost distracting. I have a voracious curiosity. But I
didn't always think of it that as an asset. I thought of it as an embarrass-
ment. Girls aren't smart! I took two years of algebra in high school.
The first year I was one of a few girls. The second year I was the only
girl. I thought, socially, that was just terrible.

I felt very ignorant when I came back from Europe. I felt as if I
didn't know anything. I had a need to master information. I had to organize the world in my head.

I wasn't comfortable back in America. Paul understood the re-entry problem.

I wasn't very happy so I wrote to Paul at Yale.

He wrote back: "Come up for College Weekend!"

My mother told my Aunt Aggie about it and she sent me a plane ticket. Yale sounded good to her. I stayed at a women's rooming house and Paul paid for it! Each night he deposited me at the door.

That weekend we discovered we had always had crushes on each other. The rest is history.

***

*In the summer of 1955, the Theiles moved to St. Louis, Missouri, where Gilbert had gotten the call as a professor at Concordia Seminary, affiliated with the Missouri Synod. After living in seminary housing for several years, the Theiles eventually bought the first home of their own.*

*By the fall of 1956, Paul was living in Ann Arbor, Michigan, working toward his master's degree at the University of Michigan. Charlotte was still at Valparaiso University, trying to figure out when she could graduate. The university took a long time to determine how much of her European schooling could be translated into American college credits. An Indiana University service was in charge of accrediting foreign courses taken by American students. Charlotte would visit the registrar's office once a week and say "Any chance I can graduate now?" The answer was always "No, we haven't heard from Bloomington yet."*

***

Then in January 1957, I came back from Christmas vacation and went straight to the registrar. "Any chance I can graduate?"

"Oh yeah! And, by the way, you have 30 credits too many."

I said, "Great! Goodbye." And I packed up and went home.

***

*With her passionate interest in different languages, Charlotte thought she might be interested in a career in foreign service. She took a number of qualifying tests for US government positions and arranged job interviews with the CIA and the State Department.*

***

I have a feisty edge. I get my back up. I've run into a lot of brick walls in my life. I wanted to be in the Foreign Service when I graduated from college. I had good language skills and was really interested in political science and government. And I'm not stupid.

I took the tests for the Foreign Service, for the National Security Agency, and for the Central Intelligence Agency. I got high marks on all of them.

I got an interview with the Foreign Service in the Federal Building in Chicago. A bunch of white men from the East Coast interviewed me. We spoke German and we spoke French. We talked about the world and current events. At the end of it, they said, "Your record is really good. Your test scores are outstanding. We can see you've got a touch. You would make an ambassador a wonderful wife."

So, then I got an interview with the CIA. Some guy was going to meet me at Lambert Field in St. Louis. I would know him because he would be wearing a red rose. At the end of the interview, he said, "Really good. Fantastic. Wonderful interview. And you'd make a spy a wonderful wife."

I couldn't believe it! I got angrier and angrier as I walked away, down the hall. But there wasn't anything to be done about it, not at that time. There was no recourse.

Anyway, it was infuriating.

That was the end of that. That's why I eventually went to graduate school.

***

*In the spring and early summer of 1957, Charlotte took a bus trip south, to visit family friends in Georgia, and then stay for a while in Florida with her grandmother Emma Ernst, who by this time was a widow.*

***

Now what am I going to do? I tried to get a job but I wasn't prepared for anything. I took some lessons from the local musicologist and I played the piano.

So I decided to go on a trip to St. Petersburg. I had never been in the South. My first time in the South was on a bus. I witnessed some Jim Crow stuff which was very distressing. I saw the military police hustle a black guy in uniform off the bus at Clarksville, Tennessee. I didn't know why they were doing it; maybe they needed the seat.

We had friends in Columbia County, about 150 miles east of Atlanta. I spent some time with them. The Cartledges. He was a professor in the Presbyterian seminary in Decatur, Georgia.

The Cartledges were bothered by Martin Luther King, Jr. Mr. Cartledge said, "His father doesn't approve what he's doing. He's going way too fast."

The Cartledges were very nice people. Very Christian. I don't think they would have considered themselves racist, yet they felt the "colored people" didn't know their place.

They had suggested I go to Agnes Scott College in Atlanta but I really didn't want to go to a southern girls school.

Then I went to St. Petersburg where my grandmother lived in this wonderful old hotel. It was quite nice, with lots of widows. Many of the residents were ministers' wives from Methodist, Presbyterian, or whatever churches.

Grandma had a nice room and a big closet. In the closet, she had a hatbox. In the hatbox was a bottle of bourbon. Every night before dinner she'd call me to come to her room—I was staying in another room—but first I should go to the kitchenette on her floor and get a bucket of ice.

"But be discreet," she'd say.

So every night at about 5 o'clock I would creep out into the hallway and tiptoe down to the kitchenette—along with all the other women who were doing the same thing!

I stayed with her for a couple of weeks. We would take the bus miles to go to a liquor store so nobody would see us to get the bourbon and bring it back to hide in the hatbox.

\*\*\*

*While Charlotte was away studying in Valparaiso, her family had moved from St. Paul, Minnesota, to St. Louis, Missouri. Her father, Gilbert, had been recruited to teach at Concordia Seminary in suburban Clayton, Missouri.*

\*\*\*

Paul and I were engaged by this time. He'd decided to come to the Midwest to satisfy one of the requirements for his master's degree. He enrolled in a French class at Washington University in St. Louis. I learned a lot about Paul that summer and this brought me closer to him.

We were friends, first and foremost. We shared values even though he'd come from a different Protestant background—or maybe because we'd come from different backgrounds.

Paul's father was an evangelical minister and his mother was a minister's daughter. Not being Lutheran, they were horrified that their son was going to marry one. Of all the people they knew, I'd learn later, they felt the Lutherans were the hardest to get along with.

Paul's mother, Ruth, was a loyal supporter of six-time presidential candidate and noted socialist and pacifist Norman Thomas.

Carl Zietlow, Paul's father, had left his church during the 1930s because of fascism. The evangelicals he was involved with were becoming more and more xenophobic and intolerant. He went to work for the National Conference of Christians and Jews where he could fight fascism.

\*\*\*

*Founded in 1927, the NCCJ (now known as the National Conference for Community and Justice) originally hoped to fight the anti-Catholic bias in America that had reemerged when a Roman Catholic, Al Smith, had started to make a run for president in '28. Chief among his antago-*

*nists were German Lutherans and Southern Baptists. The NCCJ counted among its members Jane Addams and Supreme Court justices Charles Evans Hughes and Benjamin Cardozo. The organization a few years later expanded its scope to advocate for civil rights, racial harmony, women's issues and many other traditionally liberal causes. One of the things the NCCJ did was to send a "Tolerance Trio"—a minister, a rabbi, and a Catholic priest—on tour around the country where they preached religious compassion. Soon after the end of World War II, Carl Zietlow would work in West Germany helping the remaining Jews there work with Christians to spiritually rebuild that shattered land.*

***

Quite a different kettle of fish compared to my upbringing in which my father had to conceal his liberalism. Paul and I saw the world very similarly but he'd had the support of his family while, in so many ways, I was in conflict with mine.

***

*In the spring of '56, Paul Zietlow had graduated magna cum laude in English from Yale. In the summer, he had to take a few requisite language courses for his master's degree. He elected to take them at Washington University in St. Louis. He stayed with the Theiles. Charlotte was back home at the time between school years at Valparaiso. Paul would go on to attend the University of Michigan in the fall to work on his master's in Creative Writing.*

***

Paul could have taken those classes anywhere but I think he wanted to be near me.

One day we went to a Lutheran church. The minister was a very nice guy. I liked him a lot. But Lutherans believe very strongly in Original Sin. This minister preached about Original Sin and said, "We have to do good things in this world but it doesn't matter what you do; it's not going to get you anywhere. *Sola fide* (by faith alone.) No good works really matter."

***

*In other words, we humans won't be rewarded for being loving, caring, helpful sisters and brothers if we don't have faith in God. Conversely, if we have faith in God, it doesn't matter if we do good or ill, we'll be rewarded on Judgement Day.*

***

When we got outside, Paul was apoplectically angry. He said, "That's a terrible message! It's just awful!"

We talked about it at some length. I thought, "Yeah, it really is terrible. It means nothing that you do matters. That's just hard to accept."

It was a critical moment for me. I began to rethink my relationship with religion.

I was always being told you have to do good things. Be nice to people when they come to the door. My mother didn't like people coming to the door and didn't want to interact with the congregation so I spent a lot of time, being the oldest child, opening the door and welcoming people into the study, getting them a glass of water, stuff like that. That seemed to me to be what we were told we should be doing. And then, to think, well, none of it matters! So much of what I hear from churches makes me think, "What does it mean at all?"

I'm not a super scholar of the Bible but I know it fairly well. I went to parochial schools and took religion courses. I read about other religions. I think I understand why people go to churches. But theology becomes, for me, more and more, "What...?" It doesn't make sense.

At the time, I did want it to make sense. I don't really care much now. I have faith in some things. I have faith in people. I believe most people have something good in them. We all should be working on trying to find out what that is in ourselves. I have faith that if we can do that then we can make people's lives better. I'm an optimist. Maybe that's not faith.

The whole business of being a Lutheran minister's daughter is something I had underestimated. As time has gone by, I realize it was really important. I didn't deal with it. I didn't have the time.

***

*Paul Zietlow won two Hopwood Awards in English Language and Literature in 1957 for a short story and for a play he'd written. Given annually to young poets, novelists, short story writers, dramatists, and other wordsmiths, the Hopwoods are perhaps America's most prestigious American literary prizes for aspiring writers. Winners have included Arthur Miller, John Ciardi, Mary Gaitskill, Lawrence Kasdan, Frank O'Hara, and Marge Piercy. The cash prizes amounted to a treasure for the young couple.*

***

Paul won enough money to think we could afford to buy wedding rings and get married. He found a cheap apartment in the basement of a house in Ann Arbor. Forty dollars a month including utilities. So we decided to get married that summer.

On the day Paul and I got married, it was very hot and humid in St. Louis. Paul wore his own white dinner jacket. His mother had bought him that dinner jacket while he was an undergraduate and he wanted to be married in his own clothes. I made my own wedding dress—I used the Turkish lace from my mother-in-law's wedding for the bodice. The only thing air-conditioned was the funeral limousine my father had wrangled from someone for us.

My father gave me away and then he went into the office to get into his vestments and then, together with Paul's father, co-officiated the ceremony. Paul was sweating and he dripped on the floor. I looked down and saw this puddle on the floor. Paul looked at it and then he looked at me and we started giggling. My sister Harriet, who was my maid of honor, saw us and thought we were crying and so she started crying. Then my cousin Rosemary who was a bridesmaid started crying and pretty soon everybody was crying except us. We were still laughing.

It was a good start.

# 5

# Somebody Had To Do It

Shortly after we were married, I think it was in December, my brother Mark had a psychotic breakdown and was hospitalized. Mark was tall, 6-foot-7 and very smart. He was the valedictorian of his high school class. He was diagnosed as schizophrenic. There never was anything normal about our relationship after that. His breakdown was there and it was part of our lives for years and years until he died in 2000.

My father was teaching at the seminary and still didn't have any money. Insurance didn't cover mental health care at the time. Our rich relatives helped. Mark first went into a private sanitarium in Jacksonville, Illinois. They filled him with thorazine. Then he was just dopey. Louie and Aggie got him into Payne Whitney Psychiatric Clinic, a very fancy hospital, in Manhattan. He was there for a while and then the doctors said, "We've done what we can." So, he went from hospital to hospital. He was in various state hospitals, in and out.

There were terrible, explosive scenes with my parents. Mark scared us all. He was big! And very smart and very clever and very nasty. He knew how to get to people, psychologically. It was very, very sad.

I remember coming home from college one summer. I really worked hard at Valparaiso; I took 18 to 25 credit hours a semester and did well so I could get out of there. Mark—he was very frightening—said, "What do you know? You're in college now. Are you an expert on anything? Do you know everything there is to know about German literature?"

I said, "No, I don't. I'm learning a lot but I don't know a lot either." I've always said I learned, in college, what I didn't know. I learned about my ignorance. So I've always continued to try to learn some more.

But it didn't mean I knew nothing, which is where he left me on several occasions: If you don't know everything, you don't know anything.

Paul and I didn't have children for five years because I was afraid something terrible would happen because of Mark. I saw how my parents suffered; they didn't know how to handle Mark, ever.

When we did have children, we did not see much of him. It was always very volatile. I thought, "We've got a family here and I've got to protect them. And I have to protect *me* from his verbal assaults."

In the middle of 1967 or '68, I don't remember which, he was very supportive of the Vietnam War for reasons only he could understand, so he decided to join the Army. The Army, in its infinite wisdom, accepted him. They sent him to basic training and he opted to join the paratroopers. They must have been quite desperate. They sent him to paratrooper school and he went AWOL.

He was in the Army long enough to qualify for a medical discharge. From then on, the Army took care of him. My parents were lucky; that removed the financial burden from them. It would be the Army's problem. They sent him to Jefferson Barracks Veterans Administration hospital in St. Louis. He would be either in the hospital or released to some crummy apartment that the VA paid for from then on. But they should never have taken him.

Mark made me very conscious of mental illness and what happens to people who are mentally ill and what doesn't happen to them through lack of care and lack of understanding. And the stigma! And the families.

I never thought that what happened with Mark could happen with me, but I was depressed at times. I went through depression and self-doubt. Toward the end of the '60s, the war was frightening to me. I found it threatening. I didn't want to watch the television. I didn't want to hear the news. Just leave me alone. It was enough to make me worry. I worried about not being cheerful around the children. I worried about bringing darkness in the house.

In Bloomington, at the time, there was one psychiatrist and he wasn't so good. So I went to Larue Carter Hospital, the psychiatric center for the university in Indianapolis, for talk therapy for a couple of years.

Sometime toward the end of this therapy the psychiatrist said, "I want you to come back next week and tell me what you think you can do well."

I had this sense of never being able to do anything right. I was shy and lacking in confidence. I came back and said, "What I really love to do well is make dinner parties on the spur of the moment for ten, fifteen, twenty people."

He said, "That's pretty good."

"Besides that," I said, "I'm really good at being cheerful." I laughed.

He said, "That's an interesting thing. Think about it."

I've always been pretty playful. It's in my nature. That's one of the things Paul and I had in common.

\*\*\*

*The Zietlows settled into their humble basement apartment in Ann Arbor. Paul had finished his master's degree in August 1957, the same month he and Charlotte were married. He'd earned an appointment as a teaching fellow for the 1957-58 school year back at the University of Michigan. Charlotte wondered, on occasion, what she might do with her life. She'd soon be able to pursue one passion—travel.*

\*\*\*

The first summer after we were married, Paul's parents rented a station wagon and took us, his brother and his wife and their one-year-old daughter to Mexico. I had never thought of going to Mexico.

We drove down the Pan-American Highway and none of us spoke Spanish. We went to Tula, a Mesoamerican site, the capital of the

Toltec empire that had recently been excavated, and Teotihuacan, another major Toltec city, and Mexico City. We went to Oaxaca with its two ancient sites, the Zapatec and the Mixtec, then down to Cuernavaca and Taxco. Then we went over to the west and came up along the coast.

It was a revelation, to see the ruins, those fascinating places.

***

*After Charlotte and Paul returned to Ann Arbor to begin the fall 1958 semester, she found some doors opening for her.*

***

I was thinking, "I don't know what I'm going to do here but I'll take some classes." I just went in and said, "I want to take some classes." They said, "Sure!" It's funny, in retrospect. The University of Michigan has never been that easy to get into.

I didn't even think about that when I went in there.

So, I found myself in some German and French classes because I didn't know what I was going to do. I didn't know at the time that I'd get my master's degree in German.

I didn't know how to type. That was another thing I didn't do, purposely—I was not going to learn to type. Everybody in high school learned to type. I was not going to get stuck being a typist.

Now, all of a sudden, I had to type. I taught myself to type. I got a typing book and I just worked my way through it. Eventually, I took a test for a secretary position at Michigan. Fortunately, someone in the German Department suggested I become a teaching fellow instead. So, I started teaching.

I've never had a long-term strategy. I've never thought, "What am I going to do over the next so-many years?" I've played life as it comes.

I tried. I applied for jobs, real jobs, but the employers weren't interested in me. That had a lot to do with me being a woman. So it wasn't so easy to plan my life. I didn't know what my options were; there weren't many! So I've sort of rolled through life.

***

*Young, nearly broke, living a bohemian life, Charlotte and Paul accumulated adventures and memories rather than wealth. Their home was a make-do affair just down the street from Michigan Stadium—"The Big House"—at the time the largest sports stadium in the world.*

\*\*\*

We lived in this basement apartment. It had rough-hewn walls. The primitive bathroom was across a passageway that all the other tenants could walk through. The toilet and tub were raised on a little platform so the pipes could be installed beneath it. We lived in one big room with a little kitchen off to the side. At first, the kitchen had no windows that opened. They were painted shut. The housing inspector came by and said, "The landlord has to put in new windows or you'll have to get out." So the landlord put in new windows.

We lived near the football stadium. Every Saturday afternoon, we watched two hundred thousand legs go by. But the apartment was very close to campus and it was cheap. We didn't have much money so there we were.

The walls that were put up to make the apartment were old windows, just patched together. It was very romantic initially. Then it got a little old.

In 1959, two years after we were married, we had this friend. Playing handball, Paul had got acquainted with a fellow English Department student named Whitney Buck. A very nice guy but a little lonely.

So we started feeding him. He would bring wine or beer because he had money and we didn't. He'd come from a well-to-do family. I would make pork neckbones and sauerkraut. We all got to be really good friends.

So at the end of the school year we all decided to go to Mexico. It was cheaper for us to travel to Mexico than it would have been to stay in Ann Arbor. We sublet our basement apartment.

We spent a couple of months in Mexico. Whitney had an Oldsmobile 88, very big. He had enough money that we could depend on if we got into a scrape. We made it a ruins tour.

We rented a plane in Villa Hermosa, which was described in *The Power and the Glory*, the Graham Greene book. We flew into Palenque which, at the time, you couldn't reach except by plane or train. It's amazing we survived.

The flight was an ordeal. There were four of us, we three and the pilot. Plus a number of great big plastic bags of frozen fish, melting. It was very hot. The airfield was filled with cows so we buzzed it. As we came closer on our second pass, the cows ambled to the side and we landed.

There was one hotel; it had rooms by the hour. We rented a room for several hours so we could take showers before and after we visited the ruins.

The site had recently been excavated. It had been a wonderful Maya temple. Inside there was a jade god. It was a spectacular sight that few got to see because the place was so hard to get to.

Then we went back to the hotel, took showers and had something to eat. We were told the train that would take us into the Yucatan would be coming soon and we'd better be ready to be jostled because it would be overflowing.

We went to the railroad ticket office in the early evening but it was closed. As we waited for it to open, more and more people just kept on coming. The people were settling in, starting fires and cooking. It got later and later. The ticket office wouldn't open.

We were the only non-Indians there. We didn't have anything to eat or drink. Pretty soon it was midnight. A train came at 2:00am. It had freight cars with armed guards at the doors. There was straw on the floors with men sleeping on it. It stopped and then went away.

Finally, at four in the morning the passenger train came. We found a facing set of seats and quickly claimed them.

On the train, women started changing their babies' diapers and hanging them out the window. We came to a river. We got enough out of the discussions swirling around us that it wasn't clear the bridge could hold the train up. But then the real reason we stopped became apparent—a bunch of Indians came out of the jungle and started selling tamales and plantains to the passengers. We didn't know if the food was clean but we had to eat so we bought some.

We ended up in a town called Campeche. We had to stay there a couple of days because we were sick from the food.

After the Yucatan we went back to our car. We parked it in a Tehuantepec hotel lot and took the bus up to San Cristóbal de las Casas, up in the hills on the Guatemala border. At the time, the Cuban revolution was going on. By this time, Paul and Whitney had grown beards. The kids ran down the streets after us yelling "Castro! Castro!"

We had some real scrapes. One night in San Cristóbal, Whitney couldn't sleep so he went out walking and he got mugged, losing his wallet and his identification card. Soon it was time to come back down from the hills on the bus. When we got on, we found out the driver had been trying to get his station on the radio. Whitney saw what the problem was so he showed him how to switch band frequencies. It ingratiated him with the driver.

Down the hill, the *Federales* stopped the bus in the middle of nowhere and wanted to see everyone's papers. Of course, Whitney didn't have any papers so they wanted to arrest him.

Paul and I said, "No, you can't do that! We're not leaving him behind!" Somehow everybody on the bus understood. They all started saying, "No! No! No!"

Then the driver—we understood him—said, "You're not going to keep that man!" While this was all going on, Paul slipped Whitney his Michigan ID. We got out of there but it was nip and tuck. That was scary.

We ended up spending a week in Mérida, the capital of Yucatan, always sick. The whole time at least one of us had some sort of Montezuma's Revenge. We'd brought along a big jar of bismuth and we would eat the powder as needed. So that was Mexico.

***

*Back in Ann Arbor, the Zietlows move from a basement to an attic. Paul worked toward his doctorate and Charlotte narrowed her own focus, embracing the academic discipline she really loved.*

\*\*\*

When we got back home, the woman we'd sublet to asked if she could stay there. We said, "You can have the apartment if you can find us something better." She did. She found us an attic.

It was a really nice attic. It was a bright, cheery attic. Paul would watch the squirrels in the trees.

I got my master's degree in German and French Literature. Then I did a stint, briefly, in Comparative Literature. Then I moved entirely into Linguistics. That's what I really bore down on.

We each had teaching fellowships. I was teaching German 101 and Paul was teaching English Composition. It was a meager living, enough to live in an attic.

We had bicycles. We did not have a car. We did not have children. We ate frugally. We ate well but we ate pork neckbones and sauerkraut, tuna fish and broccoli, green spaghetti and an occasional cut of meat. We would turn our milk bottles in for cash and then go get ice cream cones at Miller's on University Avenue.

We lived very frugally—and we saved money! To this day I don't understand how.

\*\*\*

*Charlotte and Paul's first child, Rebecca, wouldn't come along for another couple of years. Charlotte learned first-hand how difficult it was at the time for a married woman to plan her pregnancies. The oral contraceptive— "the Pill"—only recently had been approved for use in the United States.*

\*\*\*

I never did take the Pill. When Paul and I decided to get married, we agreed we were not ready to have children. So we needed to have birth control. We did some research; there wasn't much available at the time that was reliable. But there was the diaphragm.

Just before we were married, I went to a Lutheran doctor in St. Louis. He examined me and then I asked him to prescribe a diaphragm for me. He would not do that.

"You're a Lutheran!" he said. "You're healthy. You have broad hips. We need more Lutherans. It's your duty to have children!"

I was angry and upset. Really upset.

I went home just fuming. I told my mother about it even though I didn't usually discuss things much with her.

She said, "I've heard about this place called Planned Parenthood downtown." So I called them and told them the situation. They said, "Oh, of course, we can help you. Just come down. Bring your fiancé if you want. We can take care of you." And they did.

In Ann Arbor, they didn't have any family planning services available. We had to go for supplies—tubes of spermicidal jelly, as many as we could get—to Buffalo or St. Louis. That's why I'm a strong advocate of Planned Parenthood. It helps people have children when they need them, when they want them, and when they're able to take care of them. That's the way it should be.

\*\*\*

*In the summer and fall of 1960, an exciting, young, charismatic Democratic senator from Massachusetts ran for president. He touched Charlotte.*

\*\*\*

The reason I was interested in John F. Kennedy was there was a lot going on that wasn't being paid attention to. Some people were doing well but a lot of people were not.

I had done a little bit of social work. The summer after my second year at Valparaiso, I worked for the Lutheran Children's Friends Society in St. Louis. They dealt with adoptions and foster children. I was a case worker

At the time, I didn't drive. I didn't even have a driver's license. When I applied for the job, they asked, "Can you drive?'

I said, "Sure!" I only had a beginner's permit.

The first day at work they handed me the key to a Chevrolet in the garage in the alley. They told me to pick up these children in northwest St. Louis. I took the keys, got in the car, and found it was a manual transmission. Well, I knew something called a clutch existed, but that's all.

Somehow I got the car out of the garage, backing up into the alley. Then I had to get it going forward—and I did! I found myself on King's Highway, a major artery, going north, hoping I wouldn't have to stop and that there wouldn't be any hills.

I got to the place and I got the kids.

I made them sit in the back seat because I thought it would be safer. I took them from their temporary foster home to a permanent one.

I—we—survived.

I learned how difficult so many lives were. I learned about life on the streets in St. Louis. I decided I wasn't tough enough to be a social worker. I worried I wouldn't be able to step away from people's lives enough.

Then something strange happened. After I decided social work wasn't the way I wanted to go, my mother decided that's the way she wanted to go!

I'd told her about the broken families at the dinner table all that summer. I didn't recall her reactions but it turned out she'd been listening.

When fall came near, I had to leave the job and go back to Valparaiso. The Society needed someone to replace me and, without my knowledge, my mother applied for the job and got it.

Anyway, I knew there was a lot of poverty in St. Louis. And I already knew there was a lot of poverty in St. Paul.

I said before, St. Paul is built on hills overlooking the Mississippi River. The disparity between the poor people down low and the middle class up high was evident. Later, under Kennedy, with his housing programs, they really cleaned up and built some wonderful housing projects up on the hills. Really beautiful and well-taken care of. They'd pretty much cleared out the housing on the river flats and built ware-houses and manufacturing plants on stilts so that when the river flooded there would be protection for them. And the people weren't dispossessed—they were moved up higher. The Twin Cities did a lot of innovative stuff like that. But that hadn't happened yet when Kennedy was running.

And health care was a big issue. In our own circumstances, we didn't have health care but we were in graduate school—we were young and healthy. We were never going to get sick.

Kennedy made me feel as if I could make the world better. He was very inspirational. He came to Ann Arbor in the early morning after his famous TV debate with Nixon, the one where Nixon looked so awful. We were there when Kennedy arrived. We were on the street in front of the Michigan Union, hundreds of us. There was a platform set up in front of the Union so he could say a few words. He said he was so happy to finally be in Ann Arbor because he "could get some sleep." We roared. He called Michigan the "Harvard of the Midwest." We roared again.

We just thought: Here's this man, he was vibrant, exciting. There was a lot to be hoped for.

***

*By the time Charlotte and Paul got up in the middle of the night to help welcome JFK to Ann Arbor that September day, she'd already tossed in her lot with the candidate.*

***

I felt pretty strongly about Kennedy, also about Nixon. I talked about him—them—all the time. A friend, maybe tired of hearing me go on and on, said, "Well, if you feel so strongly about it, go out and do something!"

I said, "What can I do?"

"You can knock on doors and talk to people."

"I can't do that! I'm too shy."

"If you're going to talk about it, do something. Otherwise, shut up."

So, I volunteered. I got a list of people to go and talk to. In Ann Arbor, there was a lot of low-income housing right in the center of town for students and senior citizens. So I knocked on doors and I talked mostly to senior citizens, because they would be home.

I would tell them about Kennedy and they said, "Oh, I really like that young man." They were so scared that they would get sick and they wouldn't be able to pay for any care. One person after another. And Kennedy was talking about doing something about it.

But then they went on to say, "But we can't vote for him because he's Catholic."

I would say, "My father was a Lutheran minister. I went to a parochial school. I'm going to vote for him. If I can do it, you can do it."

I changed votes. I'd say I changed about 40 votes. Kennedy won Michigan by about 3000 votes, less than a vote per precinct. Without a hundred people like me, he might have lost Michigan and the world would have been different.

At the time, when you looked at the poverty rates, the poorest people were the seniors. That's not true anymore. The percentage of impoverished senior citizens is way down and it's because of Medicare and Medicaid.

***

*Medicare had been proposed during the Eisenhower administration but Kennedy made it a top priority, both during his campaign and into his presidency. Medicare became law in 1965 under President Lyndon Johnson who'd pledged to carry forward Kennedy's goals when he took office after the president was assassinated.*

*In the spring of 1961, Ann Arbor would hold a primary election for local races. Party organizers remembered Charlotte.*

***

I'd learned a big lesson: If you volunteer for something and you do it, that's very unusual. It attracts attention. I've told people, if you want to be noticed, do what you say you're going to do.

It was noticed that I'd really worked hard during the Kennedy campaign. I'd turned my little lists of voters in and asked for more.

So they said, "There's a city election coming along this year. We would like you to be a precinct captain."

My area, south of the campus, was a typical college town neighborhood. Lots of big old houses cut up into apartments. Our attic was in a three-story house with three apartments, one on each floor. That was typical.

Nobody had ever really worked those houses. Washtenaw County was allowing graduate students to vote for the first time.

Paul and I talked about it. We decided I would do the door-to-door work and he would keep the records. He was good at that. He'd keep records on different colored 3x5 cards, indicating who was who and who was what. We registered people to vote. I'd found people who we knew and who lived in the precinct and asked them to help. Pretty soon we had our own little organization.

We were going up and down stairways and into basements, talking to people and registering them. We got to the point where we really knew what the likely vote totals, the numbers, would be.

We had a pretty good person in charge of the city party. His name was Gerhard Weinberg. He was a German Jew whose family left Germany in 1938. He was an historian on the Michigan faculty. He wrote some important books about the Nazi period and he became a senior scholar in residence at the Holocaust Memorial Museum. He was precise. We had to do things in order, so we did.

That year, Austin Warren—a noted literary critic, a professor, and an eccentric—lived next door to us. He lived in a nice old house. I knocked on his door and talked to him. I'd taken a class from him so it was a little awkward but he was a southerner so he was dapper and polite.

We knew to a person what the outcome would be in the '61 primary. On the day of the vote, we were taking people to the polls, we had somebody counting them off as they came in. We knew who'd gotten there and who hadn't. The polls closed at eight in Michigan; it was a labor state and the rules favored working people. It was late and Austin Warren hadn't gotten to the polls yet. I went down and offered him a ride but he said no, he would go by taxi. He went everywhere by taxi.

One of the candidates we were supporting was a woman, a professor, Dorothy Pealey—as far as I can remember, that was her name. She was very smart. She would have made a wonderful mayor. But she was a woman and had a lisp and was Jewish, so she had a lot of things going against her.

Austin Warren finally came to the polling place. He was sent back to those big mechanical booths with the curtains and the big levers. You could stand in there behind the curtain and flick every little lever all you wanted. You could change your vote a hundred times. It would be registered when you pulled the big red lever that opened the curtain.

I said, "Do you need anything before you go in? You know how to work the machine?"

He said, "Everything's under control. Don't worry about it. I can do it."

Austin Warren went in the booth and he was in there for a long time. He was in there... and he was in there... Everybody's waiting. We're whispering, "What's happening? What's going on?"

Finally, he pulled back the big red lever, the curtain opened and he said in a dramatic, deep voice, "I cannot find the name of Mrs. Pealey."

Well, it was down on the lower left but it was too late. He'd pulled the lever and his vote was registered.

Mrs Pealey tied in our precinct! She would have won our precinct with his vote.

The Democrats did not carry Ann Arbor that year. It was still a highly Republican town. It was a lot like Bloomington at the time.

Real estate interests and banking interests sitting on the city council.

But I learned that organizing, finding the voters, getting them informed, getting them out to vote, is what creates wins. If you don't work, that won't happen.

We've kind of lost that. Not only the Democrats but the Republicans. We've become enamored with the computer. We think it can do the organizing for us. There's a certain amount you can do on the internet, with social media, that sort of thing. It's easier. You can sit in your living room and you don't have to move. I've given long speeches to Democratic Party officials here, saying, "Door to door is still the best way to do it!"

\*\*\*

*1961. The man who inspired Charlotte to think she could make the world a better place took the presidential oath of office. She set her sights on helping people attain lesser, local offices. She earned her first graduate degree. And she left the country.*

\*\*\*

I finished my master's degree. In the summer, Paul was offered a job, an exchange position, at the University of Mainz in Germany. But it was all iffy.

There were a lot of things going on in our lives and I was feeling hemmed in and not happy. I was seeing a therapist. Ann Arbor was one of the hotbeds of talk therapy.

I decided that if we were going to Europe, I would go by myself ahead of time, pick up a car, and meet Paul there. I was going to go off for the summer and he was going to come at the end of the summer.

I'd been taking linguistics courses—morphemics, phonemics, very basic stuff, syntax. Michigan's Linguistics Department was very much an applied program. It wasn't theoretical. Noam Chomsky was just coming into vogue but he was more theoretical. The people who taught at Michigan were, generally, from the field. A lot of the people came from the Summer Institute for Linguistics, which was a Christian group. Their goal was to go into benighted tribes and convert them to

Christianity, but to do that they had to learn how to talk to them. They were very good at it. They developed systems for analyzing the structures of languages. They were really good teachers and their tools were really wonderful. So, I'd been taking courses with them.

Just before I left for Europe, I got a letter from my morphemics teacher. He had married a Thai woman. He offered me the opportunity to do a crash course in Thai, learn the language, and then become a teacher in the Peace Corps. I would be teaching Peace Corps people Thai.

But I was on my way to Europe. I didn't take the offer seriously. That would have been total change in the direction of my life. It would have meant leaving Paul and staying in the United States.

That was really a turning point for me. I think I would have done fine because I'm really quick at languages. But I took the other path. No going back, there.

I reserved a stateroom on the USS Rotterdam. Paul was going to drive me to the ship in New York. When Aggie and Louie heard about our plans, they were horrified. They thought we were going to get divorced. They insisted, "Come by Nantucket on your way to New York."

While we were there, Aggie and Louie scolded me. Then they gave us a chunk of money to go to New York City and stay in a nice hotel and eat a good dinner before I got on the ship. So we did that.

During the course of our stay in the city, I decided I really didn't want to leave alone. It was eight o'clock in the morning and the ship was going to sail at noon. I called the Holland America Line and told them that my husband and I had had a reconciliation. I wondered if I could get a rain check on my passage.

They said yes! I must have been persuasive.

So, there we were in New York and we didn't know what to do with ourselves. I called Aggie and Louie and said, "Okay, your little plot worked! Now, can we stay in your house in Montclair while we figure out what we're going to do for the rest of the summer?"

They said, "No, that doesn't work. The house is all locked up and closed down. Why don't you just come and spend the summer here in Nantucket?" So we did.

I'll tell you why it worked. Two months before, I'd earned their respect and they earned my trust. My cousin Rosemary, Louie's daughter, the one who wouldn't let me play with her toys, got married in April. She'd invited me to be her bridesmaid. So I went out to Montclair for the wedding.

They were putting up a tent in the backyard that was as big as the house I live in now. They were waiting on a delivery of 10,000 geraniums.

But Aggie and Louie and Rosemary were totally kaput. They were just frazzled, every one of them. As soon as I got there, the doorbell was ringing and ringing and they couldn't even get up to answer it.

I said, "Should I get the door?"

"Yeah, would you do that please?"

Pretty soon, I was in charge. I answered the door. I answered the phone. I thanked the people for the presents that were delivered. I took the presents that Rosemary didn't want back to the shop. I drove Rosemary's little Mercedes convertible all over Montclair to do the things nobody else could get themselves to do.

I took charge because somebody had to do it.

What I did made a big difference. They suddenly realized, and I did too, that I was pretty competent. I didn't unruffle in a crisis.

When I got back home, they wrote to me and called me and thanked me multiple times. They got a new sense of me.

# 6

# It Sounded Like The End Of The World

*Her doubts and fears allayed, Charlotte and Paul's marriage became stronger than ever as the couple spent a year in the homeland of her—and his—ancestors. Little more than 15 years after the end of World War II, Mainz, the capital of the Rhineland, was ever so-slowly being revived. In this ancient, historic, crippled city, Charlotte would learn how important it was to eat cucumbers properly in Germany.*

***

The University of Michigan and the University of Mainz had an exchange agreement. Mainz was a big old city, 2000 years old. Still in bad shape from the bombing in World War II. It was in the French zone but the French didn't have any money to rebuild it. Weisbaden, which was fine by then, was just across the Rhine in the American zone.

There was a professor in the American Literature Department at Mainz. Hans Galinsky. He was a piece of work. There were all sorts of rumors about him including that he'd been a Nazi or at the very least he was a sympathizer. Professor Galinsky noticed the French weren't putting any money in their zone and the Americans were pouring money into their zone. So he aligned himself with the American occupation people, telling them he was an expert in on American literature. He set up this exchange arrangement with the University of Michigan, where he was a visiting professor.

He was an opportunist. He was a phony. He was clever. Paul's job was to be the American in his department. Paul despised him.

We did end up going separately. Paul's travel expenses were paid for by a Fulbright grant while I used my deferred ticket from June. I picked up a new car, a red Beetle, at the Volkswagen factory in Wolfsburg and then visited some distant relatives in northern Germany. After that I drove to Bremen and picked Paul up when his ship arrived. Then we went to Mainz.

We had to find a place to live. Mainz was really expensive. It was crushed in March of 1945 by bombing. When we got there, housing was difficult to find. We ended up finding an apartment in a little tiny wine town, Bodenheim, just south of the city. It was on the Rhine in the middle of the vineyards. We could take the train into the city in 20 minutes.

\*\*\*

*Ironically, for a country that had so recently attempted to "purify" its population, post-war Germany was home to people from many countries and cultures. Many of them were compelled to live near one another and learn about people different from themselves.*

\*\*\*

The apartment was in a two-story owned by a couple who owned the surrounding vineyard and several other houses. She was the landlady and he was a bank teller. They lived next door in a modern villa. An American couple lived across the street from us and yet another American couple lived upstairs from them, both in a house owned by our landlady and her husband. I have forgotten their names.

The husbands of both couples across the street were in the US Army. The couple upstairs were black; the husband was a private. The couple on the first floor were white and the husband was a captain. They were from the hills of eastern Kentucky, coal country. They weren't educated.

So many things going on. I learned so much. The landlady was very nice to us. She and her husband were generous. They invited us to their home.

Although she was nice to them, the landlady found it difficult to touch her black tenants. She always washed her hands after being with them. I think it was a learning experience for her, too. They were the first black people she'd ever been around. She learned it was okay to touch them even if she did have to wash her hands afterward.

These two couples had difficulty finding housing and wound up in the vineyard. Neither couple ever had interaction with people of a different race but they were brought together and found they liked each other as human beings. In fact, the Kentucky woman would look out for the black woman when they went shopping together. The townspeople gawked at the black woman and the Kentucky woman would say, "Don't stare at her!"

The landlady told us stories about what happened during the war, the bombing raids, and where they went when the sirens went off, and how difficult it was to find food at any time.

I got this insight that despite all the terrible things that came with war, it was the most exciting thing that ever happened to these people. It was the most vital, vibrant thing. Being in the middle of a disaster is something you can treasure because you survived it. That's an accomplishment.

They talked about coming out of the cellar after an air raid and they felt *alive*.

I had made a friend in the University of Michigan German Department—Renata Kepler—she was a direct descendant of Johannes Kepler, the 16th Century astronomer and mathematician. There were very few women in the graduate courses then. She became my best friend in graduate school. She came from a distinguished family in Kassel, right in the middle of Germany, in the Hesse state.

I don't believe her family were Nazis although she was a Hitler Youth because that's what one did. Kassel was badly bombed but they were able to maintain a place to live. She spent a lot of time as a child, 8 or 9 years old, going along the railroad tracks and picking up coal. She was very smart and very clever. She would forage for fuel and food, and because she was young—she was kind of forward, even fearless—she was able to help maintain the family. She would talk about that excitedly. She actually felt she had kept the family alive, warm and fed. The terrible experiences empowered people, even little girls like her.

I have a Steiff bear in my dining room. Margarete Steiff and her nephew Richard invented the teddy bear more than a hundred years ago. It's a valuable bear. Renata gave it to us for Rebecca when she was born. She had kept it all during the war. That was a huge gift. She gave it to us because she had decided she would never bring a child into this world. She had seen war.

\*\*\*

*The fall of 1961 was a dangerous time for Germany—and the world. The devastated nation was still teeming with armies from four major powers. Two of them, the Soviet Union and the United States, faced off that October in Berlin: lines of opposing tanks staged precariously close to one another, their muzzles pointed at each other in Berlin as the East Germans erected the Berlin Wall. All-out war seemed a slip or a trip away. American soldiers needed to learn to speak a rudimentary German in a hurry.*

\*\*\*

We got to West Germany in September of 1961, right before the Berlin Wall went up. It didn't take the East very long to seal the border between what were then the two countries.

The days were short and it was very cold. Mainz is on the 50th Parallel, very far north, as far up as Newfoundland and Labrador and farther than Mongolia. Our apartment was cold.

We didn't have much money so I went off to seek my fortune. I went to the University of Maryland offices in Mainz and they didn't have anything for me to teach. But they referred me to Weisbaden Air Force Base. I got a job there teaching in-service German classes.

I taught several classes for the Air Force. Some of the students were civilian employees who wanted to learn more German. One class was a unit of pathfinders. These particular pathfinders were radio operators and the only paratroopers in the Air Force at the time. Their job was to go in behind enemy lines and set up radio operations before an invasion. They were kind of a covert group and always doing practice maneuvers in the fields. Farmers would see them parachute in and wonder what was going on. I taught them how to explain to the farmers that they were innocent, that it wasn't an invasion, just maneuvers.

They were a very tough group. They would come to class after a volleyball game all beaten up and broken. But they were putty in my hands because I knew German and they needed to learn.

They all seemed to be from the South. They were scared to death to go to bars outside the immediate area around the base. They were uncomfortable going out into "the economy," which was what they called the German world they'd been assigned to live in. They felt they weren't wanted, which was probably true. I had to help them through that.

I got paid enough to keep us in food. Paul was getting paid by the University of Mainz, which was insufficient. We lived on very little for a long time; we became very good at it.

In February, 1962, all the Fulbrights in West Germany were offered the opportunity to go to Berlin. We gathered in Darmstadt near Frankfurt and headed northeast via the autobahn. Our bus was full of American graduate students, some of them with children.

***

*Now, Charlotte and Paul were to motor into a city where World War III had almost started three short months before.*

*Work on the Berlin Wall had begun in August '61 and the massive project still hadn't been completed by the following February. But the border between the two Germanys already had been effectively sealed. Berlin, itself divided, was surrounded by the Soviet-dominated East Germany.*

*The Wall was known in the East as the* Antifaschistischer Schutzwall *or Anti-Fascist Protection Rampart—the West, in the eyes of the East, being fascist capitalists. Conversely, West Berlin Mayor Willy Brandt, dubbed it "The Wall of Shame." By either name, it closed off the border between the two Berlins. Those wishing to escape to the West often were shot in the back as they leapt, climbed, or otherwise attempted to traverse the barricade.*

*The US had beefed up its military presence in Berlin. A 110-mile long column of US Army personnel in full battle gear had traveled up the Autobahn through East Germany into Berlin during the late summer of '61. After a series of confrontations between East German border guards and Western diplomats trying to enter East Berlin, US and Soviet tanks faced off on either side of the newly-built wall in late October. Only after President Kennedy and Secretary Krushchev had negotiated through back-channels did the Berlin Crisis cool down.*

***

We got to the border of East Germany. A sign said, *Halt! Hier Grenze* (Stop! The Border Is Here.) It was our first encounter with the East.

We all had our passports ready. Our bus driver who was pretty savvy had arranged us in our seats in alphabetical order to make things easier because he knew what an ordeal the crossing could be.

The uniformed guards from the East got on board and told us, *No, you have to be in chronological order by date of birth*. We could see they were just making things up as they went along.

Well, we were there at the crossing for ten hours, with no food or water, just sitting there. We waited for the guards to decide what next thing they could do to harass us. There was nothing we could do. So we moved around the bus and read books and did whatever we could to pass the time.

It was scary.

We finally were allowed to go through on the autobahn. The guards warned us, *Don't stop. No pictures. Don't even look out window too long. Just go straight to your destination.*

We went on to Berlin, not very far, just a three or four-hour ride. Then, when we got to the Berlin border, it took us another 11 hours to pass out of East Germany!

We had a wonderful time in Berlin. It was exhilarating. It was vibrant. It was supercharged. It was an exciting time in West Berlin. Willy Brandt had a special reception for us Fulbrights in city hall. He was the John F. Kennedy of West Germany.

We did go to East Berlin, twice. There were only a couple of places where we could enter the walled-off city. Checkpoint Charlie was one. That's where American and Soviets tanks had faced off in September and October.

We took the U-bahn, the underground railway, to *Friedrichstrasse* and got off the train. We had to check in at a booth to get into East Berlin. That was very scary too.

There were three of us, Paul and I and a friend of ours. We got off the U-bahn train and had to walk through this totally dark station next to unused tracks. There was nothing there! You could hear your footsteps echo.

We crossed over the tracks into a daunting-looking station where we had to deposit our passports through a slot in a window. But we couldn't see the person who took them.

We wondered, "Will we ever get out of here again?"

It took a long while before they processed our passports. Eventually we did get upstairs. East Berlin was pretty desolate.

We went to the Pergamon Museum, one of the major assets of all Berlin. It had an entire Greek temple inside. It had portions of the Wall of Ninevah. It was fantastic.

There were lots of Russians around. One of them asked me for a match, and I understood him! I was so excited about that.

The second time we went into East Berlin, we went to the theater founded by Bertolt Brecht and his wife Helene Weigel. We saw Brecht's anti-Nazi play, *Furcht und Elend des Dritten Reiches* (Fear and Misery of the Third Reich).

Then, of course, we had to go back to Mainz. We all piled back on the bus but this time brought lots and lots of provisions. We were prepared for another siege and that was a good decision because it was another 10, 11 hours to get out of Berlin and into East Germany and the same thing to get back out of East Germany and into West Germany.

So we spent several days on that bus. We were being treated arbitrarily. Totalitarians can do whatever they want. It made me realize rule of law matters.

***

*Both Charlotte's parents had come from long lines of Germans. Still, she had a lot to learn about Germans. And she didn't particularly like what she found out—or how it made her feel.*

***

There's nothing but German in my bloodlines.

Our whole year in Germany, the people we met kept accusing me of being German. I spoke good German and my name was Zietlow. I would tell them I was an American but they didn't buy it. They said, "In your heart, you're German."

We disappointed the Germans a number of times. They thought I was German and therefore should know the rules. The rules included things like *Never drink water while you eat cucumbers.* Things like that; lots of 'em!

It was not pleasant. They didn't just say, calmly, "You know, you really shouldn't eat cucumbers with water." It was, "Don't do that! I'm going to take your cucumber out of your hand if you continue to do it!"

It was a command. It was annoying. I felt hemmed in by it.

They were used to rules that were arbitrary and unfounded. And they just drove us crazy. I really got to be anti-German while we were there. I developed a *post*judice as opposed to a *pre*judice.

I feel that's unreasonable and I should get over it. I'm trying. But I sure felt it! I thought, "These people are impossible!" They were so hidebound and they were very angry with us on several occasions.

We planned to go to France at Christmas time. We had a friend living in Montpelier in a big apartment. He invited us and we thought it would be exciting. We would drive down through France to Montpelier, way down on the Mediterranean in our little red Beetle.

Our German acquaintances said, "Ugh, you're going to France. It's dirty. The food is terrible. It'll be really expensive. The French are impossible. Christmas is a German holiday; you're betraying your heritage. What's the matter with you?"

I would say, "No, no, no. We're not German."

So, we went to France. It was a wonderful trip. We had a great time. We had all sorts of terrific experiences, including staying at our friend's unheated apartment. He hadn't told us about that when he invited us.

On the way down, we drove along the Rhone and passed through Avignon and Arles. We stayed in a little *auberge* in Besançon. We ate there and the food was superb! There were several courses and they brought out this basket with 20 different cheeses in it. And it wasn't very expensive.

Then, the next day we were in the mountains. It was 30 degrees Fahrenheit and there was frost on everything so it was all kind of shimmery and sparkly. The sun was shining and it was magical.

We went down through a small town that had an outdoor market where they sold fresh oysters and then went into Montpelier.

When we headed back, we went up through Dordogne and went to see Lascaux. These caves with the Upper Paleolithic-era drawings of horses had just recently been discovered. It was just a few days after Christmas and the little town was deserted. But we found a young man who took us down into the caves so we actually saw the drawings!

Then we drove up to Paris where we spent several days before we went back into Germany. It was a great trip.

When we got back to Mainz, our German acquaintances all said, "Wasn't that awful?"

So how does this happen? How do all these groups of people say you can't eat cucumbers while drinking water? Or, France is horrible, if you're a German, you belong in Germany during Christmas?

It happens because so many of the people grew up with this whole set of rules or traditions that had become sacrosanct.

I started saying to them, "Why do you do that? Why wouldn't you drink water with cucumbers? Does any of that make sense? I don't think it makes sense so I'm going to drink water with my cucumbers; watch me and see what happens!"

While the people were very nice to us and very welcoming, I just got the sense that I could not live in Germany. I hadn't been sure how I felt about Germans but now I knew—and I didn't like 'em.

I've had trouble getting over that.

Several years ago, Paul and I hosted an ambassadorial scholar from Germany. Her trip here was sponsored by Rotary International. She was a pianist. We invited her to come over and play the piano. She did that a lot. Paul was retired by then and he and she struck up real friendship. I would be off working and he would be here listening to her play and he loved it. She helped me get over my distaste for Germans a little bit.

I lot of the young Germans I've met since Mainz aren't quite the same as the old hidebound ones. I'm really leaving that behind me.

\*\*\*

*After the 1961-62 school year and before returning to America, Charlotte and Paul traveled east and south—to the "cradle of democracy"—in their little red Beetle. Their life together would never be the same after that trip.*

\*\*\*

In the spring we decided we would drive to Greece. We went through Vienna and the rest of Austria and then down through Zagreb and Belgrade. Yugoslavia was an eye-opener; it was in such bad shape, poor and depressing. We ended up spending three weeks in Greece.

We came down through Thessaloniki and down that coast. Larisa and then Athens. We went to Corinth and to Delphi and way over to Pilos and to Olympia. We went to the bottom of the Peloponnesus. It was one interesting adventure after another.

And I got pregnant.

By that time we had made up our minds. I was 27.

\*\*\*

*Later that summer, the Zietlows returned to Ann Arbor and the University of Michigan. Charlotte continued work in her Linguistics graduate program and tutored graduate students studying French and German. Paul worked on his PhD and was bumped up to a lecturer position with a raise in pay.*

\*\*\*

We had a good friend who just could not handle German or French. He was very smart, a really capable person. He'd been in the Navy, but he just got all crazy when it came to foreign languages. He couldn't do it!

I found that was true of a lot of the graduate students.

I became a tutor for a lot of them. Mostly I held their hands and soothed them—"Let's just find the verb. Then we'll find the subject." Just enough to erase some of their fears and get them through their language exams. That's all it was; they had psychological blocks.

I earned some money tutoring so that worked out really well.

Paul had been given something more than a teaching fellowship. It offered more money and some benefits, but he had to make the commitment to finish his doctor's degree. He decided to do it when we were in Europe. He had been wavering.

So we had a little bit more money. He went back to school in Ann Arbor and we rented a garage that had been converted into a little cottage.

\*\*\*

*Almost as soon as Charlotte and Paul came back home, events in the Caribbean, in Washington, and in Moscow threatened to explode. Liter-*

*ally. The Cuban Missile Crisis dominated everyone's thoughts. Soviet nu-clear-tipped missiles had been deployed in Cuba and aimed at key cities in the United States. America threatened to invade Cuba, the Soviet Union insisted on building more missile sites on the island nation, and an angry Fidel Castro urged Nikita Krushchev to launch a nuclear at-tack on this country.*

***

We had come back from Europe. I was pregnant with Rebecca. And this time we had a car, the little red Beetle. We brought it back from Germany.

Now, we were right outside of Detroit. It would have been a target. We knew that. So, the question was, "What do we do about this?"

I kept thinking, "Just let this baby be born."

Paul, always level-headed, said, "Charlotte, we can't do anything about it. Just go about your normal life."

But it didn't even make sense to stock up on water and food. We would be obliterated right in our own home!

We went about our normal business. One day, during the worst of it, I got a phone call from a woman I'd been working with in the De-mocratic Party. She was married to one of Paul's professors. She was hysterical. We talked for a long time.

I said, "We can't do anything about this. We don't know what's go-ing to happen. Just take a deep breath and try to go on."

She asked me if she should make dinner. I said, "Make dinner. I'm going to make dinner."

She said, "I don't know if we'll make it that far!"

I said, "I don't either, but we should behave as if we will have dinner tonight." I think I talked her down. Then I went to the refrigerator and opened it. I thought, "Should I make dinner?"

We had a hanging lamp in the kitchen. It was a glass globe with a lightbulb in it. While I was standing there in front of the open refriger-ator, the globe slipped out of its setting—I don't know why; maybe it got too hot. The glass exploded and a shard sliced my face. It wasn't deep enough for stitches but I bled.

I thought, "Well that's it. I'm making dinner. I can't manage this war but I could have screwed that globe in better!"

There it was. Right there at home I could have been killed or badly hurt. It was an object lesson. I was worried about global things and then the little things go wrong. So why bother about the global things?

The same kind of thing happened just the year before, when I was bridesmaid for my cousin Rosemary. I was going to fly out to Montclair, New Jersey. I hadn't flown in years and years. I was nervous about it. I was going to fly on a Thursday. I was on my bicycle, riding along and worrying about flying in a couple of hours that afternoon when the front brake calipers came loose and fell into the spokes. I was thrown from the bicycle and hit my head. They rushed me to the university health center. I had a concussion. I had to stay overnight.

It was the same thing—I was worrying about flying and here I got hurt on a bike! It was a lesson: Don't worry about the big things when you should be taking care of the little things.

***

*The Cuban Missile Crisis was resolved peacefully. Two months later Charlotte's baby was born.*

***

I had natural childbirth with Rebecca. We'd spent our last month in Europe in Paris where the Lamaze technique was the generally accepted method of childbirth. There were ads in the Métro for it. I read a lot about Lamaze, and an English obstetrician, Grantly Dick-Read. He'd written a big book, *Childbirth without Fear*. I still have that book. They had a different attitude toward childbirth in Europe. We had much more a medical approach in America. I decided I was going to go the European way.

I found a good coach in Ann Arbor. Rebecca was born in the women's hospital where they really loved to give spinal blocks. I wanted nothing. My coach kind of held the doctors off. Rebecca was born quite readily.

My obstetrician had been a tight end for the Detroit Lions. He was very good at catching passes. And when Rebecca was born, he caught her like a football—that's how Paul and I imagined it.

*\*\**

*Charlotte may have learned to accept the vicissitudes of global events. She continued to take care of the little things. Her life went on. But the world has a way of intruding. Her heart was broken one November afternoon.*

*\*\**

I was upstairs in our garage cottage. I was babysitting Jesse Buck. Our old friend Whitney Buck had married a woman who had this little boy just before we left for Germany. Jesse was downstairs where the TV was on. He called up to me, "Charlotte! Charlotte! The president's been shot!"

I said, very calmly, "Now, Jesse. That's not possible. You just didn't see that right."

I still feel terrible to this day. All the hope, all the excitement—everything sort of stopped.

LBJ was unsavory and a boor but he would have been a great president if one ignores Vietnam. He did great things. I worked for him, knocked on doors out on Hartstrait Road in '64. He was elected but it wasn't as exciting as 1960. Then came Medicare, Medicaid, one thing after another. The War on Poverty. Terrific. What would we have done without those things? He knew how to deal with Congress. He was a very good politician in the best sense of the word. He was good at rounding up votes and talking people into things and getting his way without making them feel bad.

I would say, that's a good politician and politicians are not bad. Politics is messy. It's inefficient. But it's bringing different ideas and people together to try to get something done. Now we have 300 million people, all of 'em different. That's why I continue to work.

\*\*\*

*As the year 1963 drew to a close, Charlotte had finished two of the three preliminary exams she needed to complete before becoming an official doctoral candidate. Paul, meanwhile, was still working on his dissertation.*

*The Zietlows had been living together in Ann Arbor for more than seven years. Charlotte was certain the future held some surprises for the couple. In December, Paul attended the Modern Language Association job market in Chicago. He met recruiters from university English departments from all over the country. One of those meetings turned out to be a life-changer for him and Charlotte.*

\*\*\*

We weren't going to stay in Michigan for the rest of our lives. We were going to go to some really wonderful, exciting place, and Paul would have a terrific job, no doubt somewhere way outside of the Midwest.

I'd lived in Minnesota, Wisconsin, and Michigan—maybe we'll get to go someplace exotic.

He went to the MLA and came back with the most exciting invitations. The University of North Carolina was very interested in him. Illinois offered him a job. But then, he was invited to visit this one university.

The English Department there was vibrant. The university was growing. Paul said the department was vital and fresh, as opposed to a lot of the other departments in the country that were kind of traditional.

He'd talked to people at this university who said when they got an idea to teach something else, they could do it. Sure, there were some old guard still around who held on dearly to their Shakespeare classes but there were a lot of young faculty. It looked like an interesting place for him to be.

So he took the job... in Bloomington. Burrowed deep in southern Indiana. It sounded like the end of the world.

That's what I'd heard. I thought, "Now, we're going to this godforsaken place?"

But Paul was very excited about it and so we came.

# 7

# There's So Much We Don't Understand

*Charlotte and Paul settled in Bloomington. The town in 1964 boasted a population of about 35,000. Although it was not part of the South, the town was home to plenty of folks who might have felt awfully comfortable in Little Rock or Selma.*

*Just four years earlier, Indiana University had elected its first African American student body president, Thomas Atkins, who'd go on to earn his law degree at Harvard University, would serve on the Boston City Council, and would represent the NAACP as general counsel. The year he was elected study body president, Atkins also got married, although he and his wife had to cross the state line into Michigan to do so; interracial marriage was against the law in Indiana. In the wake of Atkins' election, a crowd of white students had marched throughout the campus, waving Confederate flags. Perhaps Charlotte was right—Bloomington indeed seemed to be "a godforsaken place."*

*Yet, underneath the hatred and the bluster there existed hope for someone like Charlotte, When the anti-Atkins marchers passed the sole women's dormitory on campus they were pelted with nail polish bottles, shoes, and other missiles. It would take Charlotte a few years to uncover the power that resided within the women and people of goodwill in Bloomington.*

\*\*\*

Rebecca and I came down here to look for housing in June of '64. We drove to St. Louis first, to visit my parents, and then we headed east through Illinois and into Indiana. That was a pretty drive, starting in Terre Haute on State Road 46. I began to feel a little bit better about the move. Driving through Spencer, I thought, "Well, at least they have hills around here."

I was seven months pregnant with Nathan when we moved down here.

We found an unfurnished house for rent in the Sunny Slopes neighborhood. It was the first time we'd lived in a place that was originally meant to be lived in. It was nice: airy and light, with huge windows. We had a great big backyard that was fenced in so Rebecca could run around in it.

The university was really booming at the time. There was a lot of construction going on around the campus. The English Department had ten new members, including Paul, that year. For him, it was a really exciting thing.

The Tulip Tree high-rise dorm had just been built. It was the tallest, biggest building in town. Right across from that were all these temporary buildings, put up right after World War II, these little apartments to accommodate returning GIs. There was a village of green trailers between 14th and 17th streets, also temporary housing. A lot of graduate students and some young faculty lived there.

So we thought we were really lucky. We had three little bedrooms and a bathroom and a nice living room and a kitchen that looked out over the greenery. It was pretty.

Except that we were all the way on the edge of town. There were no sidewalks. And we had one little Beetle.

To get to Sunny Slopes, we would come in on Winslow and High streets. That whole area was undeveloped. No sidewalks, no storm sewers, none of that.

I thought: This is really a sleepy town. It didn't have the amenities that even the tiny little villages in Wisconsin and Minnesota had. We really hadn't known what we were getting into.

There were very few restaurants, only one that was really good. Sully's Oaken Bucket. It was on the square.

The square itself was dismal. A lot of stores that were closed or closing and a lot of storefronts that were not in good condition. Kahn's Men's Store was pretty good but it had a grumpy owner. There were two or three drug stores. Kresge and Woolworth. Thrasher Hardware, which had wooden floors and the clerks would take you up and down the aisles. Tovey's and Smith's shoe stores. And Vogue, an upscale woman's clothing store. They had hats. I bought a white felt hat there in about 1970. It was perfect; a really good hat. That started me on hats. Once you've got one, you have to have more.

There was a small store where they sold some records. In February, it was Paul's birthday, and the store was having a sale, two records for the price of one. I found two Deutsche Grammaphone records, classical music, and brought them up to the front. The clerk told me, "No, you can't buy both of these."

I said, "Why? It's two for the price of one!"

"Yes. But if you buy these two, we won't have any more of them."

I finally talked him into selling me the records.

Kahn's was fairly large. They sold sort of a middling style of men's clothes. We had a friend who also was new to Bloomington that fall. He told us he bought Jockey shorts at Kahn's when he arrived. He really liked their fit and so he went back to get some more. The owner told him, "We don't carry them anymore."

He said, "That's too bad. They were really nice."

"Yeah, everybody liked them. There was so much demand and it took so much time to re-order them that we just discontinued carrying them."

That was a common mentality among the shopkeepers here.

So that was downtown. There wasn't much; it was a pokey downtown. Not only couldn't we buy things, but we were limited in what groceries we could buy. On Walnut Street, there was the A&P and there was Feris Market. On East 3rd Street, there was Bartlett's. You could go to Feris or Bartlett and order a leg of lamb but you would not find one at the A&P. Feris and Bartlett's delivered and they ran tabs. They catered to well-to-do people and fraternities and sororities. Feris was known for good meat and Bartlett's for good service. When we wanted to be really fancy, we went to Feris or Bartlett's.

We couldn't buy things. We couldn't go out to eat. So lots of people cooked and there were lots and lots of dinner parties among our new friends in the English Department. We had some friends who'd also come down from Ann Arbor who were really serious cooks. I had always cooked. We ended up preparing a lot of complicated meals together. There was a tremendous amount of entertaining at different homes. People here were very hospitable and welcoming. English was one of the larger departments here, filled with smart, interesting people from all over the country. They formed a sort of sub-group within the IU community that lasted for a long, long time.

I cooked with such zeal that, eventually, a couple of people became afraid to invite us over. I asked one of them why they didn't have us over. The wife said, "Oh, you're such a good cook. I don't want to cook for you. I'll never be that good!" That was embarrassing.

Still, it was a hard adjustment, being a faculty wife, which was totally new to me. You know, you'd go to the faculty wives club but I just wasn't ready to settle for coffee and tea. There were a bunch of very smart, interesting women in that group, but that aspect of their personalities didn't emerge much. Eventually I got to know them and appreciate them, but it was slow.

I was working on my dissertation. There was another woman, Mary Ellen Brown, who was working on hers. Otherwise, the faculty wives were not in academia. Our friends who'd moved down here from Ann Arbor were in the German Department. I could talk German with them.

Meanwhile, I had my cooking coterie. Mary Ellen Brown and I candied violets. I'd always been interested in cooking but that first year here in Bloomington I got into cooking more and more.

One of our friends from Ann Arbor, Karl Magnuson, was a very good cook. Karl was a very, very smart guy. He was a pianist. He'd entered the Michigan music department as a performer but then he got really interested in German poetry so he transferred into the German Department there.

Karl had a male partner. They were the first gay couple we'd ever had anything to do with. It was never mentioned that they were gay; it just was, that's all. The two of them cooked a lot.

The three of us would get together and do a lot of serious cooking. We made *galantine*, where you bone a duck and try to remake its original form by filling it with a chicken. We did stuff like that.

I went to Indianapolis and bought snails. I got home with this big brown bag full of them and looked snails up in *The Joy of Cooking*. I put them in the refrigerator but I didn't tie the bag. And so we had snails crawling all over inside our refrigerator! It turned out to be a three-day process to get them ready to eat. By that time we were tired of the idea of snails. I would never have done something like that except I was bored.

In September, Nathan was born. Here we were, in Bloomington, Indiana, only three months, not sure where we were quite yet. We're living on a street that doesn't have any sidewalks. It's the end of the Earth. We can't buy anything, and there's one obstetrician in town, Dr. Charles McClary.

He was very traditional and our friends who'd gotten to know us well enough told us they didn't think we'd want to go to him. I wanted natural childbirth again and our friends knew that wouldn't happen with him. He shared an office with two other general practitioners, both of whom I'd seen since we'd arrived in June. They were all open-minded.

My whole thing was, *I would like to do this my way, the Lamaze method. And I don't want you to get in the way*. I asked them, "Do you agree to that?"

They all said, grumble, grumble, grumble..., "as long as nothing out of the ordinary happens." But they all stressed: *Do not go to the hospital until you absolutely have to.*

***

*In Bloomington, there were no Lamaze coaches but Charlotte had kept all her Lamaze literature and manuals from her pregnancy with Rebecca and so went it alone when her second child was ready to come into the world.*

***

I was never inside Bloomington Hospital until the day Nathan was born. He was quite late. He was born two weeks after his due date.

One morning I woke up—it was a Friday—and something was going on in my body. So we took Rebecca over to some friends' and then I went to McClary and he said, "Well, I think you may be beginning to go into labor but it's going to be a while. Just go home. Come back when you feel something's different. Come here to the office."

Paul and I went back to the house and watched television. I lay on the rug and he massaged my back while I drank A&W root beer. About three in the afternoon I thought, "Yeah, something's changing." So we went back to McClary's office.

He checked me and said, "I'll race you to the hospital!"

This was like four, four-thirty. There were train crossings between his office and the hospital and, of course, there was a train at what is now the B-Line trail. It was the Monon Railroad at the time.

Fortunately, I was carrying my big Lamaze card that showed the various stages of breathing. On the other side, it read, "Leave me alone—I'm busy!"

Finally we got to the hospital and it was a mess. Construction everywhere. Paul dropped me off at the entrance and then went off to park the car. I kind of waddled in, huffing and puffing, and somebody pointed me toward the right elevator. He said, "Just follow these lines and go to the top floor."

I got to the labor room, which was about as big as my living room, with five or six beds in it and they were full. The nurses wanted to do things to me but I said, "No, no. Just leave me alone. I can do this!"

McClary showed up and I told him once again things were changing inside me. They wheeled me into the delivery room—about the size of my front hall—and, sure enough, Nathan was born twenty minutes later. Just like that!

Meanwhile, this is five-thirty on a Friday afternoon, pay day. There'd been a big fight down on the Levee—that's what people called the street running next to the Monon line—at a workingman's bar on the on the corner of 9th and Morton, Covington's.

Paul had parked the car and, when he came in the hospital, he was totally confused. He had no idea where to go or what to do. Someone took pity on him and asked him what he was doing and then steered him to the right place. Amazingly, the emergency room was right next to the delivery room—on the top floor!

So there were a bunch of bloody guys in the emergency room and a lot of policemen. Some woman who Paul later told me looked like Mammy Yokum walked up to him. He looked tidy; he didn't look like somebody who'd been in a fight so she thought he might be somebody in authority. She said, "Tell me what's goin' on here! My old man was s'pposed to be out groundhog huntin' and now he got all these cuts all over his face!"

Of course, Paul had no idea what was going on. He'd only find out later.

In the middle of all this, came a nurse with a bloody baby in her arms, elbowing her way through the crowd, saying to various men, "Are you Zietlow?"

Paul raised his hand and she walked up to him and said, "This is your son."

Then she went through the crowd to the nursery down the hall and cleaned up Nathan. McClary came out not too long afterward and told Paul, "That was just great! I've never done a delivery like that before.

Wonderful! A birth in a million." And Paul was still wondering what all was going on around that floor.

They rolled me out on a gurney and the first person I saw was a policeman who said, "Are you Charlotte?"

I said, "Yeah."

He said, "I hear you done good!" And he clapped me on the shoulder.

I was thinking, "Where in the world are we?"

They wheeled me to a waiting room that had been converted to a bedroom for two because they were short of space. It was chaotic. It seemed just a terrible place to have a baby. But we were all healthy. And here we were in southern Indiana.

I wasn't going to stay here the rest of my life.

\*\*\*

*Nevertheless, Charlotte found things that drew her into Bloomington life. Plus, she had her own studies to attend to. She'd soon discover the Gothic version of St. Paul's Epistles to the Romans would be her ticket to a doctorate.*

\*\*\*

I was working on my final doctoral prelim. I would go several mornings a week to the old library at Franklin Hall. This was before the Wells Library was built. There were pigeons flying around upstairs on the top floor, in the rafters, and there I was, studying.

When I passed my third prelim I had two small children and I was hundreds of miles from my doctoral adviser, William Bennett, Distinguished Professor of German Linguistics at the University of Michigan.

I was really interested in historical linguistics and had done a fair amount of study in some Germanic languages: Gothic and Old High German and Middle High German, Low Franconian and Old Norse. I'd studied applied linguistics—techniques, syntax, morphemes and phonemes and phonetics. I'd taken Sanskrit and Old Church Slavonic and Proto-Romance, Greek and Latin and the reconstruction of Indo-

European, which I just found fascinating. I was good at it. I had good instincts for how languages worked.

Dr. Bennett really liked me and he decided I should make the earliest extant manuscripts of St. Paul's Epistles to the Romans available to scholars without them having to go through what I would have to do to read them. It was a wonderful topic because it was manageable. There was a beginning and there was an end to the project. And there was a context to put it in. So that became my dissertation.

The Codex Ambrosianus, a manuscript of Epistles to the Romans, was in Milan, Italy. It is a palimpsest, meaning it's been physically altered, many times, over the centuries. It was originally written on vellum. In the twelfth century, the vellum was scraped with pumice, turned upside down and written over in Latin. Then, in the eighteenth century in Germany it was painted with tincture of nutgall which brought out the iron-based ink and made the Gothic a bit more legible, but soon began to corrode the vellum. The manuscript was then painted with gelatin to stop the corrosion. So in the 20th Century when ultraviolet rays were used to read the Gothic under the Latin the whole page fluoresced, making it unreadable.

Only in the 1930s did some German photographers use infra-red photography to bring out the Gothic again.

It was these photographs that I was asked to read critically, noting every jot and tittle, lettered by letter, to provide an accurate reading of the Gothic. The photographs were available in a large, rare book, and this was the basis of my painstaking, eye-straining research.

That became my dissertation. I finished it in 1969. I was awarded a PhD from the University of Michigan. My very distinguished doctoral committee could not read Gothic. I was, effectively, the only person in the world who could read the text critically.

***

*The 1960s were a time of domestic upheaval in America that threatened to descend into all-out war. Charlotte would learn a lot about Indi-*

*ana and both she and Paul would eventually learn that politics can frac-
ture even the warmest friendships.*

***

The Sixties were complicated here. We had all these things going on: civil rights—we were really conscious of that; the Great Society—that was wonderful. One day I opened the *Louisville Courier-Journal* and saw Medicare and Medicaid had been approved by Congress. President Johnson did a number of wonderful things. I was excited by all this and then, not too much longer after Medicare and Medicaid came the Gulf of Tonkin incident.

I was getting mixed signals, hearing more and more about the insidious disease of Vietnam and running head-on into racism here in Bloomington.

One afternoon, early on, I took the children out for lunch. Rebecca was two and Nathan was three or four months old. We went to the Dog 'n Suds, where the Village Deli is now.

We sat down and I got the kids all organized. There was a couple sitting in the next booth, a black man and a white woman. My antenna was up; I got the sense that something was wrong. They were looking around and trying to get the attention of the waiter but he ignored them.

The waiter came right over to me and the kids and took care of us. He took my order, went back in the kitchen, brought the food out to us, and the couple still had not been served.

I called him back over. "Those people," I whispered, nodding in the couple's direction, "I think they need you."

He glanced over at them and said, "Well, I'll talk to my manager."

Immediately I understood what was going on.

I said, "Can't you just take their order?"

Again he said, "I'll talk to my manager."

I gestured toward Rebecca and Nathan and, still whispering, said, "I'll tell you what. I'll just sit here with my children until those people are taken care of. And if they have to sit here too long, they may start screaming. So I hope you'll take care of them."

The couple got waited on and the kids and I sat there until they were finished with their lunch. I was really upset by it all. I didn't want to embarrass the couple so I did my best not to let them know what I was doing but, inside, I was ready for a fight.

I went home and I called my new friend Marion Gottfried, the wife of a professor in the English Department. She eventually got on the County Council and was a wise woman. I told her what had happened. I said, "Marion, what's going on in this town?"

"Charlotte," she said, "welcome to the South."

We had a good friend from the English Department in Ann Arbor named Cesar Blake. He came down here as a guest lecturer and he wanted to see Bloomington. He was dapper and handsome, very elegant. He was a light-skinned black guy.

The Sunrise Tavern, over on North Rogers Street, about where the Cook Clinic is now, had country music and we'd been there a few times. We thought we'd take Cesar there and really show him Bloomington. There was nothing like it in Ann Arbor.

We walked in with him—and the place stopped dead. Every head turned toward us and stared. He said, in a very quiet voice, "I don't think we should stay here."

We turned around and got out of there. It was clearly the wrong place to take him. Very, very palpably the wrong place to take him.

I thought, "We really are in the South."

That taught me a lot about Bloomington that I didn't want to know.

Years later things had changed but not as much as we would have liked. When I ran for Congress Vi Taliaferro accompanied me to campaign events.

*** 

*Vi was married to George Taliaferro, a legendary running back for the IU Hoosiers football team. He was a three-time College Football All-*

*American selection and was the first African-American player ever drafted by a National Football League team. Vi went on to become the first African-American circuit court judge in Monroe County history. Between the two of them, they'd seen plenty of changes in race relations and civil rights. But those changes were slow in coming.*

*When Charlotte ran for Congress in 1974, Vi often drove her to campaign stops.*

\*\*\*

Vi and I went to coffees and met with supporters all around the district. One day I had a meeting in Ellettsville. I told her where we were going to go. She looked at me, silent for a minute. Finally she said, "I am not stopping in Ellettsville, Charlotte!" She didn't need to explain why.

\*\*\*

*Beginning in the summer of 1965 and for the next several years, the Standard Oil company funded a program for English teachers at predominantly black colleges in the South to come to Indiana University for continuing education.*

*In the Sixties, many corporations either funded or helped administer special educational programs in inner cities, poor rural parts of the country, and at colleges and universities. The companies were eager to get in on the public-private partnerships that President Johnson's Great Society had called for.*

\*\*\*

The English Department asked Paul to teach in the program. He was happy to do it. Most of the participants from the black colleges were women. Paul's job was to teach them how to teach English. The women stayed in dorms while they were here in the summer. During the winter, Paul would take short trips down South for follow-up. He got a stipend and an allowance for entertainment.

There weren't a lot of places we could go to have a good time with our mixed group. We ended up having people over or going to other people's houses for dinner. The English Department had rented the home of its chair, Sam Barber, who was traveling for the summer, for the visiting black teachers to do some entertaining. It was a wonderful house off Sare Road. It had a big living room. It had a concrete slab foundation, which was good because there was a lot of dancing there.

One afternoon some of the teachers from the South were at our house. I was changing Nathan's diapers. One of the teachers was with me and I extolled the diaper service we were using. "That must be wonderful to have a diaper service," she said.

She added, "Of course, we can't have that. There's no diaper service for us. Diaper services are only for white babies."

I thought, "There's so much we don't understand." So many insults. The teachers talked quite frankly, not even bitterly, just matter-of-factly about the way things were in the South. It was a revelation.

One winter, Paul travelled to Jackson State College in Tennessee. For his return, I went to the airport early and I sat at the bar, like all the other people waiting for flights to come in or for theirs to depart.

The bartender told me I couldn't sit there. I was a woman and state law said women couldn't sit at a bar. They had to sit at a table. So there was another insight into Indiana.

Another time, Paul flew out to South Carolina State University in Orangeburg. Paul taught a class there and met with some participants in the program.

During his time there, he realized he could tell how high up people were in the hierarchy by the color of their skin. The president of the school was very light-skinned. He could almost pass for white. The deans were a little darker. The chairs, darker still. Then came the faculty and the clerical staff. By the time you got to the groundskeepers, they were the darkest of all.

Paul found it nauseating. He told me he actually got sick and vomited on the green-painted lawn when it all hit him.

***

*A couple of years later, in February, 1968, hundreds of South Carolina State students and demonstrators marched on a segregated bowling alley and held rallies on campus, protesting the owner's refusal to allow blacks in the place. Over the course of several days, the protests became heated and the governor ordered in the National Guard. On February 8th, protesters lit a bonfire on campus. Highway patrol officers moved in with firefighters and one of them was hit by a thrown bottle. The officers responded by firing into the crowd, killing three and wounding 27 others. The incident became known as the Orangeburg Massacre.*

\*\*\*

A third winter, Paul was in Tuscaloosa, Alabama, visiting the teachers at Stillman College. When he came home he was very excited. He said, "I heard this incredible young man speaking to the students and the faculty. He was effective and he was very much against the honkies."

It was Stokely Carmichael.

\*\*\*

*At the time, Carmichael was head of the Student Non-violent Coordinating Committee (SNCC). He'd been a Freedom Rider in 1961. He'd go on to become a leader of the Black Panther Party and, still later, an advocate for pan-African nationalism.*

\*\*\*

Then we began to see changes. We saw the shift from "Negro" to "Black." A couple of years into the program, teachers from the South were beginning to say, "Why do we have to learn your English?" That signaled the eventual demise of the program. But we all learned a lot from it, and we had a good time with our new friends.

\*\*\*

*By the late Sixties, now a doctoral candidate, Charlotte returned to teaching. The Indiana University German Department offered her a job teaching a course.*

\*\*\*

In the fall of 1966, I had been told by my friends there that the German Department needed a Gothic scholar, a linguist. Well, I was perfect for it! So I wrote a letter to the department chair and told him I was interested. I listed my good credentials from the University of Michigan, which was one of the leading centers of both Germanic and linguistic scholarship in the country. I added I'd taught for six years and that my dissertation director was this world-famous leading scholar, William Bennet.

I sent the letter in the fall and didn't hear anything in response for months and months. In early April, 1967, Paul found a memo in his box, very informal, from the department chair reading, "Tell Charlotte we're trying to find something for her." It was like leaving a message on a Post-it scrap.

It was one of those awakenings, of which I've had several in my life. Being a woman—and being a wife—puts you in a special class: disposable, dismissible, not worth paying attention to. So that wasn't a very good start to my career at Indiana University.

Eventually, in late April, the chair of the department called and said they had this class that they needed to have taught in the fall: The History and Structure of German. It was a graduate class required for all Literature and all Linguistics majors. They offered me a little bit of money—$300—to teach the class.

I agreed to do it and spent all summer working on it. I tried to figure out how to make the course understandable. There was a kind of standard way of teaching it. I decided to start with phonetics because there are a lot of sound shifts in the historical development of modern languages. Some dialects had sound shifts and other ones didn't, for example. It's almost like mutation in biology. Languages have their own Darwinism.

If the students saw how these things worked the whole thing might make sense. Teaching it that way would be very uncommon. I don't know if anybody else did it but it made sense to me. I taught it that way and got rave reviews. In fact, there are people here in town right now who started out as Literature majors and then became Linguistics majors as a result of taking that class I taught.

During the semester, I went to the department chair and said, "So, this is going really well. What about next semester?"

He mumbled something. I could make out: "Well, I don't know."

Eventually, he got back to me and offered me two sections, five hours apiece, in third-year conversational German.

I said, "Okay, will you pay me twice as much, then?"

"No."

I balked at that. He raised the original pay by $75.

I thought a lot about it and decided to do it. But again, I guess I'm just not good at doing what everybody else does. Most teachers walk into the class and start talking about the weather but I didn't think that was very efficient. You want to make the language really matter to the students.

What I did was find something meaningful to talk about. I used Nietzsche. We read several of Nietzsche's works because even though his concepts were hard to understand, he used language repetitively and his constructions weren't difficult. So while we were studying the ideas of Nietzsche, trying to understand his concepts, and talking about them in German, we were really mastering the language.

It worked well.

Toward the end of the semester I went in to talk to the department chair and he said, "What you're doing is brilliant! I've never heard of it before."

Later, he circulated a memo, letting the department in on this great idea he had. "We're going to have two kinds of faculty," he wrote. "The first will be required to publish and they have to serve on committees but they won't have to teach much. They'll be our tenure-track faculty. Then we'll have a non-tenure-track faculty. We won't worry if they publish. We won't have them on committees. But they'll teach—a lot. Many, many hours. And we'd like to thank Charlotte Zietlow and Charlotte Ghurye (who, like me, was a faculty wife who also had a non-tenure teaching job) for serving in this capacity already."

The next time he saw me he asked, "What do you think?"

I told him what I thought. I thought it was scab labor. Now it's become the main way universities work. Then, the idea was just beginning to spread.

"But Charlotte! We did this for you!"

I said, "No you didn't. You did it for you! I'm not going to teach under those circumstances. I'm a professional. But students will ask me for a reference and I won't be able to do anything for them because I'll have no status. I won't do it!"

He said, "I'm just so shocked. I can't believe it."

I closed the door behind me and went home and thought: "I'm not finished with my dissertation and I'm not going to spend the rest of my life thinking it's undone. So I'm going to finish it."

And I decided I wasn't going to pursue a career in teaching any longer, at IU for sure.

I set things up so I could take Rebecca to pre-school, come home and put Nathan down for his nap, and then I'd go to work for two hours in the basement. Gradually, gradually, gradually, I would get my dissertation done. And I did so.

The chair called me a week before the start of the fall, 1968, semester was to start. He said, "We really need you. We've got three sections of German 101 to fill. Five-hour classes. We'll give you $400." With no benefits.

I was still so angry and offended that I didn't call him back with my answer until three days into to semester. I told him no. That was it.

***

*Even as Charlotte grappled with issues affecting her personally, the problems of the world at large continued to bedevil Bloomington and the university.*

***

In April,1968, there was a gas explosion in the city of Richmond, Indiana. The downtown blew up. This was right after Martin Luther King had been killed and the riots that followed. People heard about the explosion and thought the worst. Then we had the presidential primary, which was very important and very divisive here.

\*\*\*

*Even at staid Indiana University in quiet Bloomington, students, faculty, administrators, and townies argued vehemently over the Vietnam War, women's rights, civil rights—anything, really. It was a time for arguing.*

*In May, 50 black students sat down on the cinder track inside 10th Street Stadium, preventing the start of the Little 500 bicycle race, a Bloomington tradition drawing thousands of spectators annually. The protesters demanded that the fraternities sponsoring racing teams promise to desegregate. Twenty of the frats immediately pledged to do so and when the remaining four hesitated, the black students threatened to shut down the race altogether. Three of the recalcitrant brotherhoods grudgingly agreed to terms and the fourth simply dropped out of the race rather than promise to allow blacks within their midst.*

*In December, white supremacists firebombed the Black Market, an arts and crafts shop operated by African American students and faculty a block west of the campus main gate.*

\*\*\*

1968 was a bad year altogether. The Tet Offensive. At one point in April, right after Martin Luther King was shot, the city of Richmond blew up—there'd been a gas explosion. It was like all hell was breaking loose.

The university was falling apart. There was a lot of turmoil at the top of the administration. There'd been a quick succession of presidents following Elvis Stahr, who was in charge when we arrived. Then we had all the unrest and the tension between the faculty and the students and civil rights and Vietnam.

The English Department was quite torn: "How radical are you?" and "You're not radical enough; you're still teaching classes!"

This had been coming for a few years. When we were in Ann Arbor, we sat in a room with Tom Hayden. He'd just finished writing the Port

Huron Statement, the manifesto of the Students for a Democratic Society (SDS). He was sitting at a desk up on a platform, pointing at different people in the audience, saying you shouldn't be teaching while all these horrible things are going on, you should be doing this, you should be doing that. He was playing God. I couldn't stand him.

At Indiana, some professors would say, "If you even talk about politics, you shouldn't be here because this is a sober university that teaches Shakespeare." There was a lot of tension and the English Department was quite lively.

The political stuff was getting intense everywhere. President Johnson was beleaguered. The anti-war senator from Minnesota, Gene McCarthy, ran strong against him in the first Democratic primary, in New Hampshire, in March. After that, Johnson shocked the nation by announcing he would not run anymore and McCarthy won a string of primaries.

In May, McCarthy was coming to Bloomington in advance of the Indiana primary and the mood of many people in the English Department was *Hooray, Hooray!*

But, not long after McCarthy's strong showing in New Hampshire, Bobby Kennedy had entered the race and Indiana would be his first battleground.

Paul and I started to wonder: Kennedy? McCarthy? Kennedy? McCarthy?

Our friends were predominately for McCarthy. There he was: clearly anti-war. Who was Bobby Kennedy? The spoiler. They said, "He's coming in to mess things up! Who does he think he is?" They told us Bobby Kennedy hadn't always been anti-war but now he was. They told us he hadn't always been visibly out front on civil rights, but there he was, now.

Bobby Kennedy landed in Indianapolis on the night Martin Luther King was shot. He spoke eloquently and movingly. For Paul and me, that sealed it for us. We voted for him in the Indiana primary.

There were a lot of hard feelings. We lost friends. A month later, Bobby Kennedy was shot.

# 8

# Something Worth Fighting For

*The world in 1968 suffered through a series of spasms that threatened to tear apart Southeast Asia, sub-Saharan Africa, both eastern and western Europe, the ghettoes of American cities, college campuses, parliaments, congresses, city halls, and even Midwestern families gathered around their Sunday dinner tables. Young and old, people raised their voices in protest and complaint about civil rights, war, women's liberation, the police, "lawlessness," and a hundred other flash points. Even staid Bloomington had become a battleground of ideas and opinions.*

*One of the hottest tinderboxes was Czechoslovakia. The "Prague Spring" began January 5, 1968, with election of liberal reformer Alexander Dubček, who promised "socialism with a human face." Czechoslovakia's patrons in the Soviet Union reacted swiftly and strongly.*

*Events in Czechoslovakia would play significantly in the lives of Charlotte and her family.*

***

For some reason, Indiana University had always had a connection with the US State Department. Yugoslavia had had an exchange program with the English Department; two of our friends had been in the Yugoslavian program and had a wonderful time.

Now, after Prague Spring, Slovakia opened up in the spring of '68. Socialism with a human face.

***

*Dubček, a Slovak, introduced the eastern half of Czechoslovakia, the then-region of Slovakia, to the global community. Part of that effort in-*

*cluded an exchange program with American colleges and universities. The program would be administered by IREX (The International Research & Exchanges Board) founded in 1968.*

***

So there was this opportunity to go to this new place, to Czechoslovakia. We wanted to go there for several reasons. One was just to get the opportunity to go overseas. Paul and I really liked being overseas.

We signed up for the Czech exchange program and the people at IREX were very happy about it.

We were excited. I was taking Slovak lessons with a tutor. Then Nathan—he was three—announced he was not going.

He was pretty much toilet trained but he started having some setbacks. He said he wasn't going to go and he wasn't going to leave his potty chair.

I got some books from the library and I showed him some nice pictures of Czechoslovakia. But, no, he was not going to go.

I sat down and took him in my lap. I said, "Now, Nathan, we're going to Czechoslovakia and you're going along because we would not go without you. We love you."

He said, "I'm not going to go and I'm not going to learn Slovak."

I said, "The fact is, I think you will learn Slovak. But that's neither here nor there. You don't have to learn Slovak."

He said, "But you won't be able to talk to me! I won't know what you're saying!"

"What do you mean?"

He said, "You're going to talk Slovak and I won't be able to understand you."

"No, no, no! I'll talk Slovak to the Slovaks. I'll still talk English with you."

"You will?"

He really thought we were going to go and he wouldn't be able to talk with us anymore. Once we got that cleared up he went along. Reluctantly.

\*\*\*

*World events and some personal considerations delayed the trip and almost derailed it completely.*

\*\*\*

Then we decided I should finish my dissertation. And the timing was off for Paul; leaving in the fall of 1968 wasn't such a good idea considering his position at the time in the English Department. So we put the trip off for a year.

When I finished my dissertation, I found I had more time to do other things. I had to do something; that's always been in me. I asked for a volunteer job with the Red Cross and was assigned to create and run its local water safety training program.

We needed swimming pools to conduct our classes. Bloomington had two municipal swimming pools but one was off limits. The people who ran the Bryan Park pool were not interested in participating in a Red Cross program, not at all. They were not about to let outsiders do anything of the sort at their facility.

We did manage to get the city to agree to let us use the Mills pool on 17th Street but we needed another location for our program.

Sarkes Tarzian had a very nice pool behind his television equipment plant on Hillside Drive. Theoretically, it was for all the company's employees but, in reality, it was used mainly by people in management. But the company agreed to let us use its pool.

I spent the summer of 1969 hiring people and getting volunteers to teach our water safety classes and swimming classes. I'd pick them up at home and drive them to the pools at seven in the morning and then drive them home in the afternoon. That was my little fling at sports. But it was important work. We got really good enrollment in our classes that summer.

\*\*\*

*In 1968 and '69, Charlotte also served on the board of directors for the Community Action Program, a nonprofit organization that still exists. Then, as now, it helped poor people get jobs and needed social services.*

*It was originally funded by the federal government as part of Lyndon Johnson's War on Poverty.*

*Her time with the organization helped Charlotte realize that women in Bloomington had a tough time getting jobs. Those who'd dropped out of school or had only earned high school diplomas lost out on job opportunities to more well-educated women. And those well-educated women had their own difficulties. The prevailing attitude here, as well as in other college towns at the time, was they shouldn't be taking higher-paid jobs away from men so they were forced to take positions for which they were overqualified.*

***

When I was with the Community Action Program, I went to the Chamber of Commerce to talk about jobs. I was really interested in jobs, especially for women. A lot of women were unemployed or underemployed in this city. Many women with bachelor's degrees, master's degrees, and occasionally PhDs worked in retail stores at minimum wage jobs. That was all that was available to them. I'd also learned that a lot of people who hadn't finished high school were competing with highly educated women for those jobs. We had this kind of dumbbell effect—two big ends: dropouts and PhDs on either side of narrow middle. We have it to this day.

Charlie Stroh was the president of the Chamber at the time. I said, "Mr. Stroh, I'm interested in knowing what's going on around town in terms of creating jobs."

He said, "Why should we create jobs?"

"Well," I said, "many people can't find jobs here and a lot of others aren't making enough to live on."

"Oh," he said, "you're talking about faculty spouses and people who haven't graduated from high school. We don't have to worry about them. We have a job buyer's market in Bloomington. We want to keep it that way."

Again, that was the Chamber of Commerce president speaking!

I said, "Really? *Really?* I'm one of those people you just described and I need a job too!"

He basically waved me off.

I would recall this conversation when I was running for city council. I would refer to it a lot when I talked to voters.

At the time, several large corporations had big factories in Bloomington that drew in employees from around South Central Indiana. RCA, Westinghouse, General Electric, and Otis Elevator employed tens of thousands. Sarkes Tarzian's company also was a big employer although that operation was not unionized. Sarkes had developed several key parts for TVs and FM radio receivers and his plant on Hillside Drive ran three shifts a day.

These factories, at least, were mostly unionized and were providing employment with a decent wage for a lot of women who had no other options.

\*\*\*

*Later, Charlotte would benefit from the relationships she cultivated with local factory managers and workers while volunteering for the Community Action Program. But first, events in Europe would have a more immediate impact on her and her family.*

*In the middle of the night, August 21st and 22nd, 1968, some 200,000 Warsaw Pact troops and 2000 tanks crossed the Danube River into Bratislava. That army quickly spread out over the entire country of Czechoslovakia. Their aim: to wrest control back from the country's liberal reformers. Images of tanks in the streets of the Czech capital, Prague, appeared on front pages and flashed across TV screens around the world.*

\*\*\*

As all of this was happening, we started thinking that we would not be going to Czechoslovakia. We didn't hear anything from IREX for a while. Then, in February, we spoke with a friend from the IU English Department, Owen Thomas, who'd been involved in an exchange program with Yugoslavia. He'd recently been in Washington, speaking with the IREX people.

Owen came back to Bloomington and said the IREX people told him, "Isn't it wonderful that the Zietlows are going over to Czechoslovakia, even under the current conditions!"

He added. "Gosh, they're so excited about you going."

I said, "Tanks in the street? Are we really sure this is a good idea?"

Owen said, "Oh, don't worry about that! That's in Prague and they'll be gone by the time you get there. And the American Embassy will take care of you. You're going to Bratislava; that's way out on the edge of everything."

Not really. Bratislava is where Hungary and Czechoslovakia and Austria come together at the Danube. It's where the Warsaw Pact came in. They came over the bridge, going through the square on the campus of Komenského University where Paul would be teaching!

***

*Charlotte and Paul contacted the IREX people and began making plans to travel to Czechoslovakia in the fall of 1969. The IREX program coordinators tried to prepare the Zietlows for what was to come but at times it seemed even they didn't know quite what to expect.*

***

They said, "You'll be the only Americans in the city and you'll be well-treated. Or maybe nobody will talk to you. It's quite possible, that nobody will want to have anything to do with you. But we'll help you get multiple entry-exit visas so you can go to Austria any time you want to."

Vienna was 40 kilometers to the west of Bratislava. Vienna was thriving and quite safe. I'd spent several months there with my mother and siblings in 1954.

They also warned us: "Don't say anything inflammatory. Don't use the black market. Don't say anything negative about the government. You'll be safe but the people you're speaking with will not be."

Anyway, we thought it would be an adventure, so we scrambled and arranged and off we went.

***

*Fall, 1969. The Zietlows traveled by ocean liner, the MS Sagafjord, to Europe. Paul would be a visiting American professor of English literature at* Univerzita Komenského v Bratislave *(Comenius University at Bratislava) in Czechoslovakia.*

***

We drove our Beetle out east. We were going to sell it to a friend in Chappaqua, New York. We loaded it up with a lot of stuff. We were going to take a ship from Hoboken to Copenhagen.

We were to report to the American embassy in Prague first. There were still tanks on the streets of Prague well into 1969. I was worried. I said, "They're fighting in the streets of Prague!"

Paul said, "The State Department wouldn't send us any place that isn't safe." He kept trying to reassure me.

He, on the other hand, was obsessed about whether we could get our short wave radio on the boat. He was worried it was one thing too much to load on. I was very unworried about that.

I said, "Paul, we'll get the radio on the boat. Everything will get there. We'll all get there. Now, what about those tanks?"

We had this wonderful counterbalance. I worried about the cosmic things and he worried about the little details. It was a good combination.

When we got to Prague, there were no more tanks in the street and we were well taken care of by the embassy. And that radio got to Bratislava and we listened to it the whole year we were there.

We landed in Copenhagen on Nathan's fifth birthday. I stayed and made sure all the luggage got off the ship. Paul took the children and picked up a new green VW bus. Then he and the children stopped at a Danish pastry shop filled with elaborate confections. He told the children they could pick out anything they wanted. They each ended up with a *brioche*, just a simple little roll.

Then we met up and went to a wonderful department store where we bought Legos. We'd never heard of them before.

We drove south and stopped in Arzberg, in Bavaria, right on the Czechoslovakia border. We looked at some Arzberg china—the town is famous for it. We didn't know at the time if we could fully stock our apartment at stores in Czechoslovakia. When we eventually got there, it turned out we couldn't buy dishes there. We couldn't really buy anything there so we went back to Arzberg at Christmas time and got some China dishes. We still have most of them. They're really pretty, with blue teardrops geometrically arranged.

At the embassy, they had a commissary where we could buy Tang and peanut butter and bourbon. We found out bourbon was a highly desirable gift and only available to Americans. Whenever you'd visit somebody in Czechoslovakia, you'd take them a bottle of bourbon.

We spent some time in Prague with the American cultural attache. We went out to dinner and he went down the list of things we should know.

Finally we got to Bratislava.

The Ministry of Education assigned a "keeper" to us, Gajdoš (pronounced GUY-dosh). He'd come from a Hungarian family.

The Ministry provided us a two-bedroom apartment in one of the Eastern Bloc's new communities of high-rises. Each of these planned communities contained a number of high-rises. Each had its own gym, its own supermarket, its own day care center. They were like little villages. The idea was good; the execution wasn't so hot. They built the high-rises out of substandard cement so the walls were crumbling already, even though the buildings weren't 15 years old.

The whole high-rise we lived in was called "Six." *Galaktiska* 6 was the address. It was heated by a soft coal-fueled central power plant miles away. It sent heat out to several of these high-rise villages. You can imagine how efficient that was. You can also imagine how much coal had to be burned. When it got really cold, you could see the air turning a sort of green.

But we were lucky: We had our own bathroom. We had hot and cold running water. Actually, hot water sometimes.

The Czech part of Czechoslovakia was more "western" than the Slovak part. When the country was part of the Austro-Hungarian Empire, the Czechs had the factories and were the clerks to the Austrians and the Slovaks were the farmers, the peasants to the Hungarians. And both were treated accordingly. The Czechs looked down on the Slovaks. The Slovaks were the "hillbillies."

Even so, the Slovaks were not quite the bottom of the totem pole. In Czechoslovakia, there were the Hungarians and the Gypsies who were lower on the totem pole.

The Slovaks, as we found out, had a wonderful folk tradition with a strong Hungarian influence, music particularly, but also art.

Bratislava had been the capital of the Slovak region. It was an ancient city. There was a large castle on a hill overlooking the city of more than a quarter million people.

We were the only Americans in the city! We were extremely well-treated; we were treated like royalty.

You couldn't buy anything in Czechoslovakia. You never knew what would be available in the grocery stores from one day to the next.

It was ironic because we were rich.

\*\*\*

*Paul was paid through the State Department in US dollars to make up for his lost Indiana University salary. At the same time, he was paid a full professor's salary by* Univerzita Komenského *in cash, Czech korunas. When the time would come for the Zietlows to leave Bratislava, they'd have to leave their Czech currency behind; it was unlawful to take* korunas *out of the country.*

\*\*\*

We kept our money in the apartment, stashed it in a hiding place. That's what everybody did. We would go to the American Express office in Vienna if we needed dollars from our American bank. Unfortunately, there was little or nothing to spend it on.

There was a sort of farmers market a couple of times a week. The people who lived in the little villages near Bratislava were allowed to raise a certain amount of food beyond what they needed and could bring it to the markets. There we could get fresh vegetables, cabbages, and fresh meat: pork and duck and goose.

We'd been in Bratislava about a month and a half. I was home one morning. Nathan was in *detsky škola* (little children's school), Rebecca was in school, and Paul was at the university. I got a knock on the door.

I opened it to a man and a woman, both in long, black leather coats. The man said in a clipped, officious voice, "Are you TZEET-low?"

I replied in a sweet, accommodating voice, "Yes?"

"What are you doing here?"

"Well, my husband's teaching at the university. We're guests of the Ministry of Education."

The man said, "We need you to come with us."

I said, "I'm sorry, I can't come with you. I have to pick up my husband and my children. I just don't have the time. Some other time maybe?"

They were used to people cowering before them. I wasn't going to be. They were taken aback. The woman said, "We're from the Ministry of the Interior!"

\*\*\*

*In Czechoslovakia at the time, The Ministry of the Interior handled surveillance and compliance. Agents of the Ministry would be considered officers of the national police force.*

\*\*\*

I said, "How about tomorrow?"

They didn't know what to do! They looked at each other and finally said, "Okay. We'll be here at nine o'clock!" And they marched off.

I called the American embassy in Prague. There was no consulate in Bratislava. We were all alone. I was told, "Drive your own car. You and Paul. Take the children with you. Then call us when you get home. If we don't hear from you by noon, we'll follow up."

So the same two people in long, black leather coats came the next day at nine, sharp. I answered the door. The man said, "We're here. You and Mr. TZEET-loh must come with us."

I said, "The children are home for the day. They're going to have to go with us."

"Oh, no! You can't do that."

"Yes I can," I said. "I'm sorry, they must go with us."

"Then we will need another car."

I said, "No, that's okay. We'll drive our own car."

The woman said, "No, no, no! You have to go in our car!"

"No, I have to go shopping afterward with the children."

Again, they didn't immediately know what to do. They weren't ready to be rough and nasty with the only Americans in Bratislava.

So we drove in our VW bus to the Ministry of the Interior. We went in and the official at the desk said, "Let me see your passport!" And then, in a loud voice, "Why have you not registered with us? Why did you not let us know you were here?"

Paul said, "We're guests of the Ministry of Education! And Gajdoš is our intermediary. We have residency permits."

The man took our passports and we were moved into this cold little bare room. We sat there for about fifteen minutes and then another man came in. In a very authoritative voice, he said, "Come with me."

We followed him into another room. It was nice and comfortable. Someone brought in coffee and *slivovitz*, a plum brandy. The man, softer now, said, "You have permits?"

We answered, "Of course!"

"Why didn't we know about this?"

I said, "Well, we're here. And these permits have been issued by your department!"

The man looked our documents over and then began to apologize profusely. Someone else brought in cookies and chocolate for the children. And then we were sent on our way.

It was just a mistake! We were so visible. We were obviously not spies! Everybody in town knew that we were the Americans in the green VW bus! Everybody knew where we lived. I would go into a store and the clerk would say, "Oh, you're the American."

They were used to making people scared but we really weren't scared. Just annoyed and amused. They had all this surveillance and all this bugging and they couldn't keep track of the elephant in the room. It was amazing.

On the whole, we were very well-treated. Rebecca was seven years old. The Ministry of Education put her in a very desirable school where they taught English in addition to regular lessons in Slovak.

She was idolized there. She was a princess. Both students and teachers wanted to talk to her and take care of her and say nice things to her. She was in first grade and she learned to read and write in Slovak. She was a good student and the teachers just loved her.

The first graders were taught writing, dipping a pen in an ink bottle. If the student made blotches, she'd get a pig stamp. If she got too many pig stamps, she would have to go sit in a corner. Rebecca lived in terror of getting just one pig stamp. She never got one.

Then, each day, she attended *druvina*, an after-school care program. Most Slovak mothers worked so there had to be afternoon care for their children.

We'd been told before we left the United States that people might be so nervous about being around Americans that we could feel isolated. That was not the case at all.

A short time after our experience with the Ministry of the Interior, there was another knock at the door. This time it was two teachers from Rebecca's school. They said Rebecca was in the hospital. She'd been playing crack-the-whip with the other children and she hadn't understood exactly how to play. She hadn't hung on when she was at the end of the whip and she flew and hit her head. The teachers were very, very upset.

I got in touch with Paul at the university and had him pick up Nathan. Then I raced off to the children's hospital. When I got there, the nurses told me I couldn't come in because it was a Tuesday. Tuesdays were not visiting days!

I still didn't know much Slovak at that point so I spoke German. I just forced my way in. I wanted to see the doctor and Rebecca. She was in the intensive care unit with a whole bunch of children who were in terrible, terrible shape. She didn't know the language so she didn't even know where she was.

She had a slight concussion but the teachers and the doctors were being extra careful with the American girl.

The doctor, a neurologist named Nebalov, fortunately had spent time in England so he spoke English quite well. He knew who we were because he had a child in Rebecca's school.

Nebalov took charge and made it possible for me to see Rebecca and spend time with her. He was very reassuring and comforting. He told me I could come back any time; he would make sure it would be alright.

"Meanwhile," he said, "do you need anything?"

I said, "What do you mean?"

"Do you need a television?"

I said, "Well, that'd be nice."

"Okay, I'll arrange that. And I'll make sure you get the little gizmo that will allow you to get Austrian television." It was illegal to have that little gizmo but, needless to say, everybody had one.

Nebalov turned out to be a real ally and friend. He took good care of Rebecca and got her out of that hospital as fast as he could.

Later, one of Rebecca's afternoon teachers told me to call her any time I had a medical issue. "I have a lot of connections in the medical community," she said.

One day Nathan accidentally scratched the cornea of my left eye, which was very painful. I took Rebecca to school and asked to see this teacher. She said, "I'm going to take you to my uncle." We went down to the eye clinic where her uncle was the head professor.

Czechoslovakia had a tradition of very good medical care. It was a sophisticated, well-developed country, although at the time it was considered "underdeveloping"—that was the Slovak joke; they made the word up—because of all the devastation it had suffered during World War II and then under the Soviet economy.

The teacher's uncle spoke German. He looked at my eye carefully, put some salve on it, then put a patch over it.

Then he told me that when I came back to see him, I should come through the back door so that nobody in front would see me. Otherwise I'd have to wait and wait.

I went out on the street and realized there were lots of people with festering eyes coming and going. Some of them came up to me and asked where I got my patch. They asked, "Who took care of you?"

I didn't know what to say. Go see the teacher's uncle?

I realized this was an economy, a society, of relationships. If you scratch my back, I'll scratch yours. The Slovaks had a word for it, *protektion*. What we had to offer was ourselves; we were the Americans. We had to be well-treated and everybody had to go the extra mile so we would think well of the Slovaks.

We were lucky.

It was a pretty bad time in Czechoslovakia. It had been more than a year after the tanks had rolled in. Then there'd been a sort of grace period after that but now, again, the screws were tightening. The purges were beginning.

People involved in the Prague Spring were gradually moved from one job to a lesser job, to an even lesser job to no job at all. Then to jail. It was a descending spiral. The book and the movie, *The Incredible Lightness of Being*, actually portrayed that period pretty accurately.

More than 20 percent of the populace were members of the Communist Party, the highest percentage of any of the Soviet bloc countries, including Russia and East Germany. Czechoslovakia was the most "communist" country. All the professionals had become members of the Party for ideological reasons. Most of them had lived through the Nazi occupation, which was so awful that, in response to it, the Czechs went the opposite way.

But the Party turned out not to be what they'd hoped it would be. Soviet Communism was not "socialism with a human face."

Meanwhile, the economy was stymied. One thing to do, if you wanted to make money in Slovakia, was to provide scaffolding. There was scaffolding on half the buildings because they were falling apart! And bunting. They were always celebrating one Communist day or another.

The grocery stores were hit and miss. We could go to the supermarket and there'd be Russian caviar and Russian champagne and cans of *lecsó* (pronounced LAY-cho), a combination of tomatoes, peppers, and onions. That would be it! Maybe bread. Maybe butter.

I'd stand in line, take a basket, and wander around. There was so little to pick from. I spent half my fall figuring out how to buy supper. I figured out where it would be most likely to find bread. I had a car and I had time and we had oodles of money.

There was something called *Tuzex*, at the time a government-run store featuring specialty and imported foods. There was something like it in every Eastern Bloc country. If you had western currency, you could buy things there. It was their way of getting dollars and francs and marks and pounds into their economies. Of course, it was illegal to have western currency in those countries. But it was one of those interesting contradictions we ran into a lot there. Crazy things, Kafkaesque.

The *Tuzex* stores were always full of people. You could get canned goods and Rémy Martin cognac for five dollars. You could get Pilsner beer—you couldn't get it in the regular stores even though it was the national brew! You could get Danish ham and Dutch cheese.

They had wonderful crystal in Czechoslovakia. I said to Paul, "We have all this money. Why don't we buy some crystal?"

So we went into this lovely store with beautiful things in the window. I pointed at some beautiful goblets and asked the proprietor, "Can I get six of those?"

He said, "We don't have them."

I said, "Those, there. They're in the window."

He laughed. "That's for display. We don't have anything like that in stock. We just show it in the window."

The Slovaks had a saying: "*Ne nie. Nie máme. Ne existule.*" (There isn't any. We don't have it. It doesn't exist.)

We heard it over and over again. When we wanted to buy pens or a notebook for the children, *Ne nie. Nie máme. Ne existule.* When we wanted a certain cut of meat, *Ne nie. Nie máme. Ne existule.*

I went to a butcher shop, one I hadn't been to before. I picked up my basket and walked around. Very clean. Too clean. The shelves and display cases were almost totally empty. There was some lard but that's about it. I asked the butcher: "Do you have any meat?"

"*Ne nie. Nie máme. Ne existule.*"

So I went toward the door. He asked, "Are you Russian?"

I said, "No, I'm American."

"American! What are you doing here? Are you crazy?"

I said, "My husband teaches here."

"Wait," he said and ran into the back room. He came back out with a couple of brown paper packages. He put them in my basket and wished me a wonderful day.

I paid for the packages but didn't know what was in them.

When I got home and opened them up, they were a chicken and a pork roast. He gave them to me because I was the American.

We indulged the kids. We went about once a month to Vienna. Paul would take the children. First, they'd go to a pastry shop and they would get wonderful things we couldn't get in Bratislava. Then they would go to a park and play or they'd go to *Prater*, the big amusement park, and ride the *Reisenrad*, a giant Ferris wheel.

Meanwhile, I zipped around, very fast, and bought all the things we needed—and that all the people we knew needed. Before we'd leave, I'd have asked all the teachers and the neighbors: What do you want from Vienna? We would bring back lemons and diapers and meat and produce. Tampons. Anything. We would pile it all on the floor of the VW bus. At the border, coming back, the guards would ask," "Anything to declare?"

"No."

They'd be looking right at the waist-high pile covered with a blanket. "Yeah, we don't see anything." We never had any trouble with the border guards.

It was a hard year but we learned so much.

Nathan went to the *detsky škola* (little children's school) for children of Communist Party officials and other high-placed people. They cut him no slack. He had to march to their commands.

He was such a sweet little kid and he didn't want to be in Czechoslovakia in the first place. But there he was. I had to get him to the center before eight and leave him until after three. Nobody spoke anything but Slovak. He could not sit on the floor. He had to sit up straight at a table. He had to hold somebody's hand when they went out for a walk. He had to take his clothes off and put pajamas on for his nap. He was good but it was hard for him.

1970 was Vladimir Lenin's hundredth birthday. Nathan's daycare center was part of a large, citywide celebration. Thousands of little kids performed at the *Spartakiad,* the city's big stadium. They wore their little red onesies and carried white hoops. You've seen the demonstrations that Soviet kids used to do on a big field with their white hoops.

The whole city was bedecked in red. When Nathan told us about the celebration, I asked him, "Who's Lenin?"

Nathan said, "He was a nice man, a kind man. He was good to children. He took them on his lap and talked to them!"

I remembered hearing a similar story about somebody else in Sunday school.

We had a babysitter, a young woman named Katerina. She was learning English and working for us would be an opportunity for her to speak it. I associate her forever with the Beatles' Abbey Road album. It came out the year we were in Czechoslovakia. We bought it in Vienna and ultimately gave it to Katerina after almost wearing it out on our turntable.

Katerina's family had been prestigious at one time. But her father, a judge, was discouraged and browbeaten. There wasn't much discretion for a judge. The law did not prevail. Somebody would come before him and he would rule as he was told.

We became friends with one person who was still a believer in the communist ideal. His name was Fero Studeny. He was an artist, a painter, and married to one of Paul's colleagues at the university.

Fero had been a peasant in eastern Slovakia. He had fought in the mountains against the Nazis. After the war, he painted fish, and that's all he painted. He painted fish because they were the food and the symbol of the poor. He was sent to art school after the war and became a Master Painter. He became highly esteemed by the establishment. We were told he was the butt of other artists' ridicule.

Fero said, "This is a wonderful country! I was a peasant and now I am a decorated artist. Where else could this happen?"

He refused to believe anything was wrong with Czechoslovakia. He didn't sympathize with the Prague Spring. He thought the communists had done a terrific job. He told us cities like Vienna were showplaces, that they were false, that all the wealth of Austria was in Vienna to make the rest of the country look good to outsiders.

Fero lived in a fifth-floor apartment with an atelier and good lighting. He painted his fish there and never went out much.

We were very, very careful not to say anything negative about Czechoslovakia or communism in front of the kids. We didn't want them repeating anything. We weren't too worried about ourselves so much as we were worried about the people we spent time with. They could get into trouble just being in a room where negative things were spoken. It was against the law to say negative things in public. And "in public" was a group of two or more.

We would have guests over and they would start talking about the government. They'd ask us, "What do you think about Czechoslovakia?" Our standard reply was, "It's a beautiful country and the people are really nice." We said that many, many times.

We didn't want to go beyond that but many of them did! We would point toward the corner of the room, as if we knew where the listening devices were, and make shushing motions. And some of them would say, sometimes shouting, "I don't care!"

But a lot of people did care. One man who'd become our friend was named Milan Šimečka (pronounced shih-METZ-ka). He had really gotten himself in trouble. His wife, Eva, was a colleague of Paul's at the university. Milan and Eva were actually Moravian. They grew up in Brno. He was an historian at The Academy, which was analogous to Princeton's Institute for Advanced Research. The Šimečkas had been in Germany when the tanks rolled in.

There were a number of people like the Šimečkas, and Dr. Nebalov, who'd been out of the country when the Warsaw Pact invaded Czechoslovakia. They had to decide whether to go back to their country or not. The Šimečkas and Nebalov could have stayed where they were and gotten asylum but they decided to go back and make their country strong again.

Others hadn't made the same choice. We knew a Slovak couple here in Bloomington before we'd left for Czechoslovakia. She was my Slovak tutor and he was a scientist. They decided to stay in the United States and apply for asylum. They got it.

So, Milan and Eva came back to Bratislava. He'd been pretty vocal, publicly, during the Prague Spring. He was a good friend of Alexander Dubček, the president. After the Warsaw Pact came in, Milan would be called in and he would be grilled.

His questioners would say to him, "Now, you said such-and-such...." Then they'd add, *sotto voce,* "but you really didn't mean it, did you?" Some of them would even whisper, "Say no."

He'd say, "Yes I did!"

More whispering: "No! You don't want to say yes."

He'd say, "No! I believed it then and I believe it now!"

So his questioners would say, "You're a good historian and we'd hate to lose you but I'm afraid you can't talk like that anymore. We're going to move you over here." And they'd assign him to a lesser post.

Two months later they'd pull him in and go through the same thing again. He'd stick to his guns and so he'd go down another peg.

It went on that way until, among other things, his children weren't even allowed to go to secondary school.

It was death by a thousand cuts.

Another man we knew, Zdeněk Stříbrný [pronounced: STRIH-bur-nee], was the chair of the English Department at Charles University in Prague. It was founded in the 14th Century, the first university in central Europe. He and his wife were wonderful. We had good times with them. But he was eventually demoted to a streetcar conductor. His children and his wife suffered.

I'll fast-forward to the Velvet Revolution that resulted in an independent Czechoslovakia in 1989, and its eventual split into the Czech Republic and Slovakia. In the years after we left Czechoslovakia, Milan Šimečka had become very close with Václav Havel. They were part of *Charta 77* (Charter '77) that criticized the communist government for human rights violations. Many members of the group, including Havel and Šimečka, were imprisoned.

When the Velvet Revolution came about and Havel became the new leader of Czechoslovakia, he brought Milan with him to the Prague castle that would be the center of government. He offered Milan a choice; Would you like to be president of *Univerzita Komenského v Bratislave* or would you like to come with me and be part of the government? Milan wanted to work directly with Havel in Prague. He became a cabinet minister.

***

*Charlotte and Paul learned through a mutual friend soon after the Velvet Revolution that they could now safely call Milan. The mutual friend gave the Zietlows Milan's phone number—it was the same one they had for him in 1969 and '70. They called and learned he would soon be coming to America for a visit. They made arrangements to meet him and his wife. Then the mutual friend called with bad news. He said, "This is terrible. Milan finally is in the castle. He's free and can do whatever he wants. And he just died of a heart attack."*

***

We had our television and we could get Austrian TV. It was illegal to have a short wave radio but we'd got it through in our duffel bag. We weren't supposed to be listening to Radio Free Europe or the Voice of America, but we did.

One night in the spring of 1970 we listened to a panel discussion on the Voice of America. It was led by the journalist Peter Lisagore, who usually leaned to the Right. Several speakers on both sides of the issue heatedly discussed President Nixon's decision to bomb Viet Cong supply routes in Cambodia. Lisagore put the question out: *What about the bombing? There are so many things wrong with the decision; let's discuss them all.* And the first speaker said, "Here's what's wrong...." The second speaker said, "No, this other aspect of it is more wrong...." And so on.

Yet all around us in Bratislava were people who couldn't comfortably talk about their dissatisfaction with their government. They couldn't say anything negative about it in public. What we had was something worth fighting for.

For me, the lesson was this: All the uproar at home, people being defiant and personal relationships being so tense, nobody we knew was taken off to jail and "disappeared." But in Bratislava, and the rest of Czechoslovakia, it could happen to anybody.

We had some big political trials in the United States, but they were all public. In Czechoslovakia, the trials were behind closed doors. We were there, watching our new friends being purged.

***

*Nevertheless, Czechoslovakia was home to a marvelous people who carried on beautiful traditions.*

***

The first day Rebecca went to her school—she went into the first grade—the ninth-graders met the first graders at the entrance of the school. They carried bouquets of flowers and introduced themselves to all the first-graders. Then they walked the first-graders through the school and, in each classroom, sang songs and did little dances. They welcomed the new children to school.

At the end, on the last day of school, the first-graders brought bouquets of flowers and gave them to the ninth-graders. Then they took the ninth-graders through the school, into each classroom, singing songs and doing little dances. It was their way of saying goodbye to the ninth-graders.

After that ceremony, Rebecca's class went back to her room and had a farewell party for her. When she came home, she was in tears.

She said, "Mama, I wish we'd never come to Czechoslovakia."

"Rebecca, you had a wonderful time and you had so much fun!"

"I know. And it'll never happen again."

These were nice traditions. They bound the people together. When Czechs left their country to go to to United States—Cleveland or Chicago or Buffalo—they left those traditions behind. They came here and became different people with different aspirations.

The day we were to leave for home was coming near. We had plenty of *korunas* left. We couldn't take them with us. We had to figure out how to dispose of them. The best we could come up with was to buy things, many things, things we didn't even need.

We bought a boat—a rubber boat—for the simple reason that it was for sale.

We toyed with the idea of simply giving the money to some of our Slovak friends. But that would have been considered an insult. The Slovaks were a proud people. So, instead, we decided to take our friends out to expensive, sumptuous dinners.

One evening we took Professor Stříbrný, the English Department chair at Charles University, and his wife out to dinner at a famous, expensive restaurant. We had a feast. We ordered the most expensive items on the menu. We had huge snifters of cognac. We had caviar.

At the end of the meal, the waiter brought us the check. It was the equivalent of a month's salary for the professor. His wife was mortified, horrified.

"You shouldn't be doing this!" she said.

Paul said, "What else can we do? We could try to give the money to you but you wouldn't take it."

She drew herself up in her chair and said, "Absolutely correct."

Paul went on, "We decided to take you out and have a good time. It would be something you could remember forever." The professor and his wife agreed they'd remember the night as long as they lived.

We would, too. It was magic.

# 9

# Why Would I Want To Do That?

*Back in Bloomington, Paul slipped easily back into his position at Indiana University. Charlotte, though, had no clear-cut path. Little did she know, while she'd been in Czechoslovakia, events at home had created a doorway for her.*

\*\*\*

I didn't know what I was going to do. The children were in school full-time for the first time. I wasn't going to teach in the German Department. It wasn't clear to me what I wanted to do.

We got back in August. We'd spent the summer in England, decompressing basically. It was such an intense experience in Bratislava. We had a wonderful apartment near Oxford. I rode a bicycle and I did some crewel embroidery. Paul went to Wessex and did research on Thomas Hardy for a book, *Moments of Vision*, he was writing on Hardy's poetry.

And you know what? We got home and the Democratic Party had been totally revived in Bloomington!

The Party had been moribund for years and years. But the 1968 Indiana Democratic primary had awakened people to the importance of having a responsive local Democratic Party and that had carried on through '70.

It was a mid-term election, always important. Vance Hartke was running for his third term in the US Senate. He had been one of the very first senators to oppose the Vietnam War, and was quite vocal about it, back in 1965. Before that, he was a loyal liberal who supported Lyndon Johnson's Great Society programs and the civil rights movement.

In Bloomington, there were other things going on, politically, as well. In the precincts, there were many contested elections within the Party for precinct chairs. The more militant progressive or liberal Democrats were elected, by and large.

In my own precinct, a young man named Marc Haggerty was elected Chair. He was a Vietnam veteran. He was a teenager when he went to war and he had no idea what he was getting into. Got there and found out. It totally changed his life. He has been anti-war ever since. And he's never gotten over it to this day.

He's a wonderful, smart person who is fearless. He's become a good friend of mine. He's kind of kooky, not like anyone else I know. He has worked as a circus acrobat. He was a huge activist and played a large role in some anti-war demonstrations around campus. He's totally committed to justice, especially justice for people who get in trouble with the law, to see they're treated well and fairly.

Meanwhile, two new grass-roots, non-partisan groups in town were springing up: the Citizens for Good Government (CGG) and the Voters Union. They were non-partisan organizations.

The CGG focused on issues. They were doing an in-depth study of the 11 Monroe County township trustees.

***

*The idea of township government was an antiquated one, dating back from the days of Thomas Jefferson, who'd championed them. Indiana was one of the very last states in the union to retain its township form of government. Each Indiana township is presided over by an elected trustee. Indiana townships are responsible for maintenance and safety within their borders in unincorporated areas of the county. The townships distribute food or cash assistance to individuals and families in need. They can also, when needed, operate fire departments.*

*The federal Food Stamp Act of 1964 had granted assistance to some 350,000 Americans in a select number of counties and cities. The Act was part of President Johnson's—and the Democratic Congress's—War on Poverty initiatives. Eventually, even Republicans came around to supporting this particular Great Society program. Over the next decade, the program expanded to aid more than 15 million people across the country in both urban and rural areas. Still, in 1970, there remained some outposts where food stamps were resisted, including in Bloomington.*

\*\*\*

I'd volunteered to work with the CGG. One of its founders was Tomi Allison, who would become the mayor of Bloomington in the 1980s and with whom I'd have plenty to do at that time. She'd gotten together with an incredible person, Shirley Connors, a fireball, and organized the group. A lot of people had joined. A big issue in the county in the 1970 election was township trustees and food stamps.

Here in Monroe County, the issue was whether the township trustees would administer the food stamp program locally or continue to distribute commodities, like surplus cheese and flour and sugar, butter and peanut butter, pork and lard, things like that. The trustees had been distributing those things for years.

The CGG developed a thorough study and sent out canvassers to interview candidates for township trustee in Monroe County, incumbents and challengers. I went out and interviewed a number of them.

Some of the trustees I interviewed offered their reasons for not wanting to switch over to food stamps. One might say, "We've always given out commodities. I don't see any reason to change." Another might say, "Aw, you give 'em food stamps, they'll just buy terrible food or steak and caviar."

Some trustees did support the food stamps idea but it was the county government that would make the decision. The CGG supported candidates for the Monroe county council as well as its Board of Commissioners who were in favor of food stamps.

\*\*\*

*In these ways, Charlotte quickly re-immersed herself into the community and rekindled relationships with the new powers in the local Democratic Party.*

\*\*\*

A good friend of mine named Pat Gross had been elected chair from her precinct down in the Sycamore Knolls neighborhood. She—and a few other people—said, "You know, Charlotte, you've been involved in politics a long time now."

Pat was an extraordinary organizer. She'd talked to Marc Haggerty (chair of my precinct) and said, "If I can persuade Charlotte to be your vice-chair, would you be okay with that?"

And he said, "Sure, okay."

Marc was not an organizer—although he was a wonderful rabble-rouser—and the precinct needed a strong organizer.

\*\*\*

*Pat Gross made it clear that Charlotte would do the heavy lifting in her precinct.*

\*\*\*

Marc and I talked. We had some nice conversations. He liked me. And so it was okay with him for me to sort of take over the organization of the precinct.

So, I got the job. We had a big job to do.

I found a young man who was living in one of the dorms and he became my vice-vice-chair. Together, we found some other recruits, volunteers from the campus, some high school kids, and we just campaigned like wild.

He and his girlfriend helped me, very methodically, organize the precinct. We had the Green Acres neighborhood and the campus south of 10th Street, which included many dorms, about 1500 people.

I had knocked on Green Acres doors several times since we arrived in Bloomington in 1964. My job was to find out exactly who lived here, make sure they were registered to vote, and find out what their inclination was, politically.

In Ann Arbor, where I'd had really good trainers, we knew almost within a vote what the outcome would be in our precinct. That was what I'd learned: counting our votes in advance and making sure every voter that we knew would be ours would get to the polls on election day.

But that's hard in a college town; it's a transient community.

We registered everybody we could find. We tried to make sure all the permanent residents in our precinct were registered.

We ended up getting about 900 votes for Hartke in our precinct. That was important because Vance Hartke carried the state by only 4200 votes against a popular Republican Congressman.

*\*\**

*Headline in the* Herald-Telephone, *September 18, 1970:*
**Jury Indicts Hooker, Young**
*Republican Mayor John R. (Jack) Hooker and City Controller Howard A. Young had been charged the day before by a Monroe County Grand Jury with malconduct in office, misapplication of city funds, and three other crimes. The charges related to a controversial deal to buy property at the corner of Dunn and Kirkwood streets and build a combined parking garage and senior citizens apartment high-rise on the site. Hooker and Young had shifted money for the purchase from the city utilities fund. Only the city council had the power to transfer those funds.*

*The Hooker/Young deal never appeared to be a scheme to enrich the two. They saw the high-rise development as a boon for the community and, essentially, cut corners in hopes of getting it done. Hooker and Young went to trial, were found guilty, and fined $2. The whole affair, though, served to sour the community on the Hooker administration and, by extension, his local Republican Party. At the time, Bloomington's city-wide offices were solidly Republican and the city council stood at 8-1 in favor of that party. Change was in the wind both in Bloomington and around the country.*

*\*\**

After the '70 election, the Monroe County Democratic Chair, Ed Treacy, came to me and said, "Charlotte, that was terrific! Have you ever thought of running for city council?"

I said, "Absolutely not! Why would I want to do that? I don't know anything about the council."

"Neither do the people who are in the council now!" he said. He suggested I just go to a meeting and see for myself.

So, I had to find out where the city council met—I hadn't even known before this—and I went.

There were some big local issues at the time. One was a proposal to build a high-rise senior citizens apartment complex very near the main entrance to the campus where the Sample Gates are now.

The main downtown churches were backing the proposal and the mayor Jack Hooker strongly supported it.

The issue was complicated because the land the high-rise was to be built on was purchased by the city, in part, with funds from the utilities department. Mayor Hooker eventually landed in court on serious charges for that deal.

The land purchase also would be funded by the installation of parking meters in residential neighborhoods. That was not a very welcome proposal.

So, I went to my first city council meeting. It just so happened that action was going to be taken on this development at this particular meeting. The council chambers were packed with people who wanted to be heard.

But the city council wasn't in the practice of hearing from the people.

Nine men, the members of Bloomington's city council, walked in after having placed their overcoats and briefcases on the mayor's couch—they didn't have offices of their own—and sat down. All these people were waving their arms, desperately trying to get the council members' attention. They were ignored.

There was no time set aside for public comment. The way it worked was the clerk would just read the name of the ordinance, titled by year and number: for instance, 1970-26. None of the people in the gallery knew which ordinance was which. The council members knew and they already had their marching orders.

The clerk would call out each council member's name. They went around and each said "Yes…, Yes…, Yes…," to every ordinance that was proposed.

We had no idea what they were voting on!

Then they were finished and the nine men walked out of the chambers, gathered their overcoats and briefcases from the mayor's couch, and left the building.

That was it.

I thought, "This is terrible! These people are the citizens and they should be heard."

That decided me. I said, "I can do better than that."

A very nice guy, Bill McGarry, who lived on 5th Street and was an appliance repairman, had already decided to run for city council from my district in the Democratic primary. I didn't know him very well but I thought, "He hasn't any more experience than I do. Maybe there's a chance for me."

People I knew were very encouraging. So I decided to run in the primary—without much hope that I would win, I have to tell you. Nevertheless, I was going to try.

During the 1970 mid-term elections, there'd been another major issue. Being a college town, there'd always been a question as to who was a real resident of Bloomington and who wasn't—and, consequently, who could vote.

The Monroe County Clerk presided over the election board and made decisions about voter eligibility. The incumbent clerk in 1970, Ruth Poling Karsell, was very rigid. She felt strongly that unless you were a married male graduate student, you should not be allowed to vote. Women, especially single graduate students should not be allowed to vote. She was known to say, *The fewer people who vote, the more smoothly the election goes.* That became an issue in the '70 campaign.

The Democrats ran this bigger-than-life person, Jamie Murphy, against Karsell. She was big and tall, strapping, and spoke in a loud voice. Very smart. She was the wife of a retired army colonel who'd worked in the Labor Studies Department at IU. She said, "I think everybody should vote!"

Jamie won the election for Monroe County Clerk in 1970. This was a year before the ratification of the 26th Amendment to the US Constitution—the 18-year-old vote. Those new voters, potentially, would play a big part in Bloomington's next local election

Meanwhile, the CGG had a counterpart, the Voters Union (VU). It was created by a bunch of very smart Indiana University guys at what would become the Wrubel Computing Center. They were very early computer geeks.

Led by a guy named Al Towell, they had analyzed the voting in the '68 primary. They concluded that the Democrats could win subsequent elections in Bloomington. To this point, the city and county elections had gone staunchly Republican. The VU found that the Democrats could win because there'd been a number of issues—housing, for one—that had been neglected under the Republican administration. The VU was very pragmatic: They analyzed the number of votes, where they came from, who candidates and canvassers should be sure to contact, who might be persuadable. They were very organized and kept good records. It was like what I was trained to do in Ann Arbor under Gerhard Weinberg.

We had a number of precinct people here who turned out to be really good at that kind of work, and they taught a lot of other precinct people how to organize.

The Voters Union went beyond even that. They had an agenda. They clearly supported Vance Hartke. They supported the county officials who endorsed food stamps. It was a liberal agenda and the VU was becoming very influential.

There was a lot coming together in the 1970 election. It all came to fruition in the 1971 election.

*\*\*\**

*The revitalization of the Democratic Party in Bloomington and Monroe County had led to a plethora of mostly young dynamic candidates for citywide office. In addition to the 37-year-old Charlotte Zietlow there were:*

**Frank McCloskey**, *32, a recent law school graduate, awaiting the results of his bar exam. He'd run the previous year for state representative and lost, but had done so well in Bloomington that he thought he could win in a citywide race. When the campaign began, he was one of the few people to hold that belief.*

**Grace Johnson**, *candidate for City Clerk. In her early 30s, Johnson worked as a secretary and was married to an Indiana University faculty member.*

**Brian de St. Croix**, *23, a social worker and community organizer, running for city council along with...*

**Dick Behen**, *a shoe store manager in his early 40s, was the most establishment-friendly of the new breed.*

**Rod Fawcett**, *also in his early 40s, Fawcett was a telephone company lineman who hoped to challenge the west side's other working class candidate, Republican Jack Morrison, about whom more later.*

**Wayne Fix**, *slightly younger than Behen and Fawcett, was a land appraiser and, unbeknown to his fellow candidates, a law student.*

**Al Towell**, *mid-30s, was a computer expert working at IU's Wrubel Computing Center. He also was one of the founding forces behind the Voters Union.*

**Jim Ackerman**, *late 30s, was a Presbyterian minister and and Old Testament scholar. He taught religious studies at IU.*

**Hubert Davis**, *late 30s, was a Methodist minister who served as a chaplain at the university's campus ministry.*

**Sherwin Mizell**, *well into his 40s, was the elder statesman of the group. He was a professor of gross anatomy at IU and one of the founders of Beth Shalom, a local Jewish temple.*

*Although the upstarts were viewed as a singular bloc, either a cabal to be feared or club of saviors, Charlotte only really got to know these folks during the campaign. "We were strangers before that," she says.*

***

I had not paid a lot of attention to our local government before this. When I sat down to think about it, I realized we had a typical small-town council: there was the banker, the insurance guy, several real estate men, the guy who ran the dairy, the guy who ran the grocery. They were active in their churches. They were heads of committees, members of the United Way and Chamber of Commerce, Rotary-type guys. A bunch of good old boys.

They were all white men, of course. Most of them were "mature." They were decent people; they gave a hundred dollars to this charity and a hundred dollars to that one—never a thousand dollars. They weren't rich men. They were upstanding citizens.

Town leaders were not receptive to women. For example, the United Way in 1968 brought on its first female board member. She was listed as Mrs. Donald Gray.

It's hard to imagine now. Those days were unbelievably different.

Mrs. Donald Gray had been a supporter of Jack Hooker in the 1967 mayoral election. She campaigned for him wearing a big sash across her chest reading "Hooker." It was all so innocent; nobody thought twice about what that looked like.

Now that I was a candidate, I had to ask myself, *Where do I begin?*

I knew what needed to be done if I would win: Allow the community to participate in government and help the people understand things.

That was the polar opposite of what we'd seen in Bratislava. I knew those things should be perpetuated locally.

I was not fully up on all the real estate issues and negotiations. I found out that the big issues in small towns were who owns the property and what do we let them do with it.

That was the burning issue as I started my campaign. We had "spot-zoning" in Bloomington and, because of it, the central core of the city was being decimated. You might even say it was being desecrated.

Spot-zoning is changing the zoning on a single piece of property in an area that's already zoned for something else—typically taking a single-family residential property and making it multi-family.

Paul and I had looked for a house to buy in 1966. I wanted an interesting house that wasn't out of a cookie-cutter. I wanted something with character. There was this wonderful place on South Fess Avenue. I really, really liked it. It had good light and a nice big backyard. Our real estate agent took us there and, before we got out of the car, she said in a very quiet voice, ""Don't buy it!"

I said, "Why not?"

She said, "They're going to spot-zone on the next block. There'll be a big apartment building there soon." Sure enough, that's what happened: sixteen units on a plot where a single-family home had been before—no parking, no green space, no accommodation for storm water runoff.

I would go up and down these streets when we first came to Bloomington and see these nice neighborhoods with beautiful homes. But things changed in a few short years. Suddenly, all these apartment buildings were tucked and crammed in between single-family homes. I thought, "This doesn't make for a nice town."

During the campaign as I went from door to door, I made it very clear the big difference between me and the incumbent in my district, Harry Day, was he voted for spot-zoning every single time it came up. There'd been hundreds of them! I went back and checked the minutes of the city council meetings. I told people I wouldn't do that.

Again, that face-to-face meeting with the voters, that hard work, was what I'd been trained to do in Ann Arbor and I was doing it in Bloomington.

A typical encounter:

> Me: Hi, I'm Charlotte Zietlow. I'm running for city council. I think we need more citizen participation in our government. I've spent a fair amount of time in other countries and I've learned we need to preserve our democracy here.
>
> Voter: Okay. So why should I vote for you? Do you have any experience?
>
> Me: I haven't been in government but I have taught a lot and I've traveled a lot. I have two children. I feel strongly attached to this community.
>
> Voter: Well, who are you running against?
>
> Me: Harry Day.
>
> Voter: Harry Day! He's a nice man. He goes to my church. He's going to be hard to beat.
>
> Me: I know. I know he's a nice man and I know he'll be hard to beat. But I have to tell you, I think this spot-zoning is ruining the core of our city. There were over a hundred spot-zoning ordinances in the last two years and Harry Day voted for every one of them.
>
> Voter: He did? Really?
>
> Me: Yes, and I wouldn't do that.

That's what I would say. It wasn't negative. It was not derogatory. It was factual. Then I'd say, "I hope you'll support me."

When I'd walk away from their doors I'd have a feeling about them. We recorded all those contacts on 3x5 cards. We had white cards for Republicans, blue cards for Democrats, and orange cards for the ones we weren't sure about.

It was pretty primitive. We kept the cards in a file box in the living room. Knocking on people's doors is hard work! But it's the best thing to do.

I didn't have a job. I had more time to campaign than my opponents. It became kind of my full-time job. I ended up going to lots and lots of events and speaking engagements, meeting people. I defeated Bill McGarry handily in the primary.

\*\*\*

*Then it was on to face the incumbent Republican, Harry Day, in November.*

\*\*\*

Studying the minutes of past city council meetings was very important for me. It's how I learned what was going on. It's how I learned a little bit about Harry Day.

At one of the council meetings the previous December, Harry Day had got up and said something on the order of, *You know, we have a lot of problems in this community. We could solve them if only we'd all go to church together on Christmas Day.*

Now that I was a candidate, I needed to get more information about jobs and economic development, I made appointments with the heads of the big companies in town—GE, RCA, Westinghouse, Otis, Sarkes Tarzian. They, of course, just thought I was a somewhat inferior, goofy woman.

I asked them what they were doing about providing jobs for people who needed them. They said, "Well, we don't need 'em right now but we do have some problems with turnover here."

I said, "Can you just tell me what the situation is for your workers about getting to work and what happens to their children and do you know about their healthcare? Do you know about these things? We can talk about them with the workers but I want to know what you know about these things."

They didn't know much.

As I campaigned, I quoted Charlie Stroh's line—"We have a job buyer's market in Bloomington. We want to keep it that way." I said, "I think we need jobs and this is what the Chamber of Commerce line is!""

***

*Times were changing.*

*In 1970, with the Vietnam War in full swing under the Nixon administration, many young people were clamoring for the vote. They argued if 18-year-olds were old enough to die for their country, they surely were old enough to vote for their leaders.*

*Responding to public pressure, President Nixon signed an extension of the 1965 Voting Rights Act in June that contained a proviso allowing 18-year-olds to vote in national elections. In March 1971, Congress approved the 26th Amendment to the United States Constitution calling for lowering the voting age for all elections, including state and local ones. The Amendment moved through the states for ratification quicker than any in history. On July 1, 1971, the Amendment, approved by three-fourths of the states, was signed into law. Now, people as young as 18—even Indiana University freshmen—could vote.*

*Bloomington's November 1971 election for mayor, clerk, and city council would be the first in the nation to feature the more youthful electorate.*

*National press coverage followed. The* Chicago Tribune, Los Angeles Times, New York Times, Louisville Courier-Journal, Wall Street Journal, *and* Washington Post *all sent reporters to Bloomington in the lead-up to the election and on the day of the vote itself.*

***

From the time all of us Democratic candidates came together, particularly after the primary, we worked together. We came from different backgrounds and had different priorities but shared important values. The biggest values we shared were the need for more citizen involvement and better communication between elected officials and their constituents.

We met regularly. We kind of divided the labor, with everybody responsible for their own precincts. The at-large candidates were responsible with Frank for the whole city. We became really well-organized.

We had many, many forums. We had many, many coffees. We talked to people constantly. The newspapers and the radio gave us all sorts of coverage. People were more aware than usual that there was a local election. There was a lot at stake.

The unions came out strongly for us—and the unions still had some clout.

Bloomington had two newspapers at the time, the *Herald-Telephone* and the *Courier-Tribune*. The *Courier-Tribune*'s editorial policy was more conservative than the *Herald-Telephone*'s but it had really good reporters. They were curious. They were young and they were kind of inspired by us. I would guess almost all of them voted for us.

But both newspapers endorsed our opponents. Their editorials pretty much said *Beware! These people are scary!* That and, *The students are coming! They're going to take over!*

The people who'd been living here forever, they thought, "Who are these people? These are strangers! They're not one of us."

That was kind of true.

That didn't matter. I began to get a feeling that something major was happening here. We piqued people's interest. We were energetic. People were friendly. They listened.

\*\*\*

*Election day, Tuesday, November 2, 1971. It was overcast and chilly with an occasional sprinkle—a typical Indiana fall day. The polls closed at 6:00pm. Described by newspapers as "the PhD housewife," Charlotte awaited the results.*

\*\*\*

There wasn't much to be done on election day. The hard work had been done in the weeks and months leading up to it. I didn't have a job—I was "the PhD housewife"—so I had time to do things some of the other candidates couldn't do. Very frequently I accompanied Frank McCloskey and the at-large candidates to functions throughout Bloomington. I was all over the city.

We'd done a pretty good job of canvassing everywhere in the city. We knew where our votes were. We believed we had a good chance of winning. We also had a good get-out-the-vote operation. And we had a lawyer in every precinct because we expected some challenges. We felt the Republicans were ready to pounce if anything seemed out of order. There was this fear of all the students voting.

There was a lot of excitement in the air. We didn't know what to expect. I don't believe that people change their votes at the last minute, but they need to be reminded to vote.

The nine of us and Frank and Grace were stationed throughout the community outside the polling places. I stood outside my polling place reminding people who I was, but I wasn't going to push myself on them.

We, the candidates and volunteers, were kind of on edge all day. We spoke excitedly among ourselves: "What's going to happen? What's going on?"

There was a very good turnout. The 1970 census had Bloomington at about 43,000 people. Eighteen thousand voted. That would be a really good turnout today with our population having doubled since then.

And it was a good turnout for the Democrats. The Republicans? Not so much. In the Republican primary, Mayor Hooker just squeaked by—he won by 54 votes. The Republicans were split and the Democrats were unified and coherent. And we were organized.

The Voters Union had gone door to door the weekend before the election carrying sheets with their recommendations. They endorsed Frank and the Democratic slate, except for Jack Morrison, Republican candidate for city council district 1.

The Citizens for Good Government had taken out ads in the papers with their recommendations. They endorsed all the Democratic candidates for city council but one. On the west side, the CGG endorsed the Republican Jack Morrison. I'm reminded of Popeye when I think of him—I am what I am. He was a tough, macho guy who'd been a

Ranger in the Second World War. That meant he was a radio operator, parachuting in behind enemy lines to set up communications lines. He'd learned electronics in the Army and then when he came back from the war he started up his own electronics shop on the west side. He was very, very good at his job. He was half Sioux. That, I think, was a problem for the Republicans here. He was not "couth" enough for them. I liked him.

In any case, we had done what we could to win.

After the polls closed, I went home to eat and freshen up. Paul and I then went down to the *Herald-Telephone* building. They'd started setting up in their big hall early that morning, putting up these huge graphs on the wall labeled with the candidates' names and all the different precincts. Paul and I got there about 8:30.

There was huge crowd. There was cheering. There was elation. But I'd learned long before in previous elections that early on in the night it isn't just the number of votes; you had to know where the votes were coming from. Your strong precincts might show you ahead but what would happen when the rest of the precincts came in?

But one number went up after another and I thought, "Oh, my gosh!"

It was amazing. It was euphoric. The excitement mounted. It got better and better and better. We were getting better than 60 percent of the vote across the board!

It became clear what was happening—it would be a landslide victory for the Democrats. There wasn't the slightest bit of doubt that night.

***

*Someone, Charlotte forgets who, grabbed a microphone and called for her to step up and deliver a victory speech. That person, laughing, quoted a belittling description that'd been bandied about during the campaign by her opposition—that Charlotte was a "somehow inferior" candidate.*

*A newspaper story the next morning described a nervous Charlotte Zietlow climbing a ladder to give her victory speech. Charlotte, the paper re-*

ported, "said in a small voice trembling with emotion... 'It's a great night... a great night... How can I thank you... I had about 300 people out working for me... it is a great victory for the people of Bloomington.'" [All sic.]

The report described the roars of the crowd and the fact that Charlotte couldn't go on because she was choked up.

\*\*\*

Eventually we went home. We invited our friends, Pat and Bob Gross over. And we danced. We didn't even need any music—we just danced! It was so exciting.

We popped open a bottle of Champagne and ate caviar on crackers.

\*\*\*

Charlotte and Paul's kids, Rebecca and Nathan, 8 and 6, had been at home with a babysitter. Rebecca, now a law school professor, remembers that night. She recalls sipping sparkling water, munching on crackers with her brother in their pajamas, and giggling at the delirious adults high-stepping around the living room to the music in their own heads.

The next morning, local and national newspapers launched weeks of analyses of the startling upset. The Herald-Telegraph's headline blared: "Zietlow: The 'Somehow Inferior' Candidate Roars In A Winner."

Charlotte and her fellow Democrats had turned Bloomington on its head. They'd won the mayor's and city clerk's offices as well as eight of nine city council seats. Only Jack Morrison had broken their streak.

The man Charlotte had defeated, Harry Day, a chemistry professor at IU, had met reporters the night before at an almost deserted Republican headquarters. "It's a relief, I guess," he told them. "I'll have more time now to continue my research at the university."

For Charlotte, the campaign had been exciting, but grueling. And the hard work was only just beginning.

# 10

# Beehive

Okay, we won. Now what do we do?

We got ourselves organized. We started drafting ordinances. We started putting together committees. We mapped out committee assignments. We solicited applications for boards and commissions from the general public, not only from the Democrats.

We had a headquarters down on Walnut Street. It used to be Joe Natale's produce market but it had been closed down by 1971. It's now the 4th Street parking garage.

It was just us council members. Frank McCloskey was off being trained to be the mayor. He was being mentored, in a way, by Jim Regester, a canny lawyer, very smart, who was part of the old guard but still supported us in the campaign.

There was no orientation for incoming council members. For years that was something that I thought was needed. Gradually, there is more preparation for newcomers now.

I read things. We all read things. Newspaper coverage of council meetings. Old meeting minutes. Ordinances. Veteran people advised us, but there was no training per se.

Brian de St. Croix created a manpower task force right out of the box. He put together this ad-hoc group of volunteers who were to find answers to certain questions by the summer. How many people are working in Bloomington? Where are they coming from? What kind of training is available? What are the options for people who are retiring?

That the council took any initiative was totally unprecedented. We had read the statutes pretty well and we found we had the power to do things like that. The power just had never been exercised.

I agreed to chair the manpower task force's support services subcommittee. We had a fervor about jobs. We knew that people needed them here. We were liberal Democrats and so we were the first ones to talk about the role local government could play in economic development.

From day one after the election, we just went through one thing after another, ticking off agenda items. We just started doing things. As I look over the minutes of those pre-inauguration planning meetings, I'm surprised at how quickly we did things.

We each established our little territory. We found out what all the positions were and filled them, the ex officio appointments and so forth. Each of us had a specialty. Jack Morrison, for example, took the west side and street lighting.

Sherwin Mizell wanted to be on the planning commission. Jim Ackerman wanted to be on the animal commission, and so on down the line. We created a real, working environmental commission; Wayne Fix wanted that job.

In addition to the support services committee for the manpower task force, I also took transportation, health care, and child care.

I took the left-over assignments for ex officio commission memberships. I got the Community Action Program and the mental health center and there were a couple of other not for profit organizations which I became a member of. That got me out in the community. Nobody else wanted to do it but I actually wanted to do it. I took these posts to find out what was going on in those areas.

We began to work on ordinances in those days leading up to the inauguration. There were a human rights ordinance, an environmental ordinance, a landlord-tenant relationship ordinance and a strong housing code. We re-worked what was an existing drug commission. We started to plan how to redo the zoning ordinance. Planning and zoning was a big issue in the campaign. We talked about developing a communications council because we were kind of aware that things were changing—cable TV was just on the horizon.

We were in the tail-end of the era of patronage. We all agreed—we didn't like patronage. It was a thing of the past. We should have professional people in positions that called for professionals.

Party officials on both sides expected employees to pay into their campaign chests. Indiana still had 2% Clubs. They were funds to which it was expected state and local government employees were to contribute two percent of their pay, theoretically to go for charitable purposes but, in fact, the money was used to underwrite political campaigns. The Democrats and the Republicans had them.

Well, we just stopped that in the city. I never learned the mechanics of it—who would collect the money, who would dole it out and so forth. But I knew it was common. It was related to political hirings and firings. We stated very explicitly in the campaign and at the time we were elected that there would not be political hirings and firings.

We said we'd encourage keeping Republicans in their city jobs if they were doing good work and we did that. That did not make some Democrats happy. They still believed to the victors go the spoils.

Even when I was running, I sat down with the planning department to try to understand why they were doing what they were doing. I tried to understand the workings of the utilities department. I was one of those people who asked a lot of questions. I wasn't very well received by the heads of the departments. They were sure I would help get rid them if I won. That had been the tradition.

We stated very clearly, "Anybody who is qualified may apply for jobs and for boards and commissions. It doesn't matter whether you're a Democrat or a Republican." We did not do a wholesale house cleaning, not at all.

We had to decide who would be the president of the council, the person who would chair the council meetings. I don't remember who suggested it but somebody said, "What about you?"

I wasn't sure I wanted to be president.

They chose me mainly because I had the time. But also I was really one of the main forces in the campaign. I was everywhere. I got to know lots of people.

We urged Frank to hire a professional engineer in the public works department to oversee municipal construction and housing code enforcement. The same in the utilities department; we didn't just want somebody's uncle to head the department but somebody who had experience with water and sewer.

We wanted professionalism all around. We looked at police and fire and realized both departments needed more training for their members, a systemized training with some sort of certification.

At the same time we started urging both the police and fire departments to unionize. At that time, both police and fire were under the city council, not the mayor. He got to choose the chiefs for the departments but we set the salaries for everybody in them, the rank and file.

We encouraged the unions to come in. That made sense. It would bring order to our relationships with those departments. It would bring a structure to the relationships. Otherwise, things were much too personal, too unprofessional. The relationship between the city and the police and fire departments were run under a more patriarchal system that didn't create good feelings on either side. It had been difficult for grievances to be resolved.

Unionization would make it easier for us to work with them. It would bring a level of order. Rather than individual police officers or firefighters coming to us with problems, they could go through their unions. We thought that was very important. Later on, in negotiations, we'd be able to introduce things like physical fitness standards.

For years, ambulance service in Bloomington had been handled by the police. Police officers just loaded people into station wagons. We moved fairly rapidly toward a more professional; ambulance service under the fire department.

\*\*\*

*Inauguration Day, January 3, 1972.*

\*\*\*

It was in the council chambers. Lots and lots of people were there, four or five hundred. It was very exciting. It was a big, huge celebration.

City Hall was where the police department is now. It had been built for the police but Mayor Hooker had taken the building over. Council chambers was where the police department training room is today.

There was feverish activity for the first few months we were in office. But first things first: We had to come up with a place for council members to hang our coats. We had no offices. There was no support staff whatsoever. So we started working on that.

That wasn't easy because there was no line item for support services for the council in the city budget. John Irvine, who was like a deputy mayor or, more accurately, Frank's assistant—he didn't have an official title—was very helpful in getting us through that time. We finally located a little broom closet. Lots of old furniture was stored there. So we left our coats on old chairs. Later, we got a coat rack and some hangers.

The worst part about the building was there were no windows. It was cavelike. It wasn't a pleasant place. We found some posters of windows and put them up.

Before we took office, the building was quiet. There was no sense of activity. Once we got in there it became a beehive, people buzzing in and out.

We were doing things! We weren't waiting for things to happen. We were encouraging people to come in. They would come in saying, "I really want to talk to you about this and that. When are you going to be there?" We had to establish some sort of presence during the day so people could come in and talk. People had great ideas they wanted to share with us.

The previous council and mayor hadn't created a presence. They were out in the community doing their day jobs but as a council, it was as though they didn't even exist. They were a rubber stamp council; we were activists. We made a totally different sound in city hall. We made a lot of noise.

We were doing things and the two newspapers in town chastised us for interfering in the business flow. There's a long tradition of doing things a certain way in Bloomington, they'd write on their opinion pages. That and What did we know? and Who did we think we were?

One of the first things we did was ask that all boards and commissions and committees give us an annual report by the beginning of March, two months hence, to see if they were still alive and well.

Well, there would be no reports. I don't think any of them had anything to say. City government hadn't been a really vibrant, action thing here. It was our intention that if there were boards and commissions they should be active and fully appointed. We wanted to be sure they would be doing something and we could support them.

I think we were each paid maybe a thousand dollars a year. It was definitely part time work for most of us. We met every two weeks, just like now. But I worked pretty much full time.

Jack Morrison was the lone Republican holdover from the previous council. He was the one who'd been around. You can imagine him sitting back and saying, "Oh, you kids. You don't know what you're doing." But he very seldom did that. We treated him with great respect and he returned that respect. We recognized that he had good lines of communication with the people on the west side, with low-income people, with the African-American community. He got along well with all of them. Jack was part Lakota Sioux. He was gruff and feisty. He'd been disrespected by his fellow Republicans, they considered him unrefined.

The first thing we did as a council was to declare him Member Number 1. The rest of us said, "You're Number 1 because you have experience, you're in the first district, and we want you to feel welcome and we want to work with you."

We had our first council meeting and I'm suddenly chairing it and I'm not a master of Robert's Rules. Actually, we followed something called Mason's Manual of Legislative Procedure. Al Towell was our parliamentarian; he used the manual to guide us through our meetings.

I was not practiced and that first meeting was something. We were very excited. The room was full of Realtors and lawyers because we had several spot zonings on the agenda. The first one, as I remember, was at the corner of Washington and 10th Street for a big gray house. It's still there. The developer wanted to take it down and build an apartment building on the site.

So that came to the floor. What I already understood was the chair doesn't talk a lot, the chair makes sure the speaking order is maintained and so forth. So we got into a discussion about this big gray house on Washington. Frank Barnhart at that time was the top attorney for re-zones.

He was nervous. He didn't know what to expect from us. He made his presentation, laying out all his justifications, primarily that the building was old. He said it served no purpose and the highest and best use of the land would be to build an apartment building there. But there were no provisions for parking, nor drainage, nor green space, or anything like that.

One of us asked him when the building had been put up.

"Way back in the '20s!" Barnhart said. "It's not useful anymore."

At this, I did say something. "I just bought a house that was built back then!" I said. "I find it quite serviceable."

The room was filled with lots of real estate men who were tapping their feet and rolling their eyes. Later, they'd tell each other—and the newspapers, "They're destroying our economy! They don't know what they're doing! They're just a bunch of novices!"

We voted the re-zone proposal down. It was the first one in forever that had been turned down.

So our first meeting ended with a lot of very unhappy people. The business people left shaking their heads and tsk-tsking.

The newspapers the next day said, Boy, things are going to be different now; how are we going to survive?

Zoning issues are hard. Zoning should be based on city planning but, back then, not everybody was in favor of planning. Mayor Hooker had been willing to consider strong planning for Bloomington. The more moderate Republicans generally were in favor of it but a lot of people were not.

With city planning, you have to think about what the city is becoming and why. Bloomington did have a planning commission when we came into office, but it was not fully staffed. Monroe County didn't have a planning department at all.

Very few Indiana counties had a planning agenda. Many cities didn't either. Bloomington was kind of innovative in that sense. That was a progressive aspect of Hooker's administration.

The objection was, You're telling me what to do with my property? It was as simple as that. I can build 20 houses on my property if I want and don't you tell me what to do! That's going on in some counties to this day.

We urged much more citizen involvement on the planning board.

We went to work on a new zoning map. The planning commission drew up the map. We went out into the city, almost block by block, advertising it, and inviting people to come in and talk about what was going to happen. We had 37 public hearings in council chambers, night after night after night. Some of them were well-attended and some of them weren't.

At one point, some guys from the university came in to talk to me about the new zoning. George Pinnell, a vice president, and Charley Sturgeon, the facilities manager—high muckety-mucks—came to me and said, "Charlotte...," (because I was never Mrs Zietlow or Dr. Zietlow, always Charlotte) "we need to talk. The university has some strong reservations about these zoning maps."

I said, "What areas, particularly, concern you?"

Pinnell said, "The one south of Third Street."

I said, "Okay. We've got a public meeting scheduled for that one on such and such a day."

He responded very seriously, quietly. "No, we can't come to a public hearing. This has to be private."

I told him it would all become public eventually so why not come that night to make his case?

No, he repeated.

I said we could talk about his concerns but I'd take that information to the public anyway. He obviously thought that when I'd hear his story, I wouldn't make it known. So we had our meeting.

Our map had a special institutional designation for the university that extended to the north side of Atwater Street. The university wanted more. It wanted a whole swath, from 7th to 17th streets, with a special designation.

I told the two university men that many parts of that area contained single-family houses. "So," I said, "this is a question for public discussion."

But the university owned a lot of properties in residential areas. Many, many, many people had made arrangements to leave their property to the university after they died or had sold it to the university while they were alive. But not all the homes were university-owned.

I said, "A lot of people live in that area. I don't think that we can do what you want. You're welcome to come to the public meetings and make your case. But this all has been discussed by the plan commission and what you want is going to be difficult to pass."

Well, I never heard from these men again about this. We implemented the map as drawn up by the planning department. That was the beginning of a testy relationship between us and the university.

We worked very hard on housing code enforcement and developing a landlord-tenant ordinance. That was another bone of contention between us and the university

The university owned a great deal of student housing off-campus. The university was a notorious landlord. A lot of its properties suffered "deferred maintenance." There's a euphemism if I've ever used one! The university didn't want to spend any more money than it had to. As long as the building was standing it could make money. And it didn't want us telling it what to do with it.

Housing was a huge problem that had not been addressed in any appreciable way before us.

If you were living in a dump, if it was roach-infested or there were live wires hanging from the ceiling, you really had no recourse. You could ask your landlord, "Would you please fix this?" But there was no back-up for that. Nobody inspected the apartments. Landlords didn't have to register their units. The electrical system could be faulty but, again, there was no enforcement.

On the financial side, the landlord could retain your security deposit no matter how you'd left the place. He'd say, "Oh, things weren't like this when you came in here." There was no recourse.

Al Towell, particularly, was really into this problem. He worked very hard on it for years.

We were looking at requiring a certain amount of light in each unit, for example. When a landlord split a single-family house into units, a lot of the units wouldn't even have windows.

We said each unit had to have certain amenities and a minimum number of square feet per person. It was a quality of life issue. But the main things we concentrated on were cleanliness and whether the heat and electrical and plumbing worked. The place had to be habitable.

Rewriting the housing code ultimately was successful. The landlord-tenant ordinance was not. We had drawn up an ordinance defining the relationship; both the landlords and the tenants would have responsibilities to each other.

***

*Al Towell, John Irvine, and another attorney, Ed Pinto, negotiated with a landlords group represented by Frank Barnhart for months. Eventually they hammered out a deal. But in the final drafting of the ordinance, the council granted the landlords only three of the four concessions the group had demanded.*

***

We passed the ordinance and within 24 hours we were sued by a group of landlords. There were some very good landlords who supported the ordinance but that didn't matter.

\*\*\*

*The suit came before Monroe County Circuit Court Judge Nat Hill, who ruled that 20 percent of the ordinance was illegal. The city appealed and the Indiana Supreme Court eventually knocked down the ordinance.*

*The housing code rewrite was more successful. It passed during the new council's first year.*

\*\*\*

We added building inspectors, the enforcement would be fines, and there would be provisions for renters to make complaints, and the landlords had to get rental permits. So all the houses around here, many of which are owned by the university, all have to be registered if they're rented out. And if the renter finds something wrong in the house, they can go and complain about it.

\*\*\*

*Even as the new crowd of city council members did all this important work, many in the old guard saw them as nothing more than parvenus or interlopers.*

\*\*\*

One of the complaints the old guard made about us was we'd never had to meet a payroll. Most of the outgoing council were small businessmen. They thought we were idealistic children, dreamers who didn't know how things really worked, especially budgets.

Marilyn Schultz a few years ago wrote a testimonial years later for my 75th birthday celebration, a fundraiser for Middle Way House. "Charlotte loves puzzles. She loves to solve them."

I guess that's right.

For me, figuring out how to get people to participate, then figuring out issues. How do we solve this problem? How do we get better child care? How do we get better transportation? Do we understand the budget?

Yes, we did understand the budget! I don't think there was a moment when I didn't understand the city's budget. People get notions. I thought, Wait a minute. I run a household! We don't have an endless pile of money to do that. I have to figure out how I'm going to spend our money. Of course I understand!

Now we were going to be dealing with hundreds of thousands and millions of dollars instead of twenty and forty dollars, but it's the same idea. That was clear to me.

It was a little startling at first to realize the budget was $35 million a year while Paul's salary was $8000. But the idea was still the same.

None of those guys who criticized us for our fiscal naiveté did that at home.

We had to learn a lot about municipal budgets, how money was spent, how taxes were distributed, what our obligations were. That was all a learning curve. And we didn't have Google. I had to go to the library and dig, dig, dig. Or go to other towns and find out what they were doing.

And the university wasn't offering training for people in local government. Nobody was doing that kind of thing. The School of Public and Environmental Affairs does that now and then today but in 1971 there was no training or classes in local government.

A tax issue came up pretty early in that first year. It looked as if the city was going to owe a lot of money in state taxes. I don't remember any of the details. It was fairly complex. Everybody in the mayor's office and the controller's office was in despair. Frank couldn't quite understand it.

I said, "Can I look at it?"

Frank said, "Sure, yeah, but you won't understand."

But I did!

I figured it out. Then we had to undo things. I understood exactly what was happening.

With Brian St. Croix's manpower task force we were hoping to get a handle on the facts about our workers in Bloomington and Monroe

County—who they were, what was their nature, what were their skills.

As the task force's support services committee chair, I worked on the things workers needed to get and keep their jobs, like what kind of transportation they needed, what kind of health care, what they would do with their kids—stuff like that.

We started work on it quickly and we worked hard on those issues. We had a huge report ready by June of our first year.

When we came into office not many Indiana locales had economic development strategies. Some did. Ft. Wayne surely did. South Bend. Terre Haute had some. But that was about it among Indiana cities like ours.

In the period before we came into office, economic development was pretty much in the hands of a blue-ribbon committee that spent much of its time trying to attract national companies to set up manufacturing operations here. For example, General Electric didn't just wander in; the city lured it, through consultants. Otis and Westinghouse were here because of that too. RCA had been in Bloomington for some time before that outreach was started.

We needed more jobs so the blue-ribbon committee went out to find them. The committee's idea was always to bring in outside national and international companies.

By 1972, that kind of thing just wasn't happening anymore, not only in Bloomington but across the nation. We began to emphasize helping local operations get going. Bill Cook founded his medical instrument business in 1963 and set up his first factory on South Curry Pike, right by the Otis factory. Cook was encouraged and supported by the city and the county in various ways and the company grew.

We asked ourselves how we could entice businesses here, how to keep them here, and what we could do to make life happy here for the people who owned those businesses.

We realized quality of life was a very important factor. If we wanted to get people from the outside to come here, we'd have to make this a nice place for them to come to. They'd see there were no sidewalks and no curbs and gutters they'd think, Bah, I'm not going to bother with that place. I can go to Ann Arbor. I can go to Madison, Wisconsin. I can go to the places around Champaign-Urbana. I can go to any place else that has sidewalks. That's a big part of it.

We started Bloomington's economic development commission. We wanted to enhance the income of the people in this community. We would work with businesses so they'd know they were going to get sewer and water, they were going to get tax abatement through TIFs and other gimmicks. That all came in the 20 years after we took office.

There was so much to do! All these undone things. We just went down the list checking off each item as fast as we could.

We saw that Bloomington needed a transit system. When Paul and I moved here in 1964, there was a sort of jitney bus operation, an on-call thing with one bus. The university didn't have a bus system either.

There was a cab company and we quickly authorized a second one.

Jim Wray was Frank's head of public works. We asked him to get us information on how we could start a bus system. From that information, we made the recommendation to start Bloomington Transit. It was more than a recommendation; it was more a mandate that we gave to the mayor. We said, "We need to do something and we need to do it now."

We kicked off Bloomington Transit by July. We rolled out our first bus the next spring.

We benefitted from many of the programs that had begun as part of President Johnson War on Poverty. In health care, for example, the federal Community Action Program picked up the ball in that area and created the Health Service Bureau in Bloomington. CAP went to work with a stand-alone nonprofit called Public Health Nursing to offer home visits, mainly to low-income people.

Similarly, we eventually got to a child care voucher program. I'd learned so much about how the big employers here viewed their workers with families while I was running office in '71. I visited company heads and factory managers throughout my campaign.

Many of those people really didn't know much about what was going on with their workers and their children. A lot of factory workers were women because they had smaller, dextrous fingers, good for assembling delicate parts.

Personnel people were aware that there was a lot of absenteeism and tardiness among these women. They had to have known that had a lot to do with them taking care of their children.

The personnel man at Westinghouse said, "We developed a system for dealing with that."

"That's interesting," I said. "What did you do?"

"We had a special line put in so that women could call their children or be called if there were an emergency."

"So, does it work?"

"Well," the man said, "we took it out."

"Why did you do that?"

"Because it was being used too much!"

It was amazing.

I'd just come back from Bratislava. All the plants there had child care! You would go to work with your children. I never talked about that publicly. Czechoslovakia was a communist country; I'm not totally suicidal. But it was in my head. It made so much sense.

I did enough talking about child care, though. That was bad enough. The *Courier-Tribune* ran an editorial saying I was about to take away people's children. This was all thought to be part of the communist conspiracy.

Another thing we did immediately was start on sidewalks—and not just to foster a better economic climate here. In February of our first year, a child was killed after being hit by a car on High Street. There was no sidewalk on High Street. We built one right away on the east side of the street. We said we had to have sidewalks throughout the city, an effort that's still continuing to this day. There are still no sidewalks on the street where I lived for more than 40 years.

We created an ad-hoc traffic task force to study what the patterns were and see what we could do to make them more efficient.

The environment—there was a commission already but all the spots on it hadn't been filled. This was just a couple of years after the Environmental Protection Agency was started so there was a lot of interest in that. Recycling was just becoming big. We asked that people in city government come up with a proposal for how we could do recycling. Several groups who strongly supported recycling were right there at our first meeting and at every meeting after that. In February, Jim Wray, the public works head, came up with a recycling idea for city hall and the various departments around town. It didn't work out but he tried and it was a start.

Garbage pickup at the time was done by a private company. We had to wait for the contract to run out and then we established a city department for trash pickup.

We created an animal commission and a municipal animal shelter.

There was a drug abuse commission when we started but it hadn't begun meeting yet. But there was a problem here with heroin. Middle Way House was in existence already but it wasn't yet a domestic violence resource. Originally it was an emergency shelter, a crash pad for people overdosing. Then it started helping people with venereal diseases. The hospitals didn't deal with either the drug or the venereal disease problems.

If you had a sexually transmitted disease or had a problem with drugs, where would you go? You couldn't go to the Girl Scouts or to the Chamber of Commerce. If you overdosed, you could go to the hospital for treatment but the hospital certainly wasn't doing any education or prevention outreach.

But people knew there was this kind of amorphous thing called Middle Way House. You could go talk to someone there. STD sufferers began to trickle into Middle Way House and we wanted to help it help them. All us new council members plus Jack Morrison listened as Middle Way House people told us about their clientele. The words venereal disease entered the minutes of the city council for the first time. We listened; we didn't put our hands over our mouths in horror.

We were activists and we wanted to get the city machinery involved with all these problems and solutions. Everything became more institutionalized to the point now where we've probably reached the high point of that movement. I think we should start backing off a little bit. We were trying to be protective without becoming too bureaucratic but now things have become very bureaucratized.

We were doing all this stuff and Frank, for the most part, agreed with the things we wanted to do. He was busy, mainly, working on annexation.

New city attorney Jim Regester's feeling was it was very, very important to annex surrounding areas to the city. The city limits were like lacework. The industrial west side was all outside the city. Curry Pike was where most of the manufacturing was. That was where the tax money was.

Otis was there. General Electric. Westinghouse. RCA was down south on Rogers and Patterson. That was a huge factory. Huge, huge. When we came in, there were maybe 5,000 employees, way down from their high of 12,000. But thousands of people were still coming into the area every day from all over the five-county region to work in and around Bloomington.

And there were other, smaller ones. Cook Medical was just a teeny, tiny little thing at the time but it was outside the city limits too. You'd go up Curry Pike and you'd pass one big factory after another. Otis had just come in and that was big because it was doing custom elevators for projects all over the world. They'd go on to manufacture the elevators for the Petronas Towers in Kuala Lumpur, the tallest building in the world in the late '90s. It was all pretty exciting.

That placed a burden on all city services. We had to find a way to pay for that.

Regester's plan was to not try to do the whole thing at once. What he and Frank decided to do was break all that lacework down into separate parcels. So there were many, many annexation ordinances and that whole effort was successful. At our first meeting, Jim Regester reported that he'd been working with the law firm now known as Ice Miller, Dinadio & Ryan, the bonding agent for the state and the expert on all municipal financial arrangements. Jimmy said Ice Miller had sent invitations to all those businesses and factories on the incorporated west side, inviting them to join the city. Thus far, Regester reported, there hadn't been any acceptances.

Jim Regester and Bob McCord of Ice Miller had worked out a negotiating strategy. So, Jimmy said, we'll go after them one by one. They went and negotiated in little bits and pieces. Work on it. Figure out a way to make it impossible for them to say no. One thing they offered was that for a period of time the industries would work in lieu of taxes or at a reduced rate and then gradually their rates would go up over time. That kind of thing reduced opposition from the industries.

It was about a year and a half later, we kind of filled in the previously unincorporated areas into the city. Most of the ordinances that first year were annexation ordinances.

By 1975, the city limits looked a lot less lacy.

A month into our first year, the issue of Vietnam came up. We had a resolution on the war in Indochina. Of course, it wasn't binding. The President of the United States was not going to change because of us. In any case, we were Democrats, we had strong feelings about the war, so we put it on the agenda and we talked about it and then we took a vote on it.

We assumed seven of us would vote for it. We thought probably Jack Morrison, the Republican, would not. Dick Behen? We weren't sure.

We had this long discussion and we came to the vote. The first to vote was Number 1, Jack Morrison.

He said, "We're talking about war here. I've been in a war. War is awful. It's terrible. I hope we never fight another war. I hate war. And I'm going to vote for this."

We were totally astonished. That validated our position. What we were doing wasn't crazy.

When my turn came, I said I'd been wondering why we were doing this and the deeper we got into the war, the more I wondered. We were following a misguided policy. We were expending incredible amounts of blood and treasure. If these young kids who were going over there and coming back weren't dead or injured, they were psychologically damaged. I knew some of them, like Marc Haggerty. We were just beginning to see the flood of veterans coming back—and for what purpose?

As time has gone by, we've learned, of course, that the policy was totally misguided. We were afraid of China coming into the war but we neglected to acknowledge that China and Vietnam have always been at each others' throats. The "domino effect" wasn't going to take place. And we had work to do here at home! The war in Vietnam took money away from the War on Poverty. President Johnson had promised we could have butter and guns—but we couldn't have both. The country wasn't ready to expend money on social services when we had a war to fight.

Dick Behen voted against the resolution.

We think we have a divided country today but I would say that at that time things were worse. Things became very personal. It wasn't just party against party.

This community had come through relatively calmly, partly because of the Hooker administration. The sheriff and the mayor had shown restraint. The university didn't provoke violence. The only real violence we'd seen was when some Ku Klux Klan members had burned down the Black Market around Christmas, 1968.

***

*A group of African-American students, faculty, and supporters opened a store on the northeast corner of Dunn and Kirkwood streets in the fall of 1968. They called it The Black Market. It featured Afro-centric books, clothing, records, arts and crafts. Less than three months later, the store was firebombed, destroying all the merchandise and artwork within. Three men were arrested several weeks later. Two of them were members of the local Ku Klux Klan chapter and the third was the regional Grand Dragon. The two men were found guilty of the firebombing and the Grand Dragon was found guilty on a weapons charge. The incident inflamed racial tensions in Bloomington*

*Events in the outside world exacerbated tensions here. In May, 1972, the Nixon administration ordered a massive bombing campaign, called Operation Linebacker, against North Vietnamese strongholds. The escalation enraged many who'd seen the United States involvement in Vietnam winding down since President Johnson ordered a bombing halt in March, 1968, leading to the start of the Paris peace talks. Several college campuses around the nation experienced disruptions, notably the University of California at Berkeley. Would campus disruptions, and even more violence, break out in Bloomington?*

***

We immediately got together and said we didn't want things to go wrong here. We called in the student government people. Jeff Richardson was student body president.

"We want to keep things at a low level," we said to the students. Together, we decided we would fan out in pairs, a city person and a student, throughout the city and collect signatures on petitions for peace. It would give us something to do. It would allow us to talk to people, to calm things down. It gave us the opportunity to work together. The students could see the city was serious and not the enemy. The petition called for a resolution calling us "The City of Peace."

People felt good about it, students and citizens working together, making our voices heard. That was good. I went out to the west side with my student partner, ringing doorbells. We agreed beforehand that if people slammed their doors in our faces, we'd just say thank you and go on to the next door.

We held public hearings. We scheduled alternating speakers, one person for followed by one person against. That became pretty tense. A lot of big, tough-looking guys told us we were crazy.

Later, I found out the police had been shadowing me for protection.

We had a big rally on the square, again with speakers on this side followed by speakers on that side. I saw a lot of law enforcement people there, milling around throughout the crowd. It went peaceably but at times things got very personal.

But, in the end, it all worked. There was no violence, there were no disruptions on the campus.

Like most college towns, there had been a real division between town and gown here. The university did not feel that it was part of the town.

But I was an academic in addition to being the first woman on the council in years. I had a PhD. My husband taught at the university. That might have estranged me from the townie part of Bloomington but during our election that whole wall started coming down.

When we campaigned, we went to every house in the city. Previously, the gown had not gotten involved in Bloomington politics. The gown wasn't much interested in things going on around town. But we talked to people about streets and sidewalks and zoning, things that were of interest to all of us, including the academics and the students. Town and gown melted together.

Still in that first year, I had a real break with Frank.

There was a gubernatorial election in Indiana in 1972. This was before the major parties chose their candidates by primary election. It was clear Otis Bowen would be the chosen candidate for governor by the Republican convention. He was very popular.

Things weren't so clear for the Democrats. There was a state fight for the nomination. There was Matt Welsh, who'd already been governor in the '60s, a very nice, gentle, Lee Hamilton-ish sort of person. He was distinguished and came from a good family, and so forth. He was the voice of the Democratic establishment. Larry Conrad was running against him. He was a legislative assistant for Sen. Birch Bayh. He was very ebullient, an energetic guy with lots of ideas. He was much less conservative than Welsh, much more willing to try new things.

Both Conrad and Welsh came down to Bloomington to talk to me and Frank. It became clear to me that the only chance the Democrats had to beat Bowen would be to run Larry Conrad. I threw my support behind him.

I talked to Frank. We had long discussions about it. Frank decided he would throw in with Welsh. Frank told me Conrad was too energetic. He wasn't establishment enough. "He doesn't look like a governor to me," Frank said.

We totally disagreed on that. We had begun to take different paths. Politically, Frank was showing himself to be more conservative than I was. He wasn't really interested in changing things. He was starting to get comfortable in the mayor's seat. He didn't want to rock the boat. He was cautious. He was going to go with the good old boys.

Welsh won the Democratic nomination and Bowen won the general election.

I was disappointed in Frank and he was annoyed with me. I was a troublemaker. That was the beginning of our disaffection.

I thought, "Gee, Frank, you're not the liberal guy I thought you were."

Frank was from Philadelphia. He'd been in the Air Force and had worked as a newspaper reporter to put himself through law school. He was very smart and he was a good writer. He was a thoughtful person, but he wanted security and the rest of us who were elected with him in '71 were no longer "safe."

In the summer of 1972, Frank had a college intern named Rob Saltzman, a Dartmouth student who was writing a paper about municipal politics. The gist of the paper would turn out to be the gap between those in local government whom Saltzman described as idealists and those he considered pragmatists. Frank, according to Saltzman, was a pragmatist. The likes of Charlotte Zietlow would be idealists, pie-in-the-sky types who were big on ideas and ideals and, consequently, less able to get things done.

Frank and I would really bump heads a short time later when the idea of running a big concrete sewer pipe down the middle of Clear Creek came up.

# 11

# The Real World

*Charlotte and her colleagues, as a group, often were criticized for not knowing how things in the "real world" work. Among the barbs thrown at them—and specifically her—were they'd never had to hustle to make sure their employees' paychecks would clear each pay period. The old guard council members were businessmen. In their minds, they—and they alone— knew how to balance a budget and pay bills. To them, Charlotte and company were naive.*

***

They told us, "You can't understand a budget until you've met a payroll." Even some of my fellow council members implied that about me. I was, after all, a mere "PhD Housewife." They forgot that I ran a home; the dollar amounts were less but all the same principles applied.

***

*Charlotte commiserated with other women who were new office-holders. Like her, they found life in a Midwest college town limiting, especially for faculty wives.*

***

There were no opportunities for women like me. There were few opportunities for women, period. In my case, I couldn't go to work as a teacher at the University because they didn't hire faculty wives for tenure-track positions. They only hired wives for fill-in jobs for a short time and for little or no money. So that was not an option.

I could have gone to work for Westinghouse, for example, but those companies wouldn't want people who were overqualified—they might ask too many questions.

Overall, women just weren't being hired for many higher-paying jobs around here. There were plenty of big employers but they wanted unskilled laborers.

\*\*\*

*Another woman in the same boat was Marilyn Schultz. She had a master's degree in Spanish and had taught French at DePauw University in Greencastle. Then she'd decided to get her PhD in Bloomington and moved to town. Here, she'd gotten involved with the Voters Union, through which Charlotte met her. They became fast friends.*

\*\*\*

Marilyn's about ten years younger than I am. But we recognized that we shared the same values—political and social values. We were interested in languages. We were interested in literature. We hit it off. She was one of the people who had interviewed me for the Voters Union when I was running for city council, to see if I was an acceptable candidate.

Marilyn decided in the middle of 1972 to run for the state general assembly. It's not a full-time job; Indiana has a citizen legislature. I supported her in the primary and helped her, organizing my precinct for her, knocking on doors, talking to people. She won the primary and then she won the general election, which was a surprise.

She was assigned to the ways and means committee, a very desirable position dealing with raising revenue for all the needs of government. She zeroed in on the school funding formula.

I wasn't completely baffled by government finances at all. Early on in my term, there was a big problem with the city's finances. Frank had all the documents and the projections but they didn't do him any good. He said to me, "I don't understand this. Here, take all this. Maybe you can make sense of it."

I read all the papers and figured it out. Apparently, the previous administration had deferred payments on money the city owed so, at the end of the year, our debt looked better than it really was. The next year, a lot of the money budgeted for accounts payable would be going toward back pay-outs rather than current pay-outs. We were going to have a huge shortfall.

I came back to him and said, "This is what the problem is." He pored over the paperwork again and said, "You're right!"

He told the city comptroller what I'd concluded and she said, "Yes, that's it!"

I understood it and then was able to explain it to the other members of the council. Still, for our critics and even some of the members of council, I couldn't understand a budget because I'd never met a payroll.

In May of '73, after Marilyn had taken office at the beginning of the year, I had her over for lunch. We had omelets, a baguette, a salad, and a bottle of wine. We talked about this and that and then I said, "So, Marilyn, how do you like working in the legislature?"

She told me she really enjoyed it but she was getting sick of all these guys, her colleagues, saying she could never understand a budget because she'd never met a payroll!

I said, "Isn't that interesting. That happens to me, too."

She said, "Most of them don't meet payrolls either, yet they criticize me." Then she added, "Why don't we meet a payroll together?"

"Yeah, let's meet a payroll. How do we do that?"

She said, "This omelet is really good. Why don't we open a restaurant?"

"What a wonderful idea," I said. "We're both good cooks. You love to cook and I love to cook."

Then we poured another glass of wine and realized something. "You know," Marilyn said, "Restaurants are a lot of work, and we're never going to be home with our families..."

"You're right," I said. "Let's not do a restaurant."

"Then what will we do?"

I asked her, "Have you ever been to Crate & Barrel? Every time I go to Chicago, I go to Crate & Barrel. I go there because I know I can always find something I need there."

You couldn't find anything here. I could never find a knife that was any good in Bloomington. I'd have to get my necessary kitchen goods by mail order.

At that time, Crate & Barrel had only one store, the first, in an old elevator factory on Wells Street in Chicago's Old Town. They still were putting all their merchandise out in crates and barrels. They had a big sign on the wall showing what ships were coming in to New York and what things would be on those ships that the store would stock.

Marilyn said, "We could certainly use something like that in this area. Nobody is even remotely close to doing anything like that. We can do it ourselves!"

We needed to have a plan. We talked to our friend Maryann Grossack, who was a Certified Public Accountant and one of the first female accountants in town. We talked to a lawyer. And we needed money.

We went to talk to a bank and the people there wouldn't give us the time of day. We figured we each could rustle up $5000. Marilyn had a friend named Ann Bron who was willing to put in another $5000. Now we had $15,000. Then I talked to my rich relatives, aunts Louie and Aggie, and they put up $30,000, which stunned me.

Now we've got $45,000. That is what we have to work with. Ann made plans to go to Germany for a year but she left her investment money here. So in the end, Marilyn and I moved forward with what we had on hand. It was enough to start but we would have to watch our pennies.

It turned out we did remarkably well considering we were ignorant and under-capitalized.

Marilyn took a business school class in accounting during the summer at the university. She said, "I'll work the books and you find out if we can get the kinds of things we want to sell and get them for the prices we can afford." We decided on three criteria for our merchandise: the things had to be useful; they had to be well-designed; and they had to be relatively affordable.

I went up to the national gift show at McCormick Place in Chicago and then I went to the Merchandise Mart. I knew some of the brands and manufacturers already but I had no idea what would be available to us, just starting out. Every time I saw something interesting, I got the catalog and I got contact information for the supplier. I collected three big shopping bags full of catalogues.

Then Marilyn and I sat down, looked everything over, and said, "We can do this!"

Still, we didn't quite know how to go about ordering. But we started the whole business up. We had a lawyer, a man, who handled our incorporation. He was one of those people who doesn't want you to understand what they're doing so they can have the upper hand. It took us a while to figure out he was treating us like infants. He would explain things as if speaking in a foreign language. "Just do as I say," he'd tell us.

We worked with him for a while and then Maryann Grossack took over as our accountant, handling a lot of the things the lawyer had—or should have. She was wonderful. She was honest and smart and she didn't try to make us feel stupid.

We had our minds firmly set on opening downtown. At the time, there were no empty storefronts around the square. One day we walked around the square three times and, suddenly, we saw people moving out of a clothing store on the south side of the square, on Kirkwood Avenue.

The building was owned by the University. It had been donated by an alumnus. As the University was wont to do at the time, nothing had been done with the building. The electrical system wasn't improved. There were other problems. But the rent wasn't terribly expensive and so we were able to sign a lease.

People thought we were crazy, but we were determined. They'd say, shocked, "You're going downtown? Oh, downtown's dead! People don't go downtown. And there's no parking!" Sort of contradictory. But shoppers were going to the new College Mall about two miles east on 3rd Street.

We'd tell them, "The only thing that's going to save downtown is stores like ours."

That was a conscious decision. The downtown is important to a community. It's the center of a community. We needed local merchants downtown and on the square. There were some—Whiteside's for clothing, the original Bloomington Hardware, Southern Sporting Goods (which even had a soda fountain), and other locally-owned businesses that provided good service and quality. Other businesses on the square included the Oaken Bucket restaurant; the Betty Jean Shop which sold cards and candy; a men's clothing store; a drugstore.

Even these downtown merchants were negative about downtown when we were opening. They couldn't see the upside of what they were doing. They complained no one was coming downtown to shop because there was no parking. That's what they told us.

We said, "People will find us. If they want to come to our store, they'll figure out a way to get here. They'll come!"

Many of the other businesses on the square were leery of us; they were strong Republicans. But we all became good friends after they realized we didn't have fangs.

They saw us working really hard and realized we were totally committed to downtown. We joined the Central Business Association, which had been moribund. We became cheerleaders for downtown.

One day before we opened, Marilyn and I and two friends, Tim Mayer and Joe Kellog, went to visit Crate & Barrel. Tim Mayer, who'd later become a long-serving city council member, was a designer. He'd come from Kansas City to teach graphic design at the School of Fine Arts. Joe Kellog was a legendary character, a huge guy, a builder, and sort of a lone wolf.

The four of us got in a car before dawn and drove up to Chicago, to the original Crate & Barrel store on Wells Street. Tim drew pictures of how the displays were set up and the kind of shelving they had. Joe assessed how they put the whole thing together.

Marilyn and I went around the store, looking at the labels on the bottoms of things, and writing down the names of the manufacturers. We were corporate spies! We were shameless. We spent three or four hours there.

We came home and Tim designed the store and Joe built it. Tim had some new ideas and he was willing to help us do this so he could try out these ideas.

We had these wooden grids that we suspended from the ceiling, as well as in the display windows, from which we hung merchandise. We got a bunch of crates that we could stack in different ways. We got these wonderful adjustable shelves made of wood and imported from Sweden. Everything was neutral in color so that the merchandise stood out.

Tim and Joe designed an island in the middle of the store for our sales counter.

We patched it all together.

Meanwhile, we had all these catalogs and we were trying to figure out what to do to get merchandise in the store. Then a sales rep I'd met on my earlier trip to Chicago dropped in. Her name was Jackie. She carried about six of the 25 lines we were looking for. She told us she'd be happy to help us figure things out and stock the place. She spent two days with us, working with us at my house.

One of her lines was Now! Designs, aprons and potholders. She asked us questions like, "Do you have any idea what a case of soufflé dishes weighs?" Of course, we didn't. We had to ask ourselves, how many people want to buy soufflé dishes and how many should we order. She helped us with all of that.

Jackie was a godsend. Through her, we got some sense of how to do things.

We really liked Chinese baskets. They were just coming into the country. We were just beginning to get imports from the People's Republic of China. But we were in a quandary. We had to search our souls. Should we order things from China? China had been America's enemy! And we were Democrats; we didn't want to be called communists. A lot of people were perfectly willing to call any Democrats communists at that time.

But President Richard Nixon had opened up relations with mainland China. So that made it okay.

These Chinese baskets came in different sizes, nested. Tim strewed them out in the windows. They looked so nice, simple. We hung some from the grids. Customers were very excited about it all. They'd never seen anything like our store!

Marilyn and I were too busy gearing up to notice what people were saying about us. The people started telling me how excited they were to see us come into the square. We had no idea of the buzz that was going on around town. And Marilyn was still in the legislature and I was still on the city council!

With the help of all these people, Marilyn and I just made this store up out of whole cloth. Our lunch, when we first had the idea, had been in May. We opened on November 3rd.

We were deluged. People just came and came and came. We hadn't thought about stocking wrapping paper and we didn't have any boxes. We hadn't realized what a big deal Christmas would be. We learned quickly.

We scrounged through our basements for wrapping paper and boxes we could use. We had to borrow tissue paper from Papagalo's women's clothing store down the block.

We hired a friend, Nancy Hardy. We agreed to hire only good people who knew how to cook and knew what they were talking about. Nancy was exactly my age, a really competent person. We would never have a lot of staff at any one time, always two or three people, but over time we hired a whole bunch of people. Just a stellar bunch.

Marilyn and I paid ourselves salaries—not a lot, and that was the last thing we paid. We paid our taxes first. That was Maryann Grossacks's mantra: "You're not getting out of bed today unless you recite three times 'I will pay my taxes first!'"

Christmas had been exhilarating. And then January came. It was a kind of a letdown but we took the opportunity to regroup. We figured out a lot more about how to make the store successful.

Bloomington Hardware was the closest thing around us to competition. They sold a few of the same things we did. They sold a Chemex coffee pot but it turned out their staff didn't know how to use it. They told their customers to go over to our store and ask what to do with the things. We were happy to help—we sold filters for Chemex. When you sell a new coffee pot you're really selling a lifetime of coffee filters for it.

At that point, I'd become a full-timer at the store, working six to eight hours a day there as a sales clerk and I always did the windows and arranged things in the store. Merchandising and selling were the fun parts. I was responsible for most of what little marketing we did. I was also pretty involved in the Central Business Association.

Marilyn and I did the ordering jointly. We loved the Chinese stuff. We wanted to order a lot of the peasant-type stuff but we had to go out and find it—not many of the distributors were supplying it. Eventually we were able to order woks and bamboo steamers and Chinese utensils. We'd get them in big heavy boxes packed in straw, straight from China.

And then our shelves didn't arrive by opening day! So we took these Chinese woven trays and strung them together with macramé yarn and hung them from the ceiling. We had these tiers of trays and baskets here and there, full of merchandise. We made do.

*** 

*By their second Christmas as shopkeepers, Charlotte and Marilyn happened to hear about a new French device for the kitchen that now was being marketed in the US. In 1973, the same year Goods Inc. opened, a couple named Carl and Shirley Sontheimer (he was an electronics wizard) had taken a machine previously sold exclusively in Europe called the*

Robot-Coupe *(pronounced ROE-boe COO) and rebranded it in this country as the Cuisinart. It was revolutionary, capable of doing in seconds what had taken cooks long minutes and even hours to do by hand. The Sontheimers had rolled their Cuisinart out at the January 1973 National Housewares Exposition in Chicago, before Goods, Inc. was even an idea. Charlotte and Marilyn knew nothing of the machine that one day would be in millions of American kitchens until an Indiana University law professor named Doug Boshkoff came in to ask for one. He was the cook in his family.*

***

Doug came in and said, "So, Charlotte, I want one of those French machines that chop things up."

I said, "What's that? Like a blender?"

"No, it's not a blender. It prepares food finely. You don't need to put liquid in it. It's called Robot-Coupe."

I'd never heard of it. We asked him lots of questions about it. He was a very smart and interesting person and a really serious cook. So we did our homework.

Research is something I can do well. There was no internet back then. We had to make phone calls. We called some of the people we'd been buying from. One of the things that distinguished us was we'd go to the gift shows and the housewares shows and the Merchandise Mart and other shows around the country and just go from booth to booth, buying something here and buying something there. So we got to know and got known by many of the manufacturers and distributors.

Most stores have a rep come in and say, "Here, choose from these products." We had more than 200 sources.

We learned we couldn't get the Robot-Coupe in this country but we could get the Cuisinart here. Somehow, we'd tracked it down.

We bought two of them. They were expensive; we must have paid $60 in those days for each one. And we didn't have a lot of capital either. We would sell them for $125.

It must have been late fall when they came in. We worried: "Who will buy these? Why would anyone besides Doug pay $125 for something like this?"

Nevertheless, I thought they were amazing machines. I told Paul all about them. I said, "They're just unbelievable. They do all these different things!"

Then one day just before Christmas, I came in and Anne Bron, who'd returned from Germany, was wrapping up the second one! I said, "We sold the other one? Gee, how exciting!"

Anne seemed a little nervous. She said, "Yeah, my husband bought it for me."

"That's amazing!"

She laughed. "It is. He never spends anything on me."

Then it was Christmas morning. I came down and under the tree was this Cuisinart that Anne had been wrapping! It was mine; Paul had bought it for me.

I spent all that Christmas day using it. I made lemon cake and a sauce and a pâté. It was so much fun!

Then I became a very enthusiastic salesperson for it. We sold many, many of them. Some people still have their old ones they'd bought from us from that time. Doug Boshkoff died in 2015 but his wife Ruth still has the one he bought from us.

As I said, we were very distrusted by the other businesses around the square at first. Then we became known as the major cheerleaders for downtown. We believed in it and they hadn't.

Marilyn was still in the legislature in Indianapolis. She'd stay up there during the week and come home on weekends to work in the store.

When my second congressional campaign was finished in November, '78, I tried to think of what I was going to do next. I asked myself, "Do I want to stay at this? Do I want to do something else?" I looked around to see what my options were but there didn't seem to be anything interesting out there.

I really liked working at the store but it seemed we need to do something more with it. Marilyn agreed. We wanted to do cooking classes and expand our inventory. But we needed more space.

We identified a really nice spot on the north side of the square, where Grazie! Italiano restaurant is now. At the time, the space had been occupied by the Ashram. The Ashram people made furniture and sold it there. They'd also built a loft in the rear of the store, kind of a story-and-a-half platform made of cherry wood. Farther back, they had a skylit garden with a tree growing right inside the store. The space was very attractive. Marilyn and I really liked it and it wasn't much more expensive than where we were.

The Ashram had built this wonderful store and we were lucky to get it. So we took it.

Once again, Tim Mayer came in and helped us design the new store. It was very raw wood-y, like the old store with the same sorts of wood shelving and lots of crates scattered around.

We built a kitchen and a huge display case that was lighted for the new glassware we wanted to get in. We did cooking classes. We got in linens and dishes. We brought in Wedgwood and flatware. We did a lot more gift-y things—Chinese and Japanese goods. We had Nambé, the high-end metal-alloy kitchenware. It was extremely stylish. We had a good time there.

\*\*\*

*The United States experienced a six-month recession in early 1980. The recovery was short-lived: the global economy tumbled the next year and the US officially re-entered recession in July, 1981.*

\*\*\*

It was the early '80s. The economy was not in good shape, both nationally and in Bloomington. The strip of 6th Street where our new store was located wasn't getting much business. People weren't walking around, shopping. Our business declined, as did everybody else's.

That's when the people from what's now known as the Simon Property Group came by and told us what a wonderful store we had.

Mel Simon was in the process of building up the biggest shopping mall empire in the nation and his company had just opened up a new mall on the east side.

They said, "Goods Inc. would so enhance our mall! It could be the jewel in our crown."

We were a little bit panicked by the recession and we got schmoozed. It was a hard decision and people were going to be mad at us if we'd leave the square but we'd gotten to the point where we were desperate to keep the store open. So we moved.

We signed a ten-year lease. We got a bigger space. We did a lot of work with it. We expanded our inventory further. We had more foot traffic and plenty of parking.

It was a mistake. We didn't enjoy the experience. It cost us more. We had to be open much longer. Our sales weren't that much greater but our expenses were.

After two years, Marilyn and I agreed we'd either have to get out of the lease or close the store.

But it was a ten-year lease and Simon had thousands of lawyers. So, our friend Tim Ellis, a Realtor who liked our store, offered to go with us to see the people who'd talked us into moving to the mall.

We made our case. We said, "You talked us into this. It's not working. We're going to have to close."

Well, they liked us and recognized it wasn't a good fit. They said, "Okay, we don't want you to go under." They let us out of our lease.

In the meantime, we'd found that the Penney's on the west side of the square was about to close. The space was significantly smaller than what we had in the mall but it would be much less expensive. And it had light! There are no windows in malls. And Marilyn and I never entered the store thought the mall. We came in through the back door and left through the back door.

It was so exciting—the Penney's space had daylight! We were so happy about that. So we signed a lease there.

We squeezed in and re-opened downtown.

\*\*\*

*Goods Inc. did well—mostly—on three sides of Courthouse Square. The store helped revitalize what had become a ho-hum shopping district. But even as the square livened up, the courthouse it surrounded became more and more decrepit—and dangerous.*

\*\*\*

The courthouse was a mess. There were two bathrooms in the back—one for men and one for women. That was where vagrants and alcoholics hung out. It was notorious and smelly. And the basement was full of raw sewage!

There was an iron staircase in the back and it was filled with boxes of files. If you wanted to leave the office section, you needed a key to get out. If you found yourself in that area and didn't have your key, you could not get out! It was a fire trap.

\*\*\*

*That courthouse would play a central role in Charlotte's political life as the 1970s turned to the '80s. But first, Charlotte's road took a few more twists and turns.*

# 12

## The Bean Lady

About two and a half years into my term on the city council, I realized how clearly important Congress was and, just as clearly, how our sitting Congressman, John Myers, wasn't doing much there. He provided good constituent services but he didn't introduce bills, he wasn't known for any particular issue.

Jim Wray, Frank McCloskey's right-hand man here, had decided to run in the Democratic primary. He was very competent in a lot of ways but he wasn't a campaigner. He was a wonderful staff person; not a good front man. His idea was to go over to Terre Haute, the power center of our district, and hang out with the powers that be there. Terre Haute at the time was a real hornets nest of Democrats, with four or five factions who wouldn't even speak to each other. It still is today.

I had a friend named Jackie Prose who'd graduated from Indiana State University in Terre Haute. She said, "Charlotte, I know people in that city. I'll take you there. But I want to warn you: Never have lunch with any one of the public officials there unless you plan to have lunch with all of them. And let each one know in advance that you're planning to have lunch with the other. You can't play favorites with any of those factions!"

Terre Haute was very turf-y and territorial. Politics was serious there; it was no game.

Anyway, among Democrats in our district, there was the thought that Jim Wray was going to do great in the primary because he knows all these people in Terre Haute and he's so smart and so forth.

He'd been out running a couple of months when, suddenly, another man from Terre Haute jumped into the race. Then a third man from Frankfort declared. It was becoming very clear that Jim Wray hadn't wrapped things up.

And then Eldon Tipton jumped in. Eldon Tipton had run in several Democratic primaries for Congress and he'd won a couple of times. But he'd never won the general election—and he wasn't going to win this time against John Myers.

All of a sudden there were five men running for the Democratic nomination after everybody had thought Jim Wray had it sewn up. But he hadn't sewn it up. His campaign wasn't gaining any traction. Tipton was not a stupid politician—he'd seen that things were wide open.

I thought, "Oh, God! Eldon Tipton'll win again. The only thing that could possibly stop him would be a woman."

A lot of my friends here were encouraging me to run, especially Bill Miller, a historian and theologian. He would go on to become a distinguished professor at the University of Virginia. Bill went out to lunch with me. He told me it would make sense for a woman to run in the primary and I was the one to do it.

I felt just sure I would get attention from the press because I was a woman—there were no other women running for Congress in the state! One woman against four men; that's a story.

So I decided to run for Congress. I filed for the primary just before the deadline. We put out an all points bulletin: Anybody who has relatives or friends or connections in any of the counties, let us know! All of a sudden I had a huge bunch of first-rate volunteers—faculty colleagues, their spouses, friends I'd made, loyal Democrats, all the supporters I'd gotten since I first ran for city council. There were all sorts of people willing to drive me here or there, to have fundraisers, to help me make contacts.

That campaign was such a blur. It went so fast. We were constantly moving, moving, moving. We did some planning but we didn't have a huge strategy—we hadn't the time to develop one. We had only three months to campaign, February, March, and April.

The district, at the time, went from Sullivan and Greene counties at the bottom and swung up to the west of Indianapolis, although it didn't include any part of the city itself. It covered all or parts of 16 counties. That was a lot of land to cover, and pretty rural.

We discovered that most of the courthouses were primarily Democratic! We thought we should be doing better in this district and John Myers shouldn't be in Congress.

I visited Terre Haute often during the campaign. I got a lot of support there; it was a union town. The Democrats there would have affairs at VFW halls a lot and all the factions of the party would be at separate tables. I would attend the events and go from table to table to chat but I'd never sit down. I didn't want to show any favoritism. Jackie Prose was right.

The other guys would stand up and say, in very dull voices, I'm so-and-so and I think we need more money for the highway department because our roads really need repair. Things like that.

So I stood up and said, in my slightly higher voice and enthusiastically, "I want to go to Washington and use the energy I have to represent the people in this room!"

And the people in the room remembered me. I was all over the district and the people got to know me quite quickly.

They remembered me—that was the important thing.

I became memorable also for my radio ads.

We decided to use radio spots on stations in Terre Haute, Bloomington, Sullivan, Crawfordsville—little radio stations. It wasn't expensive to buy time on them.

The spots featured me talking about myself as well as the difficulties facing the average housewife in district. I said, "I don't think the people of this district can afford a Congressman who spends $100,000 on his campaign while pinto beans now cost 49 cents a pound." (The price had recently jumped dramatically.)

After that, I became known as the Bean Lady.

People donated money to the campaign. Paul and I spent some of our own money, but not a lot, no more than a thousand dollars. We didn't have much at the time. It was a shoestring operation. We used free newspaper coverage as much as possible, me being The Woman. That was the big news.

A wonderful guy, Elliot Gilbert, a visiting professor in the English Department, organized a videotaping session featuring me and Paul. His wife, Sandra Gilbert, also in the English Department, helped him set up studio space and made other arrangements. They got another friend of ours named Jean Strohm to interview me and Paul. It was to be a very straightforward thing, not gimmicky at all.

Jean asked me questions like "Why are you running for Congress?" She turned to Paul and asked him, "What do you think about all this?"

Paul said, "Oh, I'm very excited by it! Charlotte would do a wonderful job. She does a wonderful job at everything."

I teared up. That was so touching. I hadn't known that. It was another step in a growing understanding between us.

We ran that videotape in ads on TV stations all around the district.

There would be gatherings in all the counties in the district, Democratic Party and town meetings, local women's functions, labor groups. We'd meet people wherever we could. The five of us candidates would be there; we each would have thirty seconds to make a case.

Labor liked me. I was more supportive of labor than the other candidates were, except for Eldon Tipton. He was a labor person too. Labor union people liked my style and my spirit—that's what they told me.

I figured out that in those 30 seconds I couldn't give the gathering many specifics but what I could show them was my energy and passion. I worked out a 30-second elevator speech that was like "Look at me! I'm here and I care about you!" That's what I conveyed. And it worked! It separated me from all these other candidates who spoke in dull, flat voices, saying, "I'm so-and-so and I come from Frankfort and I'd like to be in Congress."

I had a different level of energy. Take it or leave it, and it worked.

When I talk to young candidates now, I encourage them to get a pithy little statement and to let their energy show. I've seen too many speeches bore people to death.

As I attended more and more of these events, I got the idea that people were beginning to think I might be The One. I was very good at working a crowd. That comes from way back when I was a little girl, being the minister's daughter. I'd learned to go around a room and tell people my name and ask theirs and find out something about them. That was what I did then and that's what I would do on my campaign. When I'd meet people at these county events, I didn't tell them about me so much as ask them about themselves. It came naturally to me. It's a good way to let them know you're interested.

As a candidate, basically you're asking people to let you speak for them. So you have to give them the sense that they matter to you. John Myers, the Republican incumbent whom I was hoping to run against, was pretty good at things like remembering names and kissing the ladies with big wet smooches. Of course, I didn't do that.

I gained a reputation, being the only woman in the race, and there was a really vital women's movement at the time, statewide.

I connected with a lot of people. I'd started at the bottom and I'd come up.

I sensed I was winning among the second tier of candidates, but I thought Tipton was going to win.

Eldon Tipton was well-educated—he was a graduate of the Naval Academy at Annapolis—and he was fairly sophisticated. His wife was from Chile and he spoke Spanish with her. But he had a country bumpkin air about him. He did very well with that out in the counties.

But around here, in Monroe County, people looked down on him. People assumed he was a racist. I don't know why. His manner of speaking was completely compatible with Greene and Owen and Sullivan counties, people who worked in small factories or on small farms, people who watched their pennies.

He taught high school civics in the Shakamack school system. He was not a stupid person. But a lot of people in my "circle," university people, can be snobby. I have never liked that. I grew up with farmers and insurance people in our churches. I was taught to love my neighbors. So for me people have been people. Status is not important. In fact, I may be snobby in reverse. I'm a little leery of people with titles. I question authority.

When Eldon Tipton was a state senator, he'd voted to ratify the Equal Rights Amendment. Then he went out to the western states and campaigned for them to ratify it.

Unlikely as it seemed, I came in second to Eldon Tipton. I was not surprised. I was pleased that I did so well. It was vindicating. My efforts had made a difference. I thought, Well, I'll be able to talk to Eldon Tipton. He'll listen to me because I'd shown something. He saw it. He told people I was nipping at his heels toward the end of the primary campaign. "If there'd have been another month...," he said. He made it really clear that he kind of admired my spunk.

I wasn't depressed, I just I went back to work at Goods and at the city council.

And Monroe County Democratic officials and candidates asked me to become campaign chair for the November election. Jamie Murphy was the county party chair at the time. We worked closely together. We swept all the county races but one that year. Judge Nat Hill, who'd been in office forever, was the only Republican who won in the county.

But Eldon Tipton lost the general election to John Myers—again.

# 13

# The Big Sewer Pipe

*Late summer, 1974. Bloomington's new wave politicians have been in office nearly three years. The kinship they shared as outsider candidates back in the summer and fall of 1971 remains, but only among some of them. Mayor Frank McCloskey now wishes some of the people he rode into office with would ride out of town.*

*McCloskey, according to a story in the* Herald-Telephone *dated September 29, 1974, is "not very happy with what he sees." He sees a city council that doesn't view the city and its operations the way he does. "I'm not satisfied with the way the city is going. I'm not satisfied with the attitudes emanating from the city council."*

*He goes further: "I would be less than candid if I didn't say that dealing with the city council is the most miserable experience of my life." He adds the council members "have literally flipped me out." The council, he says, wants to become too powerful.*

\*\*\*

By now the honeymoon was over. It took maybe a year, a year and a half, for Frank to actively begin to distance himself from the council.

He stopped being generous with his communications—he would do things that we'd find out about later. He held back. When Ted Najam became his deputy, he told Frank, "Get away from them. They're not 'politic' enough. They're too far out."

From Frank's perspective, that was good advice but it was a disappointment to us. For somebody like Al Towell it was the end; no more pretending that we get along. No more even trying.

***

*Ironically, one of the city council's acts around that time was to estab-*
*lish a Utilities Services Board. Prior to this, the utilities department had*
*been answerable to the mayor and the city council so, in essence, the coun-*
*cil was weakening itself. It took the city council out of the equation. The*
*new utilities board would be an appointed body that would oversee the*
*city department responsible for delivering clean water going into Bloom-*
*ington residences, businesses, and factories, as well as getting rid of their*
*waste water. It would be comprised of a wide range of local notables. They*
*would come together, along with other powerful people in the local, state,*
*and even federal governments to discuss a pressing issue in a dramatic*
*meeting in Indianapolis.*

***

It was 1974; the sewage treatment plant here in town had to be replaced. It wasn't working; it was over capacity.

The League of Women Voters had been pushing to have utilities
run by an independent board in the wake of Mayor Hooker's problems
with the misuse of utilities funds several years before.

The League recommended the board be created, taking control of
utilities out of the hands of the city council. After some debate and discussion, we voted to create the new board. In the interests of better
government we relinquished our control over that department.

One of the members of the new board was Bill Schrader, who was
the editor and associate publisher of the *Herald-Telephone*, and another
was Bill Cook, who was just becoming known in the community.
When we were working on our zoning ordinance, we went up to
Cook's nice new factory on the west side to talk with him about it. I'd
never heard of him before that. I'd told him my contention was you
could even have factories in neighborhoods as long as you did it right.
He'd built this lovely plant on Curry Pike that did not look like a factory; it was attractive.

The utilities department directed a consultant out of Kansas City,
Black & Veech, to study some of the problems that were just on the

horizon. Black & Veech had a long history with Bloomington; it even maintained an office right in the utilities department building.

We had two waste water treatment plants at the time—as we do today, one on the north side and a larger one on the south side. Black & Veech told the utilities board our larger treatment plant was nearing capacity. The consultant recommended we build a new sewage treatment plant down near the southwestern end of Lake Monroe, near the dam at Salt Creek, which then flows into the East Fork of the White River.

That new plant would be about fifteen miles distant from the city, leaving us the question, How do we get the sewage down to the plant?

We were told we'd have to build a gravity-fed, outfall sewer pipe. It would have to be pretty big to handle the city's waste water for years and years to come—at least six feet in diameter.

We sit on limestone around here so the cost to bury the sewer pipe would be prohibitive. We'd have to build the big concrete sewer pipe above ground. The most efficient way to do that, Black & Veech advised, would be to build it in the middle of a creek flowing right to the spot where the new treatment plant would be built. That would be Clear Creek.

Now, some of the prettiest parts of Monroe County surround Clear Creek south of town. The Sassafras Audubon Society started raising concerns. The Society was led by a woman named Sarah Elizabeth Frey who everybody knew as Libby. She said the proposal was crazy. The Society's main concern was that Lake Monroe would remain a good source of clean water well into the future. We had to protect the lake.

Other people like Warren Henegar, a member of the Monroe county council, and Barbara Restle, who owned a farm near town and was some kind of biologist, agreed with her that it was crazy. First of all, it was a dumb idea and, second, it would be just terrible for the environment.

Of course, building a sewage treatment plant is very expensive. We wouldn't be able to do it ourselves. We would need financial help, lots of it, from the federal government. By then we had the Environmental

Protection Agency. Under that body's rules, we would have to conduct an environmental impact statement before we could get federal money to build the plant.

All this was brewing in the fall of 1974 when I was invited to a meeting at the governor's office. I drove myself up to Indianapolis. Gov. Otis Bowen was out of the state at the time but Lieutenant Governor Bob Orr chaired the meeting. We all sat around a big table: Orr, Frank McCloskey, Jim Wray, Cook, Schrader, someone from the regional EPA office, the Indiana Attorney General, a representative from the state bureau of the environment that preceded the Indiana Department of Environmental Management, a person from the Department of Natural Resources, and others. Everybody who had a stake in Lake Monroe.

Apparently, Bill Cook had been the driving force behind the meeting. Bob Orr called the meeting to order and said, "Okay, Bill Cook, you wanted this meeting. Why are we here?"

"We are here to talk about the sewage treatment plant," he said. He acknowledged that an environmental impact statement would say the big sewer pipe down the middle of Clear Creek was not a good idea. "So," Bill Cook said, "we're here to figure out how to bypass that process."

I was shocked. "Why would we do that?" I said.

That turned out to be one of the less welcomed statements of my career. The men around that very big table—I was the only woman present—looked at each other as if to say, "Who let her in here?"

So, they went on to describe how they were going to work at it, getting around the need for an environmental impact statement. They named names of some people who were standing in their way, making noise. Names like Libby Frey and Warren Henegar, as well as Barbara Restle. The men around this very big table agreed these people were standing in the way of progress, they didn't understand how things worked, and they weren't businesspeople.

It was very intimidating. I really was puzzled. I had a truly sick feeling, a nauseous feeling. This was not right.

It went on and on and they talked about the various things they might have to do. I could not wait to get out of there.

As I drove back to Bloomington after the meeting was adjourned, I thought, "People should know about this." When I got home, I called the newspaper. I told a reporter, "I just went to a meeting that has to be made public." I described what had happened.

That was an absolute dead end. The *Herald-Telephone* wasn't interested. The reporter didn't even want to talk to me about it. And, remember, the editor and publisher of the paper was on the utilities board. So there'd be no coverage by the *H-T*.

I called the radio station, WTTS. At that time Bloomington radio was much more active in news coverage. They would not touch it. Even the *Indiana Daily Student* didn't do anything about it.

Maybe they recognized the power structure here. This was business. The newspapers and radio station didn't want to ruffle any feathers.

And, it turned out, Bill Cook already was more powerful than I understood at the time.

So, I talked to other members of the city council. I told them what had happened. I said, "This isn't right! We need to have this discussed openly. How are we going to do that if we can't get the press to cover it?"

We decided I would deliver a report on the meeting at the next regular city council meeting. Our meetings were just beginning to be covered on television, by the predecessor of CATS (Community Access Television Services), so my report would be covered by television.

Politics, for me, has always been trying to figure out how to get people to participate, then figuring out the issues. With me, it was always, "There's a problem, we all have to solve it together."

***

*The puzzle this time was to let Bloomington and Monroe County know what the men around that very big table were considering. The ca-*

*ble TV government coverage helped but it wasn't as effective or as far-reaching as newspaper and radio coverage. So Charlotte made a fateful decision.*

\*\*\*

I always asked Paul "What should I do?" whenever it came to big political decisions. He had really good political instincts. I would never have done what I decided to do without his support.

I decided to run for mayor against Frank in the Democratic primary the next spring. I would never have considered it if it wasn't for that treatment plant issue. It was the best way to get the story out among the people.

There were those who assumed it was ambition that made me run but, as far as I was concerned, it was all about the issue. I don't even know if I wanted to be mayor. I realized that it was an uphill battle. The rule of thumb is you don't run against an incumbent. And primaries are difficult. But, I had a sense of urgency that we get this information out.

The truth is, it was not well-advised in a political sense. Paul had gone over the pros and cons of it with me but in the end, as always, he stressed it would be my decision. Frank was a first-term mayor. He was still popular. But I was popular too. There had to be some way of communicating this very important issue to the voters. A lot of people encouraged me to think about running. And a lot of other people were annoyed with me for challenging him. I told them, "This is just not right, what's going on here!"

Frank was totally supportive of the Clear Creek plan. He was a bit cowed, actually, during much of his early time as mayor, by the good old boys. Frank wanted to be accepted by them and we, the city council, were getting too radical for him.

When I told Frank my plans, he reacted with some anger and some annoyance. He said, condescendingly, "Re-e-ally?"

The whole situation was a really traumatic moment for me, a life-changer. I kept asking myself, "Why would they want to do this? Why would they want to build this ugly and dangerous thing. Who wants the whole town's raw sewage running through an above-ground pipe?"

Then, around Thanksgiving, Paul and I took the kids up to Chicago for a long weekend. We saw a movie there that had come out in the summer, *Chinatown*.

\*\*\*

*Chinatown, released in June, 1974, was an award-winning neo-noir mystery, a fictional tale based on the very real Los Angeles Water Wars of the early and mid-20th Century. The story involves corruption and murder surrounding the booming city's water rights in outlying areas and the location of its reservoirs, all of which are decided upon to the benefit of shadowy, wealthy people.*

\*\*\*

That gave me an idea. I asked myself, "What happens at the lake if this treatment plant is built there?"

I talked to Paul Levy, who was a student at Indiana University at the time. After our conversation, he went up to Indianapolis and made a list of property owners around the lake. He'd had to do that in the state capitol because the shoreline around lake is overseen by both the state and the US Army Corps of Engineers. Paul Levy found that the owners of much of the land surrounding the lake were familiar names, powerful people around Bloomington, some of whom had even attended the meeting in the governor's office.

Their land couldn't be developed because there was no sewage system in place. The few homes already on the lake had septic tanks, but they weren't easy to build because of the underlying limestone. There was no way to get their sewage uphill to our south side treatment plant. But if the new treatment plan was built right at the downstream end of the lake, you could build on sites that otherwise wouldn't be buildable. It would have opened up all of Lake Monroe to massive development.

I thought, "This really stinks!"

When I talked to Frank about it he basically waved me off.

I said, "Frank, this isn't right."

Libby Frey and the others kept pointing out the lake is our source of drinking water. It has to be protected. The lake was fragile. Did we really want a lake surrounded by private docks every 20 feet?

I concluded the best interest of the public was to preserve the lake as it was.

Were we naive, as the men around the very big table implied?

I don't think we were naive at all. They liked to think we were. Newspaper reporter Bob Hammel wrote a book, *The Bill Cook Story: Ready, Fire, Aim!* Bill Cook had eventually become the richest man in Indiana. He was worth billions. Hammel called me when he was writing the book—while Bill Cook was still alive—and said, "You know, this still rankles in Bill Cook's mind. It sticks in his craw." And this was 35 years after it happened!

I said, "I know it does."

He said, "Why did you do that?"

"Because, Bob," I said, "I was a city council member! My job was to look out for the public interest and protect the lake. Bill looked out for public interest too, as a rule, but he put that aside for what he considered a higher interest—the well-being of the landowners. So, no apologies from me."

Over the years, I bothered Bill Cook on numerous occasions; we argued over other issues anyway. One day Bill Cook told me, to my face, that I was weird. But that was one he really just couldn't get over—and it's in the book!

Over the next year after that meeting in Indianapolis, all hell broke loose. The Sassafras Audubon Society threatened to sue, demanding an environmental impact statement.

Once Black & Veech saw that, the consultant knew it would have to do an EIS, and it knew the plan wouldn't stand scrutiny. So, Black & Veech came up with an alternate plan. A site at Dillman Road and State Road 37 was chosen for the new waste treatment facility, much farther north. It was built and began operations in 1982. It can handle 15 million gallons of waste water daily. The treated water is discharged into Clear Creek. The Dillman Road plant was infinitely less expensive and much easier to build.

But that plan hadn't been announced by primary election day. The Clear Creek sewer pipe plan still was very much alive. On election night, Paul and I went to the *Herald-Telephone* to watch the results come in. The crowd was mixed, some were with me and some with Frank. I lost that primary by seventeen percentage points. Frank was not unpopular. The west side had voted for me. On the east side, a fair number of the environmentalists voted for me as well as a lot of the more liberal, Voters Union types. The populists, too. I got a fair amount of the university faculty vote but not all of it because there were powerful people who thought my running against Frank was a really bad idea. Frank got the establishment vote.

Once it was over, for me, it was over.

I'm very good at losing. It doesn't knock me out. Paul was a good political spouse. I've seen other spouses who can't take it when their spouses lose. That wasn't true for him. He would say, laughing, "Okay Charlotte, you didn't win this one but here we are, we're family, we have great kids, and we go on. You love to cook dinner and you've got a store to run." That happened more than once. I know because I got really good at losing.

I went on to do other things. I worked hard in the store. I really dug in. I took Chinese because I wanted to have another project. I wanted to know more about China and the language. I took Chinese for a year and a half at the university. I audited the class but I went every day and did all the homework. I would walk to class and then walk downtown to Goods. I kept saying to myself, "I'm fit. I'm going to be fit."

I've always thought, You keep going. There was a lot to do. There still is a lot to do.

Frank and I forgave each other, like family. By 1992, my son Nathan was working for Frank in his Washington office. Frank had become Representative in Congress from Indiana's 8th District. Nathan was counsel for the Subcommittee on Civil Service and one of Frank's legislative assistants. When I ran for Congress in 1978, Frank supported me. In 1980, Frank came to me and said, "You've got to run for County commissioner."

What I'd learned pretty early on was when something's done, it's done. I don't hold grudges. Life is short.

But Frank would disappoint me again. When I ran in the mayoral primary against Tomi Alison in 1987, he promised to stay out of it. Frank was in Congress at the time. He didn't stay out—he endorsed Tomi shortly before the primary. I lost by a handful of votes.

A few years later, while Nathan was working for him, Paul and I visited Frank in Washington. Frank said, "Charlotte, I want to take you two out to dinner. I want to apologize to you. I've done things like not supporting you when I said I would and supporting Tomi. I'm really sorry about that."

I said, "Okay, thank you very much. It's water over the dam."

We let him buy us dinner. We ordered the most expensive steaks on the menu.

I finished out my term on the city council. That was a little awkward because I still had to work with Frank. But that didn't take away from the job we had to do. From May to December, I continued on, very active. There had been a human rights ordinance in place when we took office in '72 but it had no teeth. It was only a gesture. We created a new, stronger ordinance that first year in office. It was enforceable and staffed. Then in the fall of '75, we added a new amendment to our human rights ordinance that would cover age, marital status, and sexual orientation.

My last meeting as a city council member was in December, 1975. We took up our amendment that would cover sexual orientation. This was way before its time. No other municipality in Indiana had anything like it.

This was the time when evangelicals were beginning to get politicized and organized. They came out in full force to that meeting.

Only five of us council members showed up. Five. Four didn't want to be there. They didn't want to touch the issue. Flo Davis, who'd replaced her husband Hubert on the council after he'd died, was there. Wayne Fix. Brian St. Croix. Al Towell. And me.

That was a quorum.

Brian St. Croix was gay. He came out, as far as I knew, because of this issue. What had happened was a city building inspector received a request for a construction permit from a group that wanted to remodel a storefront and open it as a gay coffee bar. He told them he would not issue a permit to homosexuals. He was very clear about that.

That group came to Brian for help. He told them, "We've got to do something about this! We've got to make it illegal for this to happen." Frank was sympathetic to them as well.

We had hired a full-time human rights attorney in 1972. That was one of the big differences between us and the previous council. If you really believe in something, if you want to get it done, you have to have staff.

Brian and the attorney drafted the amendment to the existing ordinance. It was circulated and publicized. And all hell broke loose.

People were furious. They had prayer meetings about it. They had protest rallies against it. They took ads out in the newspaper against it. One of the ads was bordered in red. They paid extra money for that. It said we would all go to hell if we passed the amendment, together with gays and gay-loving people.

Then, we had our regular meeting at which we'd take up the amendment and the five of us showed up.

We listened to everybody.

I brought my King James Bible. I read from it. John 13:34. "A new commandment I give unto you, That ye love one another; as I have loved you, that ye also love one another."

They had their Bibles, too. They read from the Old Testament and we had our New Testament. Al Towell had been a Baptist boy preacher—he started preaching when he was 11 or 12 in

Louisville—and he was happy to deliver another sermon. Brian, of course, was very eloquent. Wayne, who was a laid-back person— he normally was quiet until he had something specific to say—so when he said something everybody listened. He said this amendment was the right thing to do.

Most of the people who spoke during the public comment section were against it. But we were listening to the people who weren't there that night. And it was a matter of principle. I've always held it's my conscience and principles first, my office second, and being a Democrat third.

I can listen to the people. I can hear their voices. They can even sway me. They can convince me to change my position or at least temper it. But I don't have to do exactly as they say. I can disagree with them. They know from the get-go that I have principles, just as they do. If they don't like it, they don't have to vote for me. And a lot of them didn't!

One of the most vociferous of the speakers was a man named Don Wagner. He was an outspoken, conservative Christian who ran a shoe store in the Eastland Mall. He also served as a resident manager of the mall as a side job. He was the one who'd paid for the red border in that anti-amendment newspaper ad.

Five years later when I got to be county commissioner, there he was, now a member of the county council! So I had to work with him. And I did.

Then, seven years later, when the United States Supreme Court ruled that women had to be admitted to service clubs, Don Wagner put my name in for membership in the Rotary Club. He was my sponsor!

So, people change. You know what changed for him? His best friend had a son who was an opera singer. The son moved to New York to find work and then he died of AIDS. He had been gay.

Don and I talked about it. Don said, "My world has been opened wider. That boy was a fine person and he died." Don then talked about his role in the anti-amendment movement more than ten years before. "That was my mistake," he said. "I need to be forgiven for it."

By that time, we had become friends.

\*\*\*

*Surprisingly, the new ordinance would move Indiana University to sue the city in state court, hoping to get it overturned. The university had no quibble with the protections it offered special classes per se. IU held that the ordinance was too far-reaching, that it would impinge on the university's sovereignty. Under state law the university had extraordinary leeway in conducting its own affairs. One of the major bones of contention was that the ordinance offered protections for renters. Landlords wouldn't be able deny leases to people based on their sexual orientation, for instance. The university, a big local landowner and landlord, was loath, as a matter of principle, to have the city tell it what to do. The court action continued into the '80s.*

\*\*\*

The ordinance implied the university would have to conform to our way of doing things. The university said, no, they wouldn't do that. They got the whole ordinance overturned.

By the early '80s, the city council got around to writing a new human rights ordinance that would stand up in the state court but it lacked the gay rights part. I was long gone by then. It wasn't until the '90s that an even newer city council got around to bringing the gay rights amendment back.

There was another huge uproar over it. At that point, I was a private citizen again. There was a city council meeting with the amendment on the agenda. I wanted to be there to throw my two cents in.

A pretty raucous, angry bunch of people showed up in council chambers. The crowd was so huge the fire department made us leave the building. Phil Emerson, the minister at First United Methodist Church, gave his permission to let everybody march over to the church, en masse, and continue the meeting there. So there was about a half-hour break while the CATS television people broke down at city hall and set up again at the church. Then the meeting went on for another four hours.

I was sitting toward the front of the church, on the right side. Pat Jefferies, a Republican who ran for office a few times and lost and was a member of the church, came roaring in the side door. She saw me and walked right up to me and said, "What's going on here? Why are you all here?"

I said, "It's democracy in action."

She said, "This is a brand new carpet! We just put it in! If this carpet is messed up, there'll be hell to pay!"

I said, "You know, there are some very important principles being argued here. That's even more important than the carpet."

But she didn't care. She was very angry.

Jack Hopkins was the president of the council that year and he wanted a unanimous vote for the amendment. Republican Kirk White had indicated he was not going to be for it. But Kirk was impressed by the testimony of the amendment's supporters, which had gone on and on and on for hours. Meanwhile, the anti-amendment people sang "Onward Christian Soldiers" and other militant hymns. Kirk was very troubled by the whole thing.

At about 2:30 in the morning, Kirk stood up and asked for a recess. He went out in the hall, we could see him in anguish, and called his mother. He was the epitome of good boy. He'd been an Eagle Scout. He didn't like to ruffle feathers or rock the boat but I'd always liked him.

Kirk's sister was gay. That's mainly what troubled him. How could he not speak up on behalf of his sister? He called his mother to ask her if she would forgive him if he voted for the amendment. She told him he should do it. He came back and announced he would vote in favor of the amendment, so it was unanimous.

The meeting ended at about three in the morning. I stayed the whole time, partly because I was bound and determined to go through every pew and make sure there were no soda cans or napkins or potato chip bags left on the floor so Pat Jefferies couldn't throw that in Phil Emerson's face.

# 14

# Waving, Smiling And Avoiding Horse Droppings

*Charlotte left office on Thursday, January 1, 1976. She had her store,*
*Goods Inc., to run but she still kept her hand in the political game.*

***

Vance Hartke was running for reelection in 1976. He'd been Indiana's senator since 1959 and was hoping to gain a fourth term.

But by then he'd become kind of squirrelly, even a little obnoxious. A few years before he'd objected to proposed airline passenger screening procedures at check-ins, citing privacy concerns. The procedures became law despite his objections and soon after, when he was passing through airport screening he refused to allow guards to check his luggage. His plane was delayed and eventually took off without him. He made a big deal out of the incident and that didn't set well in people's minds.

Karl Olessker, Hartke's Monroe County reelection chair, asked me to be co-chair with him. Of course, I was familiar with Hartke already but I got a pile of materials on his Senate career, to learn more about his extensive record. He'd been a very good senator in a lot of ways. He did a lot regarding highway safety—he'd ordered automakers to equip cars with seat belts. He was the first senator to come out against the Vietnam War. He was the main sponsor of the Adult Education Act.

I thought "Boy, he's really worth supporting."

Hartke was running against Richard Lugar, the former mayor of Indianapolis and already very popular around the state. Lugar was a moderate and was known as a sensible guy. He spoke like a senator while Hartke spoke like a country bumpkin. Hartke even looked like a country bumpkin next to Lugar.

One day I took Hartke over to Foster Quad to meet the students. He did not endear himself to them. He wasn't engaging. He was totally out of synch with the kids; he wasn't talking their language. He wasn't saying anything that interested them. He was a little condescending to them. They sort of went, "Blah, what's the matter with this guy?"

It was kind of sad.

Hartke lost to Lugar in the general election by a landslide.

By then, I was beginning to think about running for Congress again.

Eldon Tipton's son ran for Congress in '76. Eldon didn't run, I think, because he was tired of losing to John Myers. Eldon was big into supporting the Equal Rights Amendment at that point, traveling around the country, especially in the western states, trying to whip up support for ratification.

I started running in the spring of '77, actually. I'd been talking to people in Terre Haute and people here in Bloomington. The two cities still were part of the same congressional district at the time. Paul and I moved into our house in 1972 and I still live there. That house has been in the 7th, 8th, and 9th districts over the years.

There was a woman in Terre Haute, Betty Blumberg, who really encouraged me to run. Betty was an art teacher at Indiana State University. She had been married to Ben Blumberg, a wealthy Terre Haute lawyer and philanthropist who'd died in 1971. Betty was a Republican but she was a feminist and pro-choice. She liked me. I'd met her when I ran for Congress in '74 and visited Terre Haute a lot because it was the largest city in the district at the time. Later, she'd get to know me even more from our work together in the bipartisan effort to get the ERA ratified in Indiana.

Apparently, Betty had been impressed with the way I ran my first congressional campaign and was happy now that I was thinking of running for Congress again. She told me she thought I would be a good potential candidate and she would support me.

Betty thought I didn't dress well enough. In her eyes, I didn't wear "fine" clothes. I made most of my own clothes. I'd get a bolt of fabric and cut out a pattern and sew the pieces together. I made dresses, skirts, and some jackets.

At that time, women didn't wear pants on the House floor. I didn't wear pants at all. The only time I wore pants was in Czechoslovakia. I got two really nice, tailored pants suits in Vienna. They were very expensive but we had a lot of money during that brief period.

Betty sent me to Meis's department store in Terre Haute. It was downtown on Wabash. Up on the second floor there was a special room where the dresser showed me different suits.

I would try one on and the dresser would decide whether or not it looked good. It was a strange experience for me. I wasn't used to that kind of treatment.

The first suit I got was plain black, really good, wool twill fabric, a plain straight skirt and short jacket with a cream satin blouse. I'd eventually get four good suits, four- and five-hundred-dollar suits. They were Betty Blumberg's gift to me.

I needed to get a handle on running for Congress again. The best way to do it would be to talk to people who'd already run their races—and had won. Indiana's House delegation in the 95th Congress was overwhelmingly Democratic. Of the 11 congressional districts in this state at the time, nine were represented by Democrats. Up until January of that year, 1977, when Richard Lugar replaced Vance Hartke, Indiana also had two Democratic senators. Birch Bayh would be in office until 1981.

I drove to Washington in March of '77 with Jean Strohm, a supporter in my '74 run for the nomination. She was the one who interviewed Paul and me for the campaign film that year. She was a friend and wanted to help me so we drove out there, and I visited the offices of every Democrat in Indiana's congressional delegation. I spoke either to the Representative or to someone in his staff.

Everybody I spoke with considered John Myers a kind of non-entity but they all acknowledged he had good constituent services.

Floyd Fithian was the Representative from the 2nd District that included Lafayette. He had run a really good campaign in '74, winning that dependably Republican district up until that year. I asked him how he won. He had run a very calculated campaign. For one thing, he was very careful about the numbers. He set up a voter identification program. This is a long time ago; we didn't have digital information yet. All the information was on index cards. He had people go into each of the counties and cull out all of the Democrats who'd voted in the primaries. He created target lists of them.

People aren't interested in who's in Congress. They're more interested in who's in the courthouse. The way to make them interested in your congressional campaign is to get them to do something for you—like sitting down and going through the voters lists. That is something concrete, something to get them involved. You're building up a commitment to the candidate. You build a committed cadre of supporters.

That's how Fithian had won unexpectedly in the 2nd District.

I met Floyd in his office in the House Office Building. He told me his political consultant, Arnold Bennett, was terrific. Floyd was a political scientist so I'm sure he had his own good ideas but Bennett had tied it all together in an effective package. He even used red, white, and blue in all of Floyd's campaign materials.

Not long after that, I hired Arnold Bennett to be my consultant.

I would travel to Washington again that spring. Betty Blumberg called me and said, "Charlotte, I'm going to send you to a workshop in Washington for women who are thinking of running for Congress. I will pay your way." It was a week-long workshop called the Getting Ready For Congress School at Mount Vernon College.

So I went out there in early June.

After I came back from Mount Vernon College, I looked closely at the map of my district. I noted who was in local office in each county. There were lots of Democrats in those courthouses and in the cities. That told me two things: There were Democrats who hadn't voted Democratic for Congress. I asked myself why that would be.

So I went out to ask them. We'd done some homework. We'd made our own targeted lists of Democratic voters. I went out to meet as many of them as I could.

I found they thought Eldon Tipton was kind of strange and they didn't think he was particularly "congressional" but they were comfortable with him and he listened to them.

They said John Myers provided good constituent service. They told me John Myers got them their Social Security checks and their Black Lung benefits. We still had a lot of coal miners in the district then.

Those checks came regularly, automatically, but sometimes they would be delayed for whatever reason. People would call Myers' office to complain. If they visited his local office to complain, he'd pick up the phone and say "Where's that check?" The person on the other end would say "It's in the mail." Myers would turn to the person and say, "It's in the mail," as if he'd made it happen.

Lo and behold the check would come in the mail within days. Smart.

I'd go back to Washington a number of times during the campaign. I'd get on the elevator in one of the House office buildings, wearing my badge showing that I was a candidate for Indiana's 7th District. People would get on with me and ask who I was running against and I would say John Myers. "Oh, really? Is he new?" And he'd already been in Congress for a dozen years! Nobody knew him! He never introduced a single bill that I can remember.

My first run for Congress in '74 was a really interesting experience for me. I liked it! I liked the people I met. They were small town people, straightforward, some of them really political and some of them not so much. I got a real taste for the district and that's why I was re-considering it for the '78 primary.

I would not consider running if Eldon Tipton was planning to run again. So I called Eldon Tipton and said, "I'm considering it but I will not run if you're running."

He said, "Oh, Charlotte, you did such a good job in '74. I hope you'll run. You're the person who can do this. And I'm not running again."

I said, "Will you be my campaign co-chair?" And he said yes.

I also needed somebody from Bloomington, an established, old-time Democrat to co-chair with Eldon. I asked Martha Regester, who was the venerable woman here in town. She was a kind of Earth mother around here, and very savvy. She was a very good real estate agent. She was alert and knew how to work with people. She was the sister-in-law of Jim Regester, the city attorney. She also was the mother of Jimmy Regester, who's in local real estate now.

Martha knew everybody in town. The Perry Township people who opened a new shelter for the homeless named it Martha's House after her. She was quite different from Eldon Tipton; they came from different places. their experiences were with different people. She was a real old-time Catholic Democrat, a Kennedy Democrat. I asked her to be co-chair and she agreed to be.

Joyce Martello agreed to be my campaign manager. She was a political novice but she was a really good organizer and manager. She worked well with people.

When the campaign got into full swing, I wasn't able to spend a lot of time with Joyce because I was on the road every day. We would have retreats and talk things over and then she would go her way and I would go mine. We both had our jobs to do.

We started working, seriously, on the campaign in the summer of 1977. It was a long campaign. I had to get to know people in 16 counties. One day not long ago, my son Nathan was in town. His friend asked him what it was like during that campaign. Nathan was 14 at the time. Nathan said, "Every morning, Mom would get up at 6:30 and be out the door at 7:30. She would get in somebody's car and we would not see her until late that night. Every day."

Paul was teaching while I was out campaigning. The children were in school during the day and he'd take care of them when they came home.

I was running against four guys who didn't present much of a challenge against me. At the last moment, it must have been around March, Eldon Tipton's cousin, John Tipton, entered the race. He was a schoolteacher who lived near Vigo County. Eldon was very angry with him and told him so. Eldon tried to talk him out of running but John stayed in.

His entrance into the race just screwed us up. We were all furious. We had to spend money to counter the Tipton name. All a lot of people would see would be the name Tipton.

Eldon urged Democrats to vote for me. We sent out mailers quoting Eldon to that effect.

I beat John Tipton easily in the primary.

Then it was on to the Democrats' old nemesis, John Myers. He was running for his seventh term in Congress. He' d been in office since 1967. He boasted that he'd never voted for a tax increase in all his years in Washington. Before he became a Congressman, he'd been a banker. After he left office, he ran a farm near Covington in the western edge of Indiana near the Illinois border until he died in early 2015. He was a whiz at raising money for his campaigns so I decided to concentrate on that in my first radio ads.

I had all the union support. Some of them were really enthusiastic. about me. The plumbers and steamfitters were big in the Terre Haute area. They really, really liked me. They assigned a guy to drive me around the city. He was named Tiny Taylor. He was about six-foot-three and weighed 300-some pounds. He liked me but we differed on guns so we talked a lot about how I might understand guns better and maybe talk about them in a way that wasn't too off-putting.

I could understand why people liked to hunt. That was not what I was concerned about when it came to guns. It was killing people.

So, when Tiny and I talked about guns, that was what we talked about. The big gun problem back then was the Saturday Night Special, the cheap .22-caliber handgun that had became such a scourge. Did people need cheap .22s to shoot rabbits?

Tiny Taylor and I learned a lot about each other. He helped me a lot.

And then there were the coalminers.

Rosalyn Carter, the First Lady, came to Terre Haute in August for a huge fundraiser. It was held in the Hulman Center, the basketball arena that the Indiana State University team played in. Paul and I rode in the armored car with her from the airport to the Katherine Hamilton Mental Health Center, where Rosalyn and I visited with the resident kids and the staff and then we went to the Hulman Center.

The coalminers had offered to be Rosalyn's escorts during her visit to Terre Haute. But the Secret Service wouldn't allow them to come near her because they'd recently gotten in trouble with the law; they'd overstepped their bounds regarding labor law and so they were *personae non gratae* with the federal government.

The coalminers were offended. They were looking forward to the honor of being with Rosalyn. They were angry. We wanted to keep them on our side. I had to make it clear that it was not my decision and they understood that.

I also had the Teamsters, the plumbers and steamfitters, the laborers, the carpenters, the steelworkers, the United Auto Workers, the machinists, and the musicians. I had 'em all. They all were, to one degree or more, enthusiastic.

I met with the machinists in the conference room on the top floor of a hotel in Terre Haute. The business manager of the Local stood up, introduced me, made a few remarks and said, "I like this lady. I'm going to pitch in $500 of my own money. How about you, Steve? And you, George?"

In five minutes they raised $3000 for me. I realized that was the way things were done.

They weren't what people here in Bloomington would think would be my support. A lot of them came from farms. People here thought of me as this sophisticated PhD housewife and didn't understand that I have a pretty good down-home touch.

I used that touch to such an extent that one day in the summer when we had a rally in Farmersburg—that's the actual name of the small town south of Terre Haute—a woman came up to me and said, "Boy, I really like you, Charlotte. I think you've got great ideas but do you have any education?"

I said, "Well, yeah. I do." She wanted to be sure I'd be okay with all those smart people in Washington.

It was a wonderful experience in so many ways. If I hadn't been running to win a campaign, I should have taken notes on everything that had happened. It was one interesting experience after another. When you're a candidate, it gives people permission to tell you how they feel, and about their lives, too. I learned and heard so many stories of people. Everybody has a story. They're mostly pretty interesting if you listen to them well. Everybody wants to do the right thing. I do believe that. Most people.

I was a woman and I was pro-choice. That wasn't a big issue in the campaign but it was an issue. It was something that was beginning to be discussed. One of my big supporters from Terre Haute, Jack Haley, owned a coalmine. He loved me. He was not a likely supporter. He was very Catholic and he had a big family. They were very well-to-do. He really had to contort his thinking to continue to support me as strongly as he did. He didn't like the idea that I would condone abortion. But he really wanted me to win. His children did too. I got money from the whole family. They took care of me in lots of different ways: they would take me out for dinner and drive me places and introduce me to people. They were just nice people.

The Sisters of Providence had a mother house at St Mary-of-the-Woods College just outside of Terre Haute. They did not like abortion. They also did not like war. They did not like guns. They were consistent in their thinking, truly pro-life. But they kind of thought sometimes things happen, that maybe God has his ways and girls become pregnant and might get abortions. They supported me strongly.

\*\*\*

*The town of Clinton is located in rural Vermillion County on the Wabash River at the far western edge of the state. The area's coal mining and brick-making industries had attracted many Italian immigrants to the town in the late 19th Century. Clinton's Italian-Americans celebrated their first festival in 1966 and have turned the affair into an annual Labor Day weekend event. It includes a midway, Italian food, live music, grape-stomping demonstrations, bocce ball tournaments, rides in a real gondola, the crowning of a Queen of Grapes, and what townspeople like to refer to as the biggest Italian parade in the Midwest.*

*In election years, the candidates turn out for the parade.*

*John Myers' hometown, Covington, was only 35 miles north of Clinton. One of Myers' best friends was Clinton's big auto dealer, who also was known as the "king of the town."*

\*\*\*

John Myers and I were invited to march in Clinton's Italian days parade. My campaign committee had not secured me a float or a car to ride in. Besides that, it was John Myers' home territory so I wasn't very welcome in Clinton. But they put me in the parade anyway. They let me walk behind a horse. And I had no signs or anything.

I thought, "What am I going to do? Nobody knows who I am but I'm here and I'd better make the most of it." So I smiled and waved. I could hear people along the way saying, "Who is that? Who is that?"

While I was walking along, I thought, "I feel like I did when I was a teenager in Switzerland and didn't know German. They may be laughing but I don't care."

I can remember that day so vividly: waving and smiling and avoiding the horse droppings. And thinking, "This is just ridiculous, I cannot feel bad about this. I have to laugh about it, too."

It turned out to be a good day. I got them talking about me.

I started having moments of hope. I knew it was an uphill battle. But I sensed I was catching up to John Myers. I was catching on. I was getting support and it was growing.

One of the sweetest things that happened was when we opened our campaign headquarters in Terre Haute. Paul and Nathan came to the kickoff party. Nathan handed me fifty dollars in cash that he had saved from his paper route. I was so touched! It was so sweet.

I didn't give the money back; I used it in the campaign.

There were some less pleasant things, too.

Floyd Fithian had recommended his consultant, Arnold Bennett, to me. Bennet liked me. But he knew everything. We got along pretty well at first but I began to feel uncomfortable because he'd sort of put words in my mouth. He would send mailers out with his words on them, words I would never say.

I'd say, "Arnold, I haven't gotten anything from you as good as my own little pinto bean speech." And he would look at me as if I were very stupid.

Just out of the blue in September or October, when it was too late to do much about it, there came a shipment of banker's boxes, each filled with 50 pounds of four-page flyers that were to be mailed or handed out.

One of the things printed on them was an attack on "big oil." I wouldn't have said the words "big oil." I was about to campaign in Clay County. They weren't talking about "big oil."

It was about $10,000-worth of stuff. I didn't have the money for it. I called him as soon as I could get to a phone. I said, "I didn't authorize this shipment. I didn't ask for it. I didn't want it. It didn't have to come here air freight. It didn't have to be printed in Washington. And now I'm not going to pay you for it!"

So he sued me.

We went to trial in 1984. Tom Berry, who been Monroe County Prosecutor beginning in the late 60s and into the 70s, was my lawyer. He was great and we became good friends. But we basically lost. I had to pay Bennett a large percentage of the bill. That was difficult and embarrassing.

Paul and I had a little bit of money and I had to ask my mother for the rest. It was the only time I ever asked her for money. She gave me $3000.

I would say I was naive in the ways of these consultants. Arnold had done a lot of good things for me but he'd also done things I didn't like. He didn't have a feel for the people around here. I did know the district and I knew how to talk to the people in it. He'd told me I was naive and stupid—and I was, but not in the way he'd meant it.

The day before the general election, the Vigo County Democratic chair, Ed Stapleton, invited me to come to his office. He had me sit outside his private inner office as he called in his precinct people to let them know who they should make sure would win. They went in one by one and each came out with an envelope. Really old-time politics. It was fascinating.

Paul and I and the children spent election night in Terre Haute in one of the married students housing apartments on the Indiana State University campus.

It took quite a while before the final results came in. You have to know where precisely the returns are coming from. People say, "Ah, you're way ahead!" Well, yeah, I'm way ahead but those are my strong precincts. What about the rest of 'em. It took a while until we got them; I would say maybe 11 o'clock that night.

I was composed all the way through. I went to the hotel on 3rd Street, Terre Haute's main drag, where all my supporters had gathered for my victory party. I thanked them all and then I called John Myers to congratulate him.

I'm a good loser. I'm gracious and I don't dwell on it. I once said, "When you run for office you have to be prepared to lose as well as to win." Vi Simpson, who'd go on to serve in the Indiana Senate, heard me say that. She said, "That's just not really a good way to think about it."

She never lost many elections. For most people, it's important to understand you may not win.

I had to be prepared to lose. I want to be able to go on. It can't be the end of my life.

Paul and I went to Aruba for three days. Just the two of us. Then we spent Thanksgiving weekend in Louisville with the children. We ate good food and we had a good time.

And then it was Christmas time and I got really busy with the store.

I lost the election to John Myers because he got more votes. He got more votes because he'd had them for so many years already. My vote total was the best showing ever against him.

I gave him the best run for his money and he knew it.

***

*John Myers would eventually serve a total of 15 terms in the House of Representatives. His Congressional career lasted 30 years from January 1966 through January 1996.*

# 15

## Who Do You Think You Are?

We ran the store in its original location through 1979. Anne did not agree with Marilyn and me about where we were to go with the store. Marilyn and I wanted to do something more. We wanted to go another step. So we started working on that. Eventually, we moved to the north side of the square. That occupied much of my thinking and time through the end of the decade.

Our house had this ugly and peeling wallpaper on our kitchen walls. It had yellow and orange flowers. I decided to take the wallpaper down. It was so old that it was just ready to peel off.

It was late winter, 1980. I was on the ladder and the phone kept ringing. This is before voice mail or phone machines. You either answered the phone or you didn't.

After a few times ringing, I got down from the ladder and answered. It was Mary Alice Dunlap. She'd been the mayor of Bloomington in the '60s. President Kennedy had picked the elected mayor, Tom Lemon, to be postmaster for the Cincinnati area in '61 or '62 and Mary Alice, the city clerk at the time, had been selected by party caucus to replace him. She held the office until the '63 election when she lost to Jack Hooker.

Mary Alice said, "Charlotte, what are you doing?"

I said, "I'm scraping wallpaper off my kitchen walls."

"No," she said, "I mean politically."

I said, "Absolutely nothing. And I don't intend to do anything politically."

"Have you ever thought about running for county commissioner?" she asked.

"Absolutely not. It has never entered my head."

Mary Alice would not be deterred. "Hanna's running again," she said. "He's a bully, Charlotte!"

Bill Hanna was a longtime Republican commissioner. And he was a bully. He pushed everybody around. He told everybody what to do—including the other two county commissioners. He ran a trucking company and had a contract with Rogers Building Supply. Rogers also had stone quarries, an asphalt plant and a cement factory with its main facility at Patterson near 3rd Street. Hanna's company had the contract to haul stone from Rogers to the county, which some people might have considered a conflict of interest.

The Democrats needed somebody to run against him. It wasn't going to be me. I said, "Mary Alice, that just doesn't make sense to me."

She said, "No, no, no. You're a good campaigner. You can win."

I laughed. I'd already gone through the process of deciding whether or not to run for Congress again in the '80 election. I chose not to because Ronald Reagan was running for president and it was already pretty clear he'd carry Indiana easily. It looked to be a landslide in this state so it would have been very difficult to run against a Republican for Congress here. Monroe County at the time was Republican even though Bloomington had become solidly Democratic. It didn't make any sense at all.

There weren't a lot of Democrats jumping up and down wanting to run in that year, especially against Bill Hanna who was a 12-year incumbent. He had a lot of money; he had the Rogers Group, the nation's biggest private producer of crushed stone and a huge national road builder, one of the big players in the county, on his side.

I made these arguments to Mary Alice but she ended the conversation by saying, "Just think about it."

I climbed back up the ladder and resumed peeling and scraping that ugly wallpaper. I thought, What a curious idea. There'd never been a woman commissioner in Monroe County. There were very few in the entire state—maybe a handful.

I was still up on the ladder and the phone rang again. Now it's Frank McCloskey. We'd gone back and forth as allies and rivals and apparently I was on his good side again. He said, "We've decided, Charlotte, you're the best possible candidate."

"You know, Frank," I said, "we haven't talked in a long time."

"Charlotte, I know. I'm really sorry. I've been meaning to...," blah blah blah. Then he launched into his sales pitch. "You could really beat Bill Hanna! We really need somebody to beat Bill Hanna! We need somebody in the county that we in city government can talk to."

There were more calls from other party people over the next several days. Vi Simpson called. She was running for county auditor. The Bill Hanna situation was a little awkward for her because her husband worked for Rogers. I kept going up and down the ladder to answer the phone. I was barraged. My wallpaper peeling suffered for it.

I was flattered. We seemed to be all back in the same family, together again for the time being. That felt nice.

Paul and I talked about it. I said, "County commissioner? What does a county commissioner do, after all?"

It's a balance, a counterweight to the county council. The commission comes up with ideas and plans. The council writes the checks. The commission is a troika, with three members. That's a balancing act too, with one commissioner in the middle, the fulcrum between the other two. "It's a hard job," I told Paul during one of our nighttime discussions.

"On the other hand," I said, "it's tantalizing."

For one thing, I like campaigning. And another, it sounded like an impossible job. I'd done a lot of things that sounded crazy.

"Maybe I can do it," I said to Paul.

So I decided to run.

I was 46 years old. Rebecca was headed to South America that summer. She was going to Brazil on a Rotary Club youth exchange.

One thing helped me a great deal. Hoosier Energy was building a coal-burning power plant about 70 miles west of us, on the Wabash River in Merom in Sullivan County. By 1980, EPA regulations had gotten a lot stricter and the smoke from coal-fired generating stations had to be treated. Hoosier Energy would need a lot of limestone for the scrubbers in their smokestacks. That limestone would come from Monroe County.

There's a railroad spur off Airport Road, down around the county fairgrounds. The plan was to load limestone onto train cars on that spur and take it down to Merom. That meant there would be 50, 75, a hundred truckloads of limestone going from the quarry to the spur every day down Airport Road.

Now, that road turned out to be lined with Republican homes. They were not very happy about it. They really raised a fuss about the plan. So, I trotted over there and started talking to them.

That turned out to be a weak link for Bill Hanna. He'd told them to go to hell, basically. His attitude was, It's gonna happen and he and his partners were going to make money at it and that's just the way the world runs. Take it or leave it.

There again, you've got a person in charge of people's lives who refuses to give them an audience. That's just not right. He could have talked to them about the trucks hauling limestone but he didn't. He just dictated.

I started going to the commissioners' meetings regularly and saw how he handled things. I saw how rude he was and nasty to people. And there weren't even public comment sections during the meetings at that time. That was one of the things that I would institute.

All of a sudden those Airport Road Republicans were not about to take him.

That turned out to be a critical factor in the election. How would you explain it otherwise? I got several thousand more votes in Monroe County than Jimmy Carter did! So I had to have a lot of Republican votes. And a lot of people had thought I was the most radical Democrat around. I wasn't; I was reasonable.

Bill Hanna didn't work very hard at campaigning. The truth is I don't think he worked very hard, period, on county business. He had his own business to run. There were a lot of things he didn't care about; he'd left a lot of things undone as a commissioner.

He was sure he had the election in the bag.

But I was the one who went out and listened to those Airport Road Republicans—his dependable base up to that time. They needed to know somebody was listening.

I didn't know anything about roads. I was a woman. But I got more votes—not a whole lot more votes, but enough—than Bill Hanna, and I won.

Everybody was amazed.

Paul and I went down to the *Herald Times* the night of the election. I ran into a woman named Margaret Tomey in the rest room. She was kind of a snippy woman. Very smart. She did scud work at the recorder's office for property closings. She ripped into me for running against Bill Hanna.

"Who do you think you are, beating Bill Hanna?" she said. She thought it was abominable.

It was startling. She really lashed out at me. My mother-in-law knew her, they were both in the American Association of University Women. My mother-in-law told me, "Well, I never liked her!"

Wouldn't you know it, Margaret Tomey and I became friends. She liked a lot of what I did as commissioner, including listening to her.

Warren Henegar, another Democrat, had gone from the county council to being commissioner and was reelected to a second term. The third seat was occupied by Phil Rogers, a Republican; his seat wasn't up for election that year. And Vi Simpson won her election, partly because she had the support of the Rogers people. That was expected.

But everybody was surprised I won. I had some real help from the mayor's office. Frank really wanted me to win. He wasn't just talking. That was one time he really came through for me.

John Goss was Frank's deputy mayor. He was excellent organizer and very politically savvy. He organized my campaign throughout the county. He gave Mike Davis and Steve Cohen, a couple of really bright SPEA students who volunteered for me, their marching orders. They recruited other student volunteers and they all went out and walked the streets and knocked on doors throughout the county. It was a grass-roots campaign.

Before the '80 election, the county commission was comprised of two Republicans, Hanna and Rogers, and the Democrat, Henegar. Now it would be two Democrats and one Republican.

Phil Rogers was this quiet fellow who worked over at Gosport Gravel, also a Rogers operation (Phil was not related to the people who ran the Rogers companies).

He was a country boy with a club foot. He had a nice, sparkling, twinkling smile. But he never said anything. Nobody had ever heard him talk at commission meetings. Hanna had treated him like dirt. I didn't. I saw that as part of the balancing act that a commissioner would have to perform.

# 16

## Fearless

*It was a late March morning in 2012, more than a quarter century after Monroe County's justice center was built. A crowd had gathered on the building's steps, spilling over onto the sidewalks—many of the women wearing hats, a nod to the honoree—at the intersection of College and 7th avenues. They were there to honor the woman who'd made it her business to get the place built. Dedicated in 1985, the justice center was testament to both the city's and county's growth in the second half of the 20th Century. Monroe County had outgrown its neo-classical courthouse in the middle of downtown. That structure had become decrepit, even dangerous, and so insufficient for the needs of the burgeoning area that county offices had to be scattered all around town. Plenty of people wanted to tear the building down even as cases continued to be heard in its three courtrooms. The old jail, too, had become a problem. Located a block south of the courthouse, it was ill-heated and falling apart.*

*It was common knowledge as far back as the early 1960s that something had to be done about the old courthouse.*

\*\*\*

The memory brings tears to my eyes.

In 2012, they named the new justice center after me. Commissioner Mark Stoops called and said, "Charlotte, we'd like to name the building after you. Would that be okay?"

I said, "I suppose I should say no..."—you know, in all humility — "but I'm not going to!"

I got off the phone and told Paul, in tears, they were going to name it the Zietlow Building. He said, forcefully, "It should be the Charlotte Zietlow Building!"

I said, just as forcefully, "I'm not going to tell them that!"

The day they unveiled it, it was the Charlotte T. Zietlow Justice Center. The number of calls and comments I got, especially from older women, was overwhelming. It meant so much to them to have a woman's name on a building. If you think about it, there are very few buildings in this country that have women's names on them. Very few. The symbolism of having a woman appreciated meant a lot to a lot of women.

Judge Francie Hill was asked to say something at the ceremony. We had some long conversations and finally, she said, "You're fearless."

I said, "Not exactly."

She said, "No, you're fearless. I admire that. You just keep on going if you think it's right even when people don't like where you're going."

She put together a little book of pictures of the ceremony, a memento for me. I was really touched. It was totally unexpected.

***

*To many people, fearless means being scared to death but still willing to act.*

***

I think that's what it was.

My county commissioner days are probably the most demanding of anything I've done. The first four years, Vi Simpson and I and to some extent Warren Henegar and to a great extent Phil Rogers, who was a Republican, and Norm Anderson, and some of the other Republicans, Carl Harrington on the county council representing Ellettsville, and Morris Binkley on the county council from Bloomington—we were able to bring the county into the 20th Century. Not the 21st, but 20th.

It was hard work, but the PCBs, the Courthouse and all that construction stuff, reorganizing the airport, creating a veterans service office—it all got done. We computerized too. That was inevitable and very painful, but we did it.

I'm really proud of the veterans service office. My predecessor, the one I defeated, Bill Hanna, didn't think we needed it but the veterans did. We listened to them and we figured it out, Norm and the rest. We figured out how to fund it. It was really necessary. It turned out to maybe being one of the best things we did.

***

*County governments are set up in accordance with statutes of the State of Indiana. The Board of Commissioners comprise the executive branch. They make contracts; they issue orders; they're in charge of all the roads and other physical property owned by the county, including solid waste landfills, the airport, the office buildings, the courthouse, and so on. They pay the county's bills. They pay county employees' salaries. The commissioners also serve as the legislative branch, writing and enforcing ordinances.*

*The county council has a more singular, defined role: it controls the budget. It sets salaries. It sets the county tax rate and it appropriates the money, with the commissioners spending it. A number of elected countywide officials operate independently of the commissioners, including the recorder, the auditor, the assessor, the sheriff, and the treasurer.*

*With the 1980 election in the books, Monroe County would begin the year 1981 with two Democrats and one Republican comprising its board of commissioners. Those three would work with the county council and the county-wide elected officials to accomplish more than had been done in decades. The commissioners got to work even before they were inaugurated on Thursday, January 1st, 1981.*

***

Warren Henegar told me, and he was probably right, that the state constitution set up county governments as an anti-government move! The framers made it complicated. They didn't want it to be easy for any one official to run any other official's business. Most of what happens in the county is under the authority of 28 elected officials. That makes it very complicated because we commissioners couldn't just walk into somebody's office and say "Okay, we're all going to do this now." No. That doesn't work.

I had to figure out what did work. I spent a lot of time with all these elected county officials, learning what they did.

There were human problems. For instance, the council has its very clearly defined mission. It's very small, very narrow. But it's important because we commissioners could only spend money that had been authorized by them. The human problem arose because the council wants to do many more things. People on the council traditionally are constantly trying to figure out how they can have more to do. A lot of council members really want to act like commissioners. So there's always that tussle.

Even among the three of us commissioners, those human problems could become time bombs if they weren't addressed quickly.

Phil Rogers was quiet and had been ignored by Hanna. He also lived outside Bloomington, "out in the county." Warren was opinionated. We kind of divvied up responsibilities. Warren was interested in solid waste. So that was going to be what he would work on. Phil would work on roads because he knew more about that than either of us. And because I could devote all my time to the work of the county (Phil and Warren had day jobs—Warren worked for the county Health Department), I sort of got everything else.

After we were inaugurated this division of labor worked well. Phil really did know a lot about roads so when he came in with a proposal from the highway department we knew it was probably a good idea. Warren would come in with his thoughts about waste and other things like that. He was a Quaker and a character. He was an environmentalist, too—mostly. We would eventually have to deal with a PCB problem that became national news—some of the first EPA Superfund sites were located right here in Monroe County. Most people still didn't know much about PCBs even after we'd been designated. Warren didn't think they were dangerous; he claimed he could eat PCBs and he wouldn't get sick at all! Long before I did my homework on PCBs, I knew that was crazy. I'd say, "Come on, Warren. Don't even talk like that!"

After the election but before our inauguration, the lame duck commissioners (meaning Bill Hanna; Phil and Warren were incumbents) were going to enter into a new contract for cable TV service in the county. Bill ran things the way he wanted and he wanted to continue the county's relationship with a local cable provider that really hadn't provided much cable for us.

I begged the commissioners not to sign another contract with the company. Steve Ferguson was the part-time county attorney. The county got around to hiring a full-time attorney a couple of years after I became commissioner. Ferguson said, "Aw, well, this is as good a deal as we're going to get."

"It's a sweetheart contract!" I said. My thoughts on it didn't carry much weight yet because I was still a private citizen. Nevertheless, I persisted: "Please put this decision off until next year when we can negotiate a better contract. It will take away our options if you do this now."

We needed more options because the cable company hadn't provided the services spelled out in the contract that was about to expire. "We haven't got enough safeguards for the county," I pleaded.

I'd started going through the minutes of the commissioners' meetings way back, at least twelve years. I found the old contract. Reading it over, I realized the cable company had never made good on its end. It hadn't provided service and it hadn't paid its franchise fees to the county.

Somehow, I'd persuaded the commissioners to put the contract off until after the first of the year. After the inauguration, we hired Guy Loftman as county attorney. He'd been a founder of the Students for a Democratic Society (SDS) chapter at Indiana University before becoming a lawyer. He read through the old contract and found that the cable company owed us a lot of money—a half a million dollars! Steve Ferguson hadn't even checked into that! Or he had and hadn't bothered to tell the commissioners about it. One or the other. Neither option was laudable.

Guy and I talked to the cable company officials. We said, "Pay us what you owe now." It did pay us. And then we opened up the bidding for a new contract.

We eventually signed a contract with another cable company and the county began to get cable in a more systematic and equitable fashion and to collect the franchise fees due us in a timely manner.

Steve Ferguson and Bill Hanna were part of a group of Monroe County Republicans who ran things the way they wanted, and good sense had nothing to do with it.

\*\*\*

*Thursday, January 1, 1981. Charlotte Zietlow is sworn in as a new Monroe County Commissioner. Warren Henagar and Phil Rogers are sworn in as returning commissioners.*

\*\*\*

We elected Warren president of the commission at our first meeting. The next year, I'd be elected president and I'd serve in that capacity all the succeeding years of my two terms as commissioner. The 1984 election turned the commission from two Democrats and one Republican to two Republicans and one Democrat, with Bob Doty replacing Warren. By then, I was well-known for saying, "Let's put party aside." That worked well when the Democrats were in the majority and would continue to work well when we were in the minority.

The Republican commissioners knew I meant what I said. So in my second term, the two Republicans made an agreement—each year one or the other would nominate me for president and vote for me. The other would abstain. That way, they wouldn't get in too much trouble with the Republicans in the county although, really, I doubt if they would have.

I took office for my first term during a very, very cold January. Immediately, we faced a problem with the jail. It was horrible. Awful.

The county jail was next door to the old city hall, what is now the Ivy Tech John Waldron Arts Center. The cells were on the second and third floors. The main cellblock was in the rear of the second floor. You had to pass through the kitchen to get to the cellblock. To get in the cellblock you had to have a key. I still have the lock from that door. You also needed a key for each of the several dozen cells in that cellblock.

The kitchen had a history of grease fires. If one of those kitchen fires spread into the adjoining cellblock, it would have been a funeral pyre. The hallway connecting the kitchen and cellblock was lined with old mattresses. It was a disaster waiting to happen.

The main cellblock had several dozen cells. It couldn't have been but a few days after I took office when the sheriff, Randy Williamson, called me, because the commissioners are in charge of the county's buildings, and said, "Charlotte, It's really cold in here. We've got to do something."

So I called Norm Anderson, the president of the county council. I still didn't know Norm very well by that point, although we would get to know each other well as time went by.

I said, "It's very cold in the jail and I'm not sure how to proceed with this. Do you have any suggestions."

First of all, let me say this was a first—a commissioner calling the county council president for advice. That never happened under Bill Hanna.

Norm, I'd learn, was an extremely competent person and a very decent guy. He said, "Maybe you could call the Red Cross and get blankets for the inmates."

"Okay, I'll do that."

Then he said, "Tell me, how cold is it in there?"

I had to call the sheriff to find out.

Randy said, "I don't know what the temperature is. How do I find that out?"

I said, "Why don't you go out and get a thermometer? You can get one at the hardware store right up the block. And make sure to get a room thermometer, not a kitchen thermometer." Somehow I knew these things had to be spelled out.

So he called me back and said it was 70° in the place. That didn't seem right. I asked, "Is it still cold in there?"

"Yes," he said. "It's really cold."

"Where'd you put the thermometer?"

This is true—he said, "I put it in the kitchen."

I took a deep breath.

"Where's the coldest place in the cellblock?" I asked.

"Well, it's over by the windows. But it's really cold there."

I said, "That's what we want to know. We want to know how cold it is there!"

He brought the thermometer nearer the windows. It read 50°.

"That's cold," I said.

I called the Red Cross and got blankets. Then I called Norm back and told him what we'd found out. He said, "We'll have to get some Visqueen and put it up over the windows." Visqueen is a thick, polyethylene sheeting material. At least it would stop the drafts from coming through the windows. Norm took care of that and made a few other temporary fixes.

But the jail needed to be replaced. And the courthouse needed to be addressed as well. I'd have to devote my full time to these and many other problems in the county even though being commissioner was considered a part-time job paying $7000 a year.

After the jail issue was settled as well as it could be at the time, I got a call from Peck McClung, the Democratic county council member from the Baby Creek area. Baby Creek is on the far east side of the county just south of Unionville. It's a little creek, not very deep but winding. Peck said, "Charlotte, you ought to come out here and see something."

Phil and Warren and I got into the county engineer's Jeep and went out to Baby Creek, where we met some residents. We learned they needed to cross the creek to get to their homes from the gravel road. We went up and down the creek to see these accesses. They were all very icy, making crossing the creek almost impossible.

Peck said, "So, what are you going to do about this?"

The county engineer was there. I thought we'd been friendly enough so far but he seemed very defensive. I asked him if this was a county road.

"Yeah," he said, "it's a county road."

"Okay, so we have some responsibility to do something about this."

"Yeah, we have responsibility."

"Do we have any plans for this?"

"No, we don't have any plans."

I asked him what we could do. He suggested we lay down big corrugated galvanized pipes, four feet in diameter, with dirt laid over them and wooden boards laid over that, so the cars and pickup trucks could cross the creek and the creek water would still flow through the pipes.

"We do that all over the county," the engineer said. "It's not inexpensive but it's not hugely expensive. And it's not complicated engineering either."

I suggested he draw us up a proposal: how it would work and what it would cost. "Will you do that?" I asked. He nodded. "And bring it to the next commissioners meeting so we have this on paper."

I turned to the residents and said, "And you come to the meeting too and talk to us so we have an official record of the problem from your point of view."

So, the engineer came to our next meeting and the residents came too. The project would cost about $8000 and we could get it done over a period of a few years. The problem wasn't insuperable.

But Warren Henegar didn't think much of our solution.

"Oh, Charlotte," he said. " You're such a patsy!" It wouldn't be the last time he'd say that to me. He went on. "These people knew what they were getting into when they bought their property! And they'll never pay enough taxes to make up for that expense."

"But Warren," I said, "that's not what democracy is all about. We have taxes so we can address the needs of the entire population. It's not just you paying your taxes to fix your own problem."

Warren laughed and laughed.

That night, the commissioner who'd never been heard before, called me at home. "This is Phil," he said. Phil Rogers? Calling me?

Phil was a Republican but that didn't matter to me. It turned out he was really concerned with trying to solve problems for people. The gravel firm he worked for was part of the Rogers group of companies (again, he was not related to the people who ran them). Rogers, the company, had a lot of power in Monroe County, even within county government. Bill Hanna's trucking company had lots contracts with the Rogers companies to transport stone and gravel and asphalt for the county. For years, Hanna had benefitted from almost every contract the county had for those materials. I'd pointed that out when I was running against him, a big reason why I'd won the year of the Reagan landslide.

The company Phil worked for also benefitted from county contracts but he hadn't been bothered at all that I'd pointed out the Rogers companies' peculiar relationship with the county.

We wound up getting along very well. We talked a lot. I even got him to talk at commissioners meetings—sometimes. We agreed on pretty much everything. And when I ran for reelection in 1984, Phil's daughter gave me some cash and told me she appreciated the fact her father now recognized that women were people too. "My father never was a feminist but he's been nicer to me and his wife than ever before since he's worked with you."

Phil's ideas about running a campaign were a lot like mine. We both believed door-to-door canvassing is the most important thing to do. During elections, Phil would partner with Jerry Bales, one of the two state representatives from Monroe County at the time. They'd go up and down county roads, knocking on doors, Phil on one side and Jerry on the other. And they both walked with pronounced limps. Phil had been born with a club foot—he'd spent some years in a Shriners Hospital as a child. Jerry had suffered some kind of leg injury. No matter what, door-to-door canvassing is effective.

Now, Phil Rogers was on the phone.

"You know, what Warren said to you this morning wasn't right," he said. "And what you said was. We're supposed to be there for everybody, to serve the people. If you make a motion on these pipes, I'll second it."

That spelled out our relationship for the next eight years. Normally, he wouldn't want to be involved in a public row. He didn't want to be knocked down in public either. And he thought Warren had knocked me down in front of those people at Baby Creek.

Warren and Bill Hanna were two different kinds of people and Phil had had to live with them for the previous four years. So Phil and I just got along.

We got to work installing those pipes. The job took a few years but the pipes still work.

I ran into some Baby Creek residents in 2018. We talked about the fix. They said, "We're going to live here forever or as long as we can." I asked if they could still cross the creek. They said they could, nearly 40 years after we'd fixed the problem.

My work was really just beginning. I had the time and the inclination. I did a bunch of things, with the agreement of the other two commissioners. I set up a bunch of committees and task forces. One was to look at how the highway department was functioning. It wasn't functioning smoothly. There were factions within the department. There was a sense that the superintendent, Jim Sargent, had favorites and that the really good workers within the department weren't among his favorites. There was a lot of internal grumbling.

So I set up a blue-ribbon committee of county residents, primarily Republicans who knew things about roads and highway management, just to look things over and make recommendations to resolve the morale problems.

Jim Sargent was really angry with me for that. His wife was even angrier. I started getting anonymous notes saying things like I didn't know what I was doing or what I was talking about. We eventually figured out who they were coming from—Sargent's wife.

We ended up unionizing the department. I called the local of the American Federation of State, County and Municipal Employees (AFSCME) and said, "Maybe unions can bring some order to our highway department and tell the workers what we can do for them." Then I went to the superintendent and said, "Let's see if the union can help. It could bring some order to the department."

AFSCME came in and won the election to represent the workers. That really settled things down but it took a while.

Jim I worked through our own problems. He made a desk chair for me, by hand, as a symbol of his affection for me. I have it upstairs.

Then I set up task forces to work on space needs for county offices, trash collection, veterans services—pretty much everything the county was responsible for. I just called in the troops, local experts, not consultants from afar.

For instance, Randy Sciscoe, a Republican, was the trustee for Perry Township. He was a country boy and he knew a lot about how things worked in the county. He had a special interest in the county's trash problem. People who lived in the county outside Bloomington did not have public trash pick up—many people just threw their trash into ravines or along the sides of roads. I appointed Sciscoe to head the trash task force. He and his committee came back with a proposal for trash drop off locations around the county and how to manage them, which is pretty much still in place.

So, a lot of things were happening and, again, some of them started happening even before I was sworn in. In November and December, between the election and the inauguration, the commissioners approved another in a series of petition drives to save the courthouse. The historic preservation people already had done two petition drives, both of which had been rejected by the county council because they weren't specific at all. The council said, each time, we're not going to deal with anything that doesn't offer a resolution to our courthouse problems.

The historic preservation people wanted to do another petition drive. I begged the commissioners not to okay it. I suggested we wait and act on it in January. I could see it was going to go nowhere again because this petition still didn't offer a plan. It just said Save the Courthouse, which was a good idea but still didn't solve the problem. But Bill Hanna wanted to pass it and so the commissioners did.

I knew the county council would say exactly what they'd said two times before—Forget about it. Nevertheless, I got a bunch of petition sheets and started gathering signatures, dutifully, just to be helpful. I ended up gathering as many signatures as anybody else.

\*\*\*

*Under Indiana state law citizens can demand, through a petition process, that a big, expensive project be done. Any group of people can begin collecting signatures—as they had twice already in recent years calling for the courthouse to be rebuilt. The process is complicated, including different paths for different types of obligation bonds that would finance the project and requiring approvals from a number of different authorities.*

\*\*\*

The third petition went to the county council in the Spring of '81. The council said, We told you, you had to have a full scale plan. You don't, so too bad.

That wasn't a total surprise but it took the wind out of my sails.

After that the newspapers, the people in the courthouse, the people outside the courthouse, they all said it was never going to happen. The courthouse would never be saved. That was the general sentiment. It became a drumbeat: We weren't going to build a new courthouse; we weren't going to renovate the old one. The conventional wisdom was nothing was going to happen.

\*\*\*

*From the time of the November, 1980 election on, Charlotte spoke with as many people as she could—looking for different ideas, trying to gauge public sentiment, consulting knowledgeable parties as well as the general citizens.*

***

People had been clamoring for a new courthouse for 20 years. Bloomington Restorations Inc. (BRI) had been passing petitions that kept getting knocked down by the county council.

The BRI people voted for me—I know they did. It was a bipartisan group and they knew Bill Hanna didn't want to have anything to do with the courthouse any more. They weren't getting anywhere with him. He'd even suggested they dig up the lawn around the courthouse and put offices there, underground. Then somebody pointed out that's solid limestone just underneath the surface so that idea wasn't too good.

During the campaign, people asked me, "What are you gonna do about it?" I said, "I don't know exactly. But I know something has to be done. There's got to be a solution and we can't stop looking until we find it." That's the best I could offer them. It was an honest answer. I promised I would work on it until we solved it—and I did! I made good on my promise.

I'd started working on getting a more complete plan to save the courthouse as soon as I got into office. But we didn't have the tools to do that. We had no consensus on what exactly we should do. We didn't have any money to do it. We had no design plan. And where were we going to put all the county employees while the work was being done?

We commissioners would be in charge of where the various departments would be temporarily housed and how they were going to work in the interim. We wanted that to work smoothly while the courthouse was being renovated or torn down. We didn't want to issue directives by fiat. That wouldn't work, just telling people what to do. We had to have input from all concerned parties. It would be a balancing act.

One of the first things I did was order panic bars to be installed so workers stuck in the courthouse after hours could get out should the worst occur.

The structure was solid and it was an historical building. It meant something to people here. It had the potential to be beautiful again. It was—and is—the center of the town. It creates a sense of community. It was worth saving.

One of the things I'm proud of is the courthouse. After two and a half years, taking one alley and then another and then another, we eventually arrived at our goal of restoring the courthouse—and ultimately building the new justice center because that had to be part of the deal. It was a very hard job that required an enormous amount of carrots and sticks and stroking and smiling and groveling. We got it done at budget and in a reasonable amount of time.

The courthouse was a horrible, awful mess and way overflowing. Space needs had been a longstanding issue. Judge Kenneth Todd had an office way back in a corner and you had to go through a courtroom to get to it—or you could come in through the window. Judge Marc Kellams was on the third floor. His office was in a bathroom, literally! The bathroom had a little anteroom that had room for a desk, and that's where Judge Kellams had his office hours. Judge John Baker was on the third floor too and he had a real office, probably the best of the judges' offices, which wasn't a surprise; he was persuasive. Judge James Dixon had the northwest corner and the ceiling was falling on him.

The question became, How do we get the momentum started toward solving this thing? We couldn't just rely on people going around with petitions; we have to get them thinking and caring about the courthouse. We want the courthouse to be saved. Norm Anderson and I got together and said, Okay, what are we going to do now?

I had already begun going throughout the county, talking to people, the lawyers and the bankers, the so-called powers that be, asking them, What do you think? So many of the really big guns said, Tear it down!

I suggested we hold a summit for county employees, come one come all, tell us what you think. So Norm and I co-chaired the summit. As you might guess, the suggestions were all over the map: I don't care what you do, just get something done! and I'm really tired of falling over boxes and electrical wires.

Next, I suggested we set up a steering committee, nine members, that I chaired. It included the publisher of the *Herald-Telephone*, Scott Schurz (he was adamant about tearing the courthouse down); Rick Zabriskie, the president of BRI (he was an adamant, to his toes, historical preservationist); Lester DeCoker, a farmer and the leader of Save Our Taxes, a group that wanted minimal public spending, and who'd run against Warren in the fall—he said, "I don't care what you do just so long as the taxpayers don't have to pay anything for it; Vi Simpson, the county auditor; Don Wagner, who'd been my antagonist in the city council against the gay rights ordinance—he was now on the county council and still a curmudgeon and very fiscally conservative; Terry Claypacs, the vice president of facilities for the university because he knew something about buildings; and a few others. Then we had Judge Dixon—his thinking was: I don't care about the courthouse; just get those people out of that old jail before they get burned up!

It was not an easy group to work with but I'd set it up to make it really hard.

We started meeting in June, '81. The committee lasted the rest of that year and all the way through the next one.

The first thing we worked on was: Do we have a problem? Believe it or not it took a while to get to that conclusion. It was, Well, I dunno. Maybe we can get along with things as they are as long as it doesn't cost anything. Or Damn right we have a problem. We have a building that's falling apart because we're not taking care of it! And Yeah, we have a totally useless building and we should tear it down! That sort of thing.

We worked our way through, step by step, until we got to a point where we agreed: Yes, we did have a problem; Yes we should solve it; Yes, we're not going to get any other things done as long as this hangs over our heads. We went through these simple things very deliberately.

The committee came to a point where we agreed it was time to get some professional advice on what our options were. It authorized Vi Simpson and me to go to Norm Anderson with a bold suggestion. What if we hired an architect to come up with some ideas about how we might deal with this? How much would that cost? And where would the money come from?

Norm and the council found the money and the committee found the professional.

We had in mind a local architect, Larry Burke, a founder of the Odle Burke firm. He was really interested in local architecture and he was an historic preservation person. We didn't emphasize that when we went through the process of requesting county money but my preference was to renovate the courthouse. We asked him for five options that would include projected operating costs for 20 years. We all agreed that's what his charge would be.

Larry went off and came back several months later with five options, including both tearing the courthouse down and doing nothing.

Then I went to Frank McCloskey, now in his third term as mayor, and said, "Will you join us in calling for a big meeting of community leaders?" It would be a second summit, a hundred and fifty people in positions of power and opinion-makers who weren't necessarily in power. He agreed to it even though he really didn't think any of this would work. He agreed to support the plan just to humor us.

One of Larry Burke's proposals was to restore the courthouse and dedicate it only to the smaller county offices that weren't growing, basically the land-use offices, and build a whole new facility for the criminal justice system.

So we went to the 150 leaders and arranged one big meeting of all of them at the IU Foundation. We gave them Larry Burke's set of five proposals and asked them to choose one. We let the options speak for themselves. There was a consensus by the end of the meeting that afternoon already. There was not a ripple of dissension, nothing audible enough to detract from the overall approval.

They picked the one I would have chosen. We would restore the courthouse and build a new justice center.

I went to Tom Hirons, who'd been active in the College Democrats and the student body vice president under future Bloomington mayor Mark Kruzan. Hirons had just opened his own public relations and marketing company—it's still in business and now has its headquarters in Indianapolis. I said, "We're going to have a fourth petition drive and this time we can't lose."

He helped line up all these other businesses. He designed a logo for us. He made up banners and posters and buttons, T-shirts and bumper stickers. It was all privately underwritten by the businesses he'd per-suaded to join in the effort.

\*\*\*

*February, 1983: As the courthouse renovation work continues, Char-lotte receives word her father has died. Gilbert Amadeus Theile was 72 years old. He died of an aortal aneurysm. Charlotte recalled him being a three-pack-a-day smoker since she was a small child. The family gathers in St. Louis for the burial and to put things in order. Going through Rev. Theile's papers, Charlotte discovered that he'd kept secret from his fam-ily—his trial for heresy.*

*After helping handle her father's affairs, Charlotte turned her atten-tion back to county matters.*

\*\*\*

Lester DeCoker said, "Alright, let's go with one of these, but don't spend any money on it."

"Lester," I said, "what do you suggest?"

He suggested we raise the cost of the courthouse renovation by fundraising rather than issuing a general obligation bond. So we had some bake sales. Lester also suggested we ask every single property owner in the county to pay up front the amount they'd have to pay for the project over time; that way they would be saving the cost of interest.

We sent out a mailing to everyone who was on the county tax rolls. We did it all with private financial contributions and services from businesses like The Rogers Group, Fine Print, and The Trojan Horse.

Our mailing to every taxpayer read, We're going to do this. It will be cheaper if you, the taxpayer, paid for it up front—then your assessments won't go up. So please put money in the return envelope and just send it in.

Some 11,000 of those letters went out.

Lester and I went to each of the largest taxpayers in the county, GE, Otis, Westinghouse, RCA, Sarkes Tarzian, and told them they'd save a lot of money by paying their share now. We told these chief executives, "It'll be a lot cheaper if you pay cash up front. That way we can avoid the interest and legal charges for bonds, which will be considerable." We had the figures, how much they'd save, and showed them. They all said they'd think about it. None of them bit.

All told we raised $11,000. My sister and I each contributed $500. She didn't have much money at that time; I don't know how she did it. I must have written a good letter asking her for a contribution.

I had forewarned Lester that I would do this with a full heart but, I said, if it doesn't work we would have to go to a petition drive.

So now I said, "Lester, I'm really sorry, but we're going to have to do something more than this. We're going to have a petition drive for a general obligation bond." By then he was beginning to feel the groundswell for saving the courthouse.

We started at the county fair in August. We had a booth and we recruited people from all over the county to man it. We figured it would cost about $2 million to gut the courthouse and rebuild it, faithfully. That was a lot of money but it wouldn't be prohibitive for each individual property owner. So I came up with an idea: on the flyers for the petition we said if you own a $100,000 home your tax for each year of the general obligation will go up seven dollars—the cost of a large pizza with anchovies.

The fourth petition drive was a steamroller from then on.

It was September when we turned the petition in. And there was no remonstrance!

\*\*\*

*One of the steps in the byzantine petition process is the option for remonstrance. Citizens have a chance to submit a counter-petition. Should that drive amass one more signature than the original petition, the proposal is effectively killed.*

\*\*\*

The newspapers and radio commentators had been saying, Oh, Charlotte, they're going to come forward. There will be remonstrance. You haven't won yet!

It seemed that everybody was saying, Oh no, it's not going to work.

Yet the day came and the day went and there was no remonstrance. At which point we got a letter from Bill Cook.

\*\*\*

*At the time, one of the new big names in Bloomington was that of William Alfred Cook, "Bill" to everybody who knew him. He'd started a little medical instruments company in the spare bedroom of the small apartment he and his wife shared in 1963. His company, the Cook Group, would become the largest family-owned medical device manufacturer in the world. Bill Cook would become a billionaire several times over and the richest man in Indiana. In 1981, he was on the rise and trying to help remake the image and environment of the town. One of his signature passions was historic preservation.*

\*\*\*

Long before we got to this point, a rumor spread that Bill Cook was going to give us $2 million. That was totally upside down. He wanted to take the money from us, he wasn't going to give us the money.

We'd been hoping to have a $2 million ceiling on the bids for the renovation project. While all this was going on Vi Simpson and I went out to lunch with Bill Cook. I said to him, "Okay, you're interested in historic preservation. Do you have any suggestions for the courthouse?"

He talked about what they'd done up in Crown Point: maybe the courthouse could be turned into a mall.

I think he felt I wasn't afraid to speak to him as an equal. I wasn't bedazzled by his celebrity. I did not feel in any way overwhelmed by him. He was used to being surrounded by people who adulated him. I thought, "You're not any help at all." Out of the blue, he said to me, "Well Charlotte, you're a weird person. You're a weird duck."

We said thank you and got up to leave.

Then, weeks after our lunch meeting with Bill Cook, we got this letter from him saying, You guys don't know what you're doing. You give me $2 million and promise not to tell me what to do and we'll do it our way. He addressed the letter personally to me but he circulated copies of it to 11 people whom he thought would be his allies in this scheme. We'd give him the money and he'd get carte blanche.

The first I knew of the letter was when local labor leader, John Lampkins, came running up to me one morning just as I was going into Goods to work that day. He was waving Bill Cook's letter as he was crossing the street and he was furious. He said, "Charlotte, you can't do this! Bill Cook won't hire union labor!"

I didn't know what he was talking about. He held the letter out before me. I said, "John, let me read it."

Okay, I read it. "John," I said, "there's no way this can happen. We don't just give $2 million to anybody to do anything! We've got laws we have to follow. We have to have a plan; we have to put it up for bids; we have to have a contract; we have to follow the prevailing wage law. There's no way we will give Bill Cook $2 million just like that. This will not happen so forget it."

I got back to my office and got a phone call from Rick Rechter, who'd risen through the ranks at the Rogers Group from laborer to eventually become chairman of the board. He hadn't liked me because

I'd opposed his buddy Bill Hanna. He said, "Come over to my office. I have to talk to you!"

I walked in and he was holding Bill Cook's letter in his hand. He said, "Now we know who has the biggest ego in the community!"

Rick had a plaque on his office wall that read something like It doesn't matter who gets the glory; it matters that the job gets done.

"That's my principle," he said. "Anything I can do to help you on this project, just let me know."

We became allies, just like that. So, you never know.

Bill Cook was another Trump-y person. Ready, fire, aim—that was the subtitle of the biography former *Herald-Times* reporter Bob Hamill wrote about him. Once Bill Cook had power, he just did whatever he damned well pleased.

We got a bid from a very reputable local contractor, Ed Goheen, for two million dollars. We were lucky; his bid was exactly what we needed.

It was late 1983, when we finally got all the financing in place for both the courthouse renovation and the construction of a new justice center. Workers gutted the courthouse and cut holes in two of the floors to restore the big original rotunda. The contractors found woodworkers and plaster workers who could replicate all the interior wood trim, walls, and pillars.

\*\*\*

*Fall, 1983. The county must move all its operations out of the courthouse and into temporary quarters.*

\*\*\*

Now we had to find some places to put everybody while the courthouse was being renovated. Space had always been an issue, from the time I took office. When I started as commissioner, we had no commissioners' offices and we had no staff. We used the highway department secretaries as our staff. The County Auditor kept the minutes for our meetings.

The highway secretaries were people we could go to for help; there were two or three of them. One of them was a really loyal person to Bill

Hanna. She did not like the idea of my being there. She didn't do much for us. So I suggested that maybe we replace her with somebody who would do more for us. And we did. I don't think I've been forgiven by her for that but I did what I had to do.

I asked the county council to okay the hiring of an executive assistant for the commissioners. We got the okay and hired a person who didn't work out. Then, at the end of 1982, city council president Tomi Allison—who'd soon take over as mayor with the election of Frank McCloskey to Congress—recommended we hire a woman named Jinnie Rose. Tomi's husband, Jim Allison, worked with Jinnie's husband in the psychology department at Indiana University.

Jinnie wasn't working at the time although she was registered nurse. She came from Minnesota where her father was a big construction contractor, so she knew a lot about things like that. She had been on the hospital and library boards and had been elected to school board. She was a community leader, very smart and very canny.

We hired Jinnie in 1983 and she turned out to be our lifesaver. She agreed with me that there was a lot that was backward in Bloomington; she also noticed many of our streets didn't have curbs or sidewalks or storm sewers.

Jinnie made all the arrangements to move county offices before the courthouse renovation began. Bill Cook's CFC Properties had recently bought Graham Plaza, the Curry Building, and the old Monon Railroad depot knowing we'd need space for county offices. So we leased a lot of space from CFC: the county council and commissioners had offices in the basement of Graham Plaza; the auditor, treasurer, recorder, and assessor offices were in the railroad depot; and the courts, the clerk, and the prosecutor's offices were in the Curry Building. Jinnie got them all moved and settled in. She got along really well with the workmen and the contractors, too. She was a gift.

She would be a gift, too, during my second term as commissioner.

It was in December, 1983, that I went to Bloomington Hardware to get a sledgehammer for a groundbreaking ceremony. I hit the wall of the third-floor courtroom with the sledgehammer. Lo and behold, we found these little posts or balustrades, the originals, behind the drywall. That was exciting. It was to be a faithful restoration.

We had the renovated courthouse open by the election in '84.

Building the justice center was a totally separate thing. While we were finishing up the courthouse, we started on the justice center. We hired the architect, Burke, to design it.

Then we had to buy land. That was a big deal. We learned that Sam Benavole, who owned a Lincoln-Mercury auto dealership at 7th and College, was thinking of closing his business down. He owned the property it stood on. We went back and forth with him on the purchase price. He raised it and lowered it and then decided not to sell. Eventually, we struck a deal.

Then we had to get construction bids.

It was really funny—we had all these people come in with slide shows and music and all sorts of stuff going on. They would have these big dog and pony shows. Then the Weddle Brothers construction company came in, just three local guys, to make their presentation. They said, "Well, here's what we do. And here's what we think we can do for you." Totally down home. And it was totally persuasive!

We got a lot more information from them than we got from all those other glitzy presentations. Phil, Warren, Norm, and I talked it over. "They're right here," we said. "We trust them. They're not going to get away with anything. They will work with us on an easy basis." We decided the Weddle Brothers were our best choice.

So we hired them as our construction manager for the justice building in '84.

Meanwhile, we were also negotiating for the old post office building at the southeast corner of 7th and College. The county didn't pay any money for the building; it was deeded to us by the Postal Service with the proviso that it be used for health services. So it's the County Health building now.

We dedicated the justice center in 1985.

*\*\*\**

*Well into the fourth year of her term as county commissioner, Charlotte was tired. She'd been elected president of the board her second year in office and was reelected to that post in both 1983 and '84. She'd led the effort to get the courthouse renovated and the new justice center built. She worked on acquiring the old US Post Office building at College Avenue and 7th Street and transforming it into a county health building. The commissioners had reorganized the Monroe County Airport. They'd started the county's first veterans services office. They'd set up local trash drop-off centers for people who lived in unincorporated areas and hired a private solid waste management company to run the county's landfill. They'd consolidated the county's insurance policies, dramaticly reducing its premiums. Her plate had been full—even overflowing—since she'd taken the job in January, 1981. Now it was time for her to decide whether she should run for reelection.*

*\*\*\**

It had been a full-time job for me, but not in terms of pay. We had saved the courthouse. We were building the justice center, we were working on plans to renovate the old post office, making plans to reorganize the airport and the landfills, there were just so many things going on.

I was tired. I thought, I don't have to do anything more, do I?

I was exhausted. People said you have to run again and I said I'm not so sure. Being county commissioner was a lot of work.

*\*\*\**

*Many Bloomington leaders, including Frank McCloskey—now a member of the United States Congress—urged Charlotte to run for reelection. They reminded her the justice center still had not been completed and the unfinished project required her leadership. She decided to run again and faced, for the second time, Bill Hanna.*

*\*\*\**

I ran for reelection kind of reluctantly because I was tired. I'd done all these things—I don't have to do anything more, do I?

I won but the outcome had been kind of iffy. The final tally was very close—129 votes in my favor out of a total of 35,005 cast. Bill Hanna demanded a recount.

Monroe County paper ballots were marked with an X. The two sides were locked in a room to count each and every X. Neither I nor Bill Hanna was allowed in the room. I had some very quick-witted people in the room, doing the counting for my side. Bob Gross, Pat's husband and a very good friend of Paul's, was my counter. Elizabeth Mann, the erstwhile judge known to everyone as Nicki, was my attorney.

Each side had to make sure the other side hadn't peeked to see who the X was for before they either accepted or rejected the ballot. I learned afterward the recount process itself was very contentious. Lester Musgrave, a Republican member of the election review committee and a man of integrity, was a great hero in the process. He made sure only the legitimate votes were counted.

Bob Gross was very smart and he made sure the other side wasn't peeking. Nicki's very smart too and the two of them prevailed for me. I won—I was reelected honestly. The final margin was 19 votes in my favor!

Bill Hanna had never, ever spoken to me—ever, ever in his whole life. He's dead now so he's never going to speak to me.

# 17

# Burn

*Certified the winner in the first week of December, 1984, Charlotte figured the heavy lifting was behind her. Little did she realize that the fight of her life was about to begin. She would be sworn in again on Tuesday, January 1, 1985. But before that she was handed a sheaf of papers, a legal consent decree, which, had it been carried out, would have changed the character of Bloomington forever.*

*One of the divisions of Westinghouse Electric Corporation operated a factory on Bloomington's west side. At its peak, the factory employed thousands of people from all over the region. Beginning in the late 1950s, the Bloomington facility manufactured capacitors, electrical energy storage devices in which two or more conductors are separated by an insulator. The capacitors contained a liquid polychlorinated biphenyl (PCB) insulator. Eventually, Westinghouse employees, area residents, and public officials became aware that hundreds of thousands of tons of the PCB had contaminated workers, solid waste dumps, the city's sewer system and water reclamation facilities, and even the soil in city gardens and surrounding farms.*

\*\*\*

At first, everybody was unaware of PCBs. Then, slowly but surely, people began to understand what PCBs were. And people started getting sick.

The EPA had begun to get concerned about PCBs. It was looking around the country for them trying to find them in places where they shouldn't have been. It was obvious to look around a plant like Westinghouse.

We really had a mess here.

The city hired Joe Karaganis, who was a smart, three-piece suit guy from Chicago, to represent it.

\*\*\*

*Joseph V. Karaganis ran his own law practice specializing in environmental litigation and energy and natural resources cases. Frank McCloskey hired Karaganis to go toe to toe with Westinghouse.*

*In 1981, the city, represented by Karaganis, filed a common law nuisance and trespass suit against Westinghouse. Two years later, the EPA designated two Bloomington landfills containing discarded capacitors as Superfund clean-up sites. The agency also filed suit against Westinghouse. In 1984, the EPA named a third local landfill a Superfund site. One of those Bloomington Superfund sites—the Bennett Stone Quarry—was characterized by the EPA as the biggest PCB dump in the nation.*

*Karaganis began negotiating with Westinghouse. Soon, the Indiana Attorney General and the EPA joined the negotiations. The meetings were held in secret.*

\*\*\*

Karaganis and Westinghouse and the EPA and the city would respond creatively to the challenge. Together, they all came up with this wonderful idea: Westinghouse would build an incinerator. It would be a totally new technology, using PCB-tainted soil as part of its fuel. It was a great deal for Westinghouse. I'm sure the Westinghouse people thought they'd develop this thing and then sell it to other municipalities facing the same kinds of problems.

So after the recount, I was certified the winner of the election. I was handed this thick sheaf of papers regarding the incinerator plan. "Okay, you're going to be in office. Here's your consent decree. Have a nice Christmas!"

\*\*\*

*The 108-page legal document spelled out the plan. Westinghouse would build an incinerator, using municipal solid waste as fuel and burning up the PCB-tainted sludge from the city's water treatment plant as well as any and all other toxic material resulting from the company's years of producing capacitors.*

\*\*\*

It must have sounded like just a great idea to all concerned. They'd kill three birds with one stone: getting rid of the PCB-tainted soil, the PCB-tainted sewer sludge, and the city's municipal solid waste.

Interestingly, nowhere in the document did Westinghouse admit to any guilt in the matter.

I wanted to know what it was all about. I took the consent decree home and, after Christmas, I sat down and read the whole thing. I had question after question after question after question. I thought, "Uh-oh!" I got more and more uneasy as I read it because I thought there were too many unanswered questions.

One thing I found: There was a preliminary paragraph that said, in so many words, We guarantee this thing will be safe. I took note of that.

Frankly, I just knew very few others would read it. I think our county attorney Jim Trulock did and the head of our health department, Steve Creech. But I was sure neither Bob Doty (a Republican who had replaced Warren Henegar on the board in the November election) nor Phil Rogers would read it all the way through.

\*\*\*

*As the PCB contamination throughout the city and county became more widely known, the idea that an incinerator might be built to take care of the problem also became common knowledge. The more some people thought about it, the less they liked the idea. Opponents began showing up at city council meetings to voice their displeasure. Many seemed well-versed in the scientific aspects of the problem, citing the biphenyls themselves, dioxins, dibenzofurans, and the dangerous toxins that would result from inadequate burning of the PCBs.*

*Meanwhile, the parties to the negotiations realized they'd left out a sixth necessary participant, another voice to join the chorus of the city, Westinghouse, the state environmental department, the Indiana attorney general, and the federal EPA.*

\*\*\*

Now let's see—we forgot something. Municipal solid waste will be the fuel for the incinerator. Where is that? Well, a lot of it is in the county's landfill. Oh my God, we're going to have to bring Monroe County into this!

The parties to the consent decree realized this as I was running for reelection.

The city lawyers said to us, the county commissioners, "We're really sorry but we're going to have to pull you in. But don't worry, we're taking care of everything. You don't have to do anything. Just sign the consent decree. Sign off your solid waste to us. It won't be a problem. Just do it."

And then I got the petitions.

\*\*\*

*The consent decree process called for all parties to hold public meetings as they considered whether to sign it or not. The first city meeting was scheduled for December 6th, days after the document's release. Six days later, the city held a second public meeting. At that session, Joe Karaganis stated that no matter what the public's comments were, there'd be no changes to the consent decree. The implication? Take it or leave it. More and more people opted to leave it.*

*The city council scheduled two meetings in March, the first to debate in public the merits of the consent decree and the second to vote on it. The day before one of the meetings another thick sheaf of papers was delivered to Charlotte. The* Herald-Telephone *reported it was a petition signed by 6,000 area residents opposing the incinerator. The petition was sponsored by InPIRG (Indiana Public Interest Research Group), a '70s-era collection of student environmental activists that had become resurgent when the incinerator was announced.*

***

The petition was addressed to all parties that had to sign the consent decree. I was told by Mayor Allison that I could ignore the petition because the people who'd signed it didn't know what they were talking about. She called the signers "instant experts." Other people from the city told me, "Don't worry about that thing!"

I read the petition. It raised the issues of health, safety, and sensibility. Very basic stuff. They were reasonable concerns.

So I randomly called about 50 people who'd signed it. I said, "You signed this. Why did you do it?"

It turned out they did know the terms of the consent decree! They knew exactly what they had signed. Many scientists had signed it. Mathematicians, chemists, physicists, and environmentalists of every sort. All of them were residents of Monroe County. Not stupid people.

I didn't fully understand everything in the consent decree by a long shot but I had read it and I was concerned about health and safety and sensibility too. I talked to the other two commissioners and the members of the county council and said, "Let's have a resolution that says we will satisfy the demands and the concerns of the petitioners. Our approval of the consent decree will be contingent on the promise that these things will be taken care of."

So now I've got this thing, this consent decree, and I've got this petition. I get a call from the city. "Everything okay? All set to sign it?"

I said, "I've still got some questions."

***

*Charlotte put the caller off—for the time being.*

***

A few days later I got another phone call asking me the same thing. "I've still got all these questions," I said.

The caller said, "Just sign it."

"But all these people who signed the petition...?"

"Oh, that doesn't mean anything. They didn't know what they were signing. Nobody understands this stuff!"

Remember, I'd called a lot of signers. They knew what they were doing.

I said, "Really? This sounds fairly straightforward to me. They want this thing to be safe. And they want it to not break the bank."

\*\*\*

*The Bloomington city council was scheduled to vote on the consent decree on March 21st. Council chambers were packed and noisy the night of the vote. Opponents of the incinerator tried to shout down the council members as they discussed the document. The din grew louder when council president Pat Gross called for a vote.*

\*\*\*

Pat Gross was all for the consent decree. Almost everybody who counted was for it because it was obviously so smart—you burn stuff and it's gone!

That meeting was very traumatic for her. She was really scared. Tempers were running very high in council chambers. It was almost a riot.

When it came time to vote, only Pat Murphy opposed it. He was the only no vote on the council. I've always had a warm spot in my heart for him because that took a lot of nerve.

\*\*\*

*Then it would be the county's turn to have a meeting and vote on the consent decree.*

\*\*\*

I didn't really fully understand the consent decree or the incinerator itself. But it sounded to me as if the consent decree said, "Oh, maybe this will work."

I was uneasy about it. What I wanted to say was, "Before you do this, there have to be some assurances."

So I came up with the resolution with multiple points, creating conditions for acceptance of the consent decree. You say this incinerator is going to be safe? We say these are things that can't happen: it can't pollute the air; it can't pollute the water; we want specifics in all the various ways it can pollute; and it can't break the bank.

It started with me sitting at my desk, writing it up, and then I talked about it with Jinnie Rose and Norm Anderson from the county council and, of course, my county commissioner colleagues, Phil Rogers and Bob Doty. We refined and finalized the resolution.

Norm said, "Yeah, this sounds good to me. Sure, bring it along to the meeting. It can't hurt."

We had scheduled a joint meeting of the county council and county commissioners to consider the consent decree. The document was big and not scintillating reading. Phil and Bob depended on me to report on it. They trusted me.

Then I talked to all these people who had drawn up the petition opposing the incinerator. They were very persuasive. They brought me piles of literature which I duly read. I did some calling around to experts. All this before the April public meeting.

I planned to introduce my resolution before the vote itself. Everybody—Norm and Phil and Bob and Jinnie—they all said, "Yeah, this looks pretty good."

We scheduled the public meeting but the city people didn't want us to talk about the incinerator. They wanted the discussion to be over. They wanted us to interpret the law the way they wanted. They were very upset. They told me, "We've already had public meetings! We've already heard all the arguments. We've had that; we've done it. There's nothing you can do about this so don't bother." But I insisted. It was my decision.

I said, "We're the county and you're the city. We need to hear from the people!"

This is when I started hearing the line, "You just don't understand, Charlotte," over and over again. There was a lot of me not understanding over the next few years.

But I had to do my homework. Jinnie Rose, I learned long afterward, was appalled by the consent decree. Jim Trulock and Steve

Creech thought it was a terrible idea. But they didn't want to stick their necks out and say so publicly. And they didn't want to say so to me because, they told me later, they didn't feel it was their place to influence me with their personal opinions.

They should have.

The members of the county council thought, by and large, that the incinerator would solve the problem. Norm Anderson said to me, "You know, Charlotte, they're just going to burn it all. That's all."

I said, "Norm! What's going to come out of the smokestack? And what are they going to do with the ash?"

He insisted, "Burning's going to take care of the whole thing."

I said, "I don't think so."

He was at least pleasant about it. And he did share my concerns.

The morning of the meeting at which we were to vote on the consent decree, I was called by Joe Karaganis, along with the lawyer from the state, the lawyer from the EPA, the lawyer from Westinghouse, all of them on a conference call. Our deputy county attorney was on the line too.

It was all these lawyers, as one, and me. I couldn't tell the difference between their voices! They were all saying the same thing.

They started right in. "Charlotte, we've read your resolution (which I'd given to them). You can't act on it. It will just mess everything up."

I said, "How will it hurt? What'll it do?"

"Well, it'll confuse things. If this gets in the record and then, later, if somebody wants to sue us, they'd have this to use. There'll be all sorts of questions raised. You just can't do this!"

"But this is what we want to say," I said. "We're concerned about this incinerator. This is important."

These five lawyers spoke with one voice. Every one of them said, "You can't do this!"

They said, "This resolution won't have any effect anyway. It won't stop the consent decree. It won't matter."

"If it won't have any effect," I asked, "why can't we just go ahead and adopt it? At least it will express, publicly, our concern."

"Well, no, no, it'll mess things up. You can't do it."

These are five lawyers, all saying the same thing. Shut up! Just behave yourself! That's what they were really saying.

The meeting was to begin in ten hours.

I got sick. That phone call made me sick. That afternoon, I had to pick up some new glasses. I remember going out to the College Mall, and I was so distressed I became nauseated.

We had a very big turnout at the courthouse. The entire county council and all three commissioners were there. Plus the county auditor, Rodney Brown, a Republican, kept the minutes. The mayor was there. The city council was there, including the president, my friend Pat Gross. The city officials did not attend in an official capacity. They were there to watch. They weren't going to say anything during the meeting.

Hundreds of people showed up, many of them holding black balloons on strings. They had become the symbol of the poison that people were sure was going to come out of those smokestacks.

It was a mixed crowd: There were well-dressed, clean-shaven people and there were a bunch of people who weren't so clean-shaven. We met in the third floor courtroom of the courthouse. It was filled with spectators and lots of police. We sat there and listened to one person after another. Everybody got their say. We asked them some questions, too—pretty rudimentary stuff. It turned out to be extremely orderly. The meeting went on for hours.

I listened carefully. The environmentalists and activists had sent me lots of materials but I hadn't gotten any technical advice from the head of the health department or the county attorney. As I said, they'd purposely decided not to talk with me about it.

But I had a lot of credibility with the commissioners and the council. I was president of the board. They were willing to listen to me because they knew I did my homework. Didn't mean they always did what I wanted but if I'd known more, I'm sure I could have persuaded all of them to vote against the incinerator.

I'd wanted both the commissioners and the council to vote on the resolution. As for the consent decree, the commissioners would be the signatories but the council would control the money that would have to be spent on it. I wanted both to vote on it.

Finally there was the vote. It was really hard for me. I thought, "I just can't do this. I can't vote for this consent decree. And it will pass because these other people haven't read it and I haven't given them a big speech about it."

The county council voted first. Seven people. Two of them—Carl Harrington and Morris Binkley, both Republicans—voted against it. The rest, I felt, were lukewarm about it but they voted for it. They must have thought, Well, it'll clear this problem up.

And then the commissioners voted. I sat there—I remember this so clearly—with all these thoughts running through my head: If I vote against it, all these people who are always saying, "Oh, Charlotte, you just don't understand..." will think, See? Told you. She's a bad girl. Doesn't behave. Just a problem child.

The thoughts kept rolling around. I can't vote for this; but if I don't Tomi Allison will hate me forever; but I just can't do it; but Pat Gross and my Democratic allies—it'll be the end of our relationship. A lot of friendships I had with people would never be the same again. They would think I was betraying them.

I voted my conscience; I voted against it.

Phil Rogers and Bob Doty voted for it. The two of them took me out afterward for a drink at the Irish Lion. We went upstairs, way in the back, so we could be by ourselves. They understood what I'd gone through. They wanted to reassure me. They apologized to me, hoping to make me feel better. They'd tried to be good kids. They'd behaved themselves. They probably thought, People have worked so hard on this consent decree; it must be all right.

But they trusted me enough to know that I had good reasons for voting the way I did.

If I had known more I could have persuaded Phil and Bob to vote against the consent decree. I could have persuaded all the county council people not to vote for it. The thought nagged at me: If I'd known just a little bit more, a little bit sooner. I still feel bad about that.

I had to make a stand there. I had to! And then I thought, "Okay, what do we do now?" One line from the consent decree stuck with me—This will be safe.

So now we had a consent decree. Now I read it again. Then Steve Creech, head of the county health department, and Jim Trulock, county attorney, came to me and said, "Charlotte, you voted the right way."

I had to laugh to myself: Why didn't you tell me before this? Why didn't you tell the rest of us?

Rodney Brown, a conservative Republican who had replaced Vi Simpson as county auditor, said to me, "Charlotte, I don't care how some of those people were dressed, they were clearly right. You did the right thing."

It was a hard thing to do but at least I was on record against it.

I huddled with Trulock and Creech. I offered a suggestion: "Let's read this thing over again. There's a guarantee that the incinerator will be safe. Let's figure out how we can be sure it will be."

And that's what got me going on a three-year odyssey. I—often accompanied by other local officials, but just as often alone—visiting many solid waste incinerators around the country, reading a lot, studying, talking a lot with incinerator operators, listening to a lot of experts, making phone calls, finding out whether these incinerators really worked, finding out if they really were safe. Trying to answer the question: Why are thousands and thousands of people in Monroe County so upset?

That was my trek.

I said to people in both city and county government, "I'd like to see how PCB incinerators work. We need to go to a site."

The people from the city suggested we go to an incinerator in South Chicago.

So we went there. We got somebody to fly us up there; I forget who. The incinerator was in one of those godawful industrial tracts. Tomi Allison and Pat Gross and seven or eight others—people from the utilities department and other city offices—were with me.

These men showed us around the place. We came to these barrels, filled with liquid, and there were labels hanging on them, filled with scientific terms and abbreviations. I lifted one and tried to read it. I said, "What is this?"

One of the men said, "That's a chemical analysis of what's in the barrel. This is liquid and we have to know what's in here so we know how to monitor what comes out after we burn it."

He explained: "We capture the emissions in the smokestack. We've got all sorts of measurement equipment up there."

I said, "Wow, that's pretty complicated."

He said, "We've got to do it. It's the only way to be safe."

"You know," I said, "we don't have liquids. We have soil."

His mouth fell open. "Oh, I don't know how you're going the monitor that!"

So I turned to Tomi and Pat and said, "How are we going to monitor what comes out of the smokestack? We're burning municipal solid waste. How will we know what to look for?"

Tomi wagged her finger at me. "The only things that'll come out of that smokestack will be carbon dioxide and water!"

I shook my head and said, "I don't know."

Tomi said, "You don't. You have opinions. I have facts."

By wagging her finger in my face Tomi was really saying, Don't you understand, you child? We're trying to do something here and you're getting in the way!

So I determined I was going to have the facts. When I got back home the first thing I did was go up in the attic where I'd stored all my college things and got out my old *General Chemistry for Engineers* textbook.

Burning things. It's a myth that's deeply impressed in people's minds—burning things gets rid of them. That's what Tomi believed. She was adamant about it.

I'd remembered that the elements don't change their essences. They may change their form; they may become vapor when they're burned. But they do not just go away when they're burned.

I sat there with the textbook in my lap and thought, "We do not know what we're doing here!"

That thought led me to plan more and more trips and visits to other incinerators.

Soon after, we commandeered the jet that the IU football team used. It was the team's offseason. About 40 of us flew to El Dorado, Arkansas, a small town where PCBs were manufactured, where, we'd found out, there was another liquid PCB incinerator.

We had a wonderful attorney here in town, Jim Cotner. He was a Republican who'd been the city attorney under Mayor Hooker. Jim was very good, really one of the smartest attorneys in town. A very decent guy. He had a daughter, Jenny. She'd married the son of a very prominent family in El Dorado.

It had been in the newspaper that we were going to go down to El Dorado. Jim called me before we left and said, "Charlotte, my daughter wants to see you when you go down there."

I met Jenny when we arrived there. Jenny and I and her husband, also an attorney, had lunch. They were part of a large group of people trying to get the El Dorado incinerator shut down.

Jenny told me children living near the incinerator were coming down with lung cancer and other cancers in totally disproportionate rates. Many of them had been admitted to St. Jude's Children's Hospital in Memphis. And, of course, the incinerator had been built in the black area of town. Jenny's people believed the incinerator had something to do with those cancers.

Furthermore, there was a young man here in Bloomington named Jimmy Ross, who worked for Indiana University as the student affairs person. He'd come from El Dorado and now he was dying of a degenerative neurological disease. It's just possible that he had been affected by the incinerator in his hometown. There were a lot of people who thought so, too. He'd talked to me about El Dorado before we left.

After I met with Jennie and her husband, our Bloomington contingent went to the incinerator in El Dorado. The people there told us what a wonderful operation it was, how clean its emissions were.

The next day, we flew to a town outside Houston, Texas—Deer Park. It was a hell spot on a river. It was filled with refineries and all these horrible plants that produced poisons. A company called Rollins operated a PCB incinerator there.

John Langley, the city's program manager for the PCB issue and who worked for the Bloomington utilities department until 2018, and I talked with the manager of the operation.

The manager asked us, "How many gallons of PCBs are you going to be incinerating?"

John said, "We're not doing liquids. We're doing soil."

"Wha-a-at?"

"Soil. Impregnated with PCBs."

"Do you know how much soil you're going to burn?"

"Oh, 600,000 cubic feet at least."

The manager laughed and laughed and laughed. He caught his breath and asked, "Do you realize that when you're finished incinerating all that, you'll have 1.3 million cubic feet of hazardous ash?"

John said, "What do you mean?"

The manager explained: "When you incinerate soil, it fluffs. It doubles in volume!"

Well, that was news to all of us.

Apparently, Westinghouse hadn't planned for that.

It was astonishing. This added another dimension to the debate, another piece in a very complicated puzzle.

We came home. *Herald-Telephone* reporters Steve Higgs and Steve Hinnefeld had already begun writing articles almost every day about the proposed incinerator. The word was getting out.

I got to work tracking down as much as I could on incinerators. Then there was public meeting after public meeting, with experts trying to educate the community. We had an IU mathematics professor give a presentation. He'd been crunching the numbers. "The numbers aren't good," he said. "This is not going to work!"

I visited incinerators in other places on my own. Paul and I went to visit our son Nathan in Brunswick, Maine, where he attended Bowdoin College. As we were driving toward Brunswick, I had a map unfolded in my lap. Paul was driving.

"Paul," I said, "can we take half a day to go over to this little town, Auburn? I think they have an incinerator."

Of course, we went. When we got to Auburn we found out the incinerator wasn't working. It had broken down.

Later, I heard there was an incinerator in Germany. I think it was in Hamburg. Somebody who'd come from Bloomington was now living in Hamburg so I called her and asked her to find out how it was working. This woman arranged for me to talk with a man at the plant. The man fudged and hemmed and hawed and eventually said, "Yeah, there are problems." He didn't come right out and say it didn't work but he provided a lot of information that indicated it wasn't running smoothly.

Pat Gross had been a very good friend. She was a really smart, interesting person. But she never forgave me for voting against the consent decree. She was president of the city council at the time. She just didn't get that this was not a good idea.

I'd reached out to her to help me at least illuminate the community, to invite EPA people and other experts—chemists and physicists—to speak at public meetings on the incinerator. She and I co-sponsored the meetings. She had been willing to get people to understand the incinerator at first and she was sure they would eventually come around to support it.

All these experts were saying, clearly, "No, this is really bad!"

There was one whistle-blower at the EPA, he came out and spoke to us. It was a meeting at Bloomington High School North called by private citizens. He felt the consent decree was a terrible agreement and that the EPA was not living up to its charge.

Then there was a nationally known attorney, a very smart guy, who had been working with people near Buffalo, New York, a place called Love Canal.

That encouraged me. That told me I wasn't crazy. That told me I wasn't smelling fish that weren't there.

Pretty soon, Pat withdrew from planning these meetings.

The county council and the other two commissioners—they came from a generally conservative Republican position—by this point believed me that the incinerator was problematic.

It's interesting: some of the most conservative Republicans in town would come up to me and say, "Charlotte, you've got to stop this thing! This is going to destroy us."

There were three young men, high school aged, sons of prominent citizens, who'd died of a peculiar kind of lung cancer in the period of time just before all this. These prominent, conservative Republican citizens believed their sons' cancers had to do with the air we already had here in Bloomington, air that had been tainted by PCBs. They told me, "You're the only one who can stop this. You've got to keep working on it!"

It engendered very odd sets of opponents and proponents. The Democrats—usually attuned to environmental concerns—for the incinerator and Republicans dead set against it. Mayor Allison was absolutely adamant the incinerator was a wonderful thing, the best thing since sliced bread. The city council people continued to say to me, by and large, "Charlotte, you don't understand...."

The proponents kept repeating, "This is the only option the EPA gives us. We have to do this!"

It turned out that was not true but they had been told by the lawyers it was true.

There were other options. Not building the incinerator, for one thing. Digging up and transporting the tainted soil to another place, for another. Nobody in authority had told the city and the county and Westinghouse that we had to burn all this stuff. The lawyers had voluntarily come up with that. And many people believed that was our only option because they hadn't done their homework as I had.

Some county people and I took another trip to look at incinerators. Four us were designated to go on this trip. It was me; Don Wagner, probably the most conservative member of the county council—in '75, he was one of the people most opposed to the gay rights ordinance and at the time he thought I was terrible but we'd been working together for years by now and had become friends; Steve Creech of the county health department; and a young woman named Stephanie Dean, who had been appointed to be the county's PCB program point person.

This trip we did in an ugly duckling car, one of those bashed-in rent-a-cars. It would take us a week. We planned to visit incinerators in St. Louis, El Dorado (a second time for me), Memphis, Nashville and Gallatin in Tennessee, and Louisville.

That trip would have made a funny movie. We had to stop every time Don Wagner saw a place that served pie. He loved pie! We took turns driving and dreaded Steve Creech's turn. He would not go a single mile per hour over the speed limit. We'd yell, "Steve, the road's wide open, you can go 52!"

"No," he'd say, "50 is 50."

This was a frugal trip. We stayed at the Drury Inn in East St. Louis the first night. Then we visited the sewage sludge incinerator in St. Louis, across the Mississippi River. We spent a morning there and found out that sewage sludge—the operators told us over and over again—could not be incinerated at temperatures greater than 1,200º F.

After you burn all the organic material out of sewage sludge, you're left with a soup of heavy metals. At temperatures above 1,200, the heavy metals become gaseous and you don't want people to breathe that.

Our incinerator was planned to burn materials at 2,100º F. The people had been operating the St. Louis incinerator for years and they knew what they were talking about. They also told us it wasn't working so well and they weren't sure what they were going to do with it.

Then we drove on to El Dorado. Jenny and her husband hosted the four of us. Coincidentally, it was the day of a big EPA hearing there on the illnesses that had been cropping up in children around the incinerator.

We spent nearly seven hours at the hearing. We listened to a litany of sad stories about the children getting sick. Local scientists and other people who'd done their homework really believed the illnesses were caused by the incinerator.

Then we went on to Memphis to see a municipal solid waste incinerator that wasn't working so well. The people who operated it told us there was a lot of down time.

From there, we moved on to Nashville, Tennessee, where, in the parking lot for the incinerator, all the cars of the officials who worked there were covered with tarps.

I asked, "Why are you doing that?"

The officials did their best to avoid answering directly.

That facility had a reputation of being a wonderful model municipal solid waste incinerator. While there, we learned it was down due to problems and repairs maybe a third of the time.

On to Gallatin, about 30 miles northeast of Nashville. The facility was a regional collector of solid waste. It was big; it had a tipping room about a hundred yards long and three stories high.

A crane moved over it on rails, back and forth, like the ones you see loading ships at a port.

"How do you monitor for things that shouldn't be burned?" I asked.

"Oh," the man there said, "our crane operators have eagle eyes! When they lower the claw that pulls up the trash to dump it in the hopper where it gets augered down into the burning chamber, they can tell immediately if something toxic is there. So they don't dump it in the hopper. They pick it up and put it to the side."

"Really?" I said. "That's amazing."

"Oh yeah, they're good. We're very proud of them."

A few minutes later, we were all sitting in a conference room, hearing more talk about how wonderful the whole operation was when, all of a sudden, there was this awful noise, an ear-shattering screech.

It turned out the eagle-eyed crane operator had picked up a 4'x8' solid steel door and dumped it in the hopper, ruining both the hopper and the auger.

That was illuminating.

We finished up visiting the incinerator in Louisville. When we got back home I said, "We've got to inform people about what we've seen!" I had someone draw up a Mylar footprint model of the incinerator. It would be three football fields long and taller than Graham Plaza, the old 10-story hotel at the northeast corner of the square. The smokestacks would be in a direct line of sight as drivers came down the big hill on State Road 37, on the way to Lake Monroe, which we were pushing as a tourist destination. "I don't think people realize that," I said.

Furthermore, the incinerator would be southwest of town. Opponents had been talking about Bloomington's prevailing winds. When I asked Mayor Allison about the prevailing wind issue, she said, "Well, there aren't any."

"Really?" I said. "That would be unique in this country. In this world!"

Not much later, opponents would stage a demonstration proving the prevailing wind would blow the incinerator's emissions over the entire city.

We needed to persuade the city government that this incinerator plan was no good. I was not going to be the one to change Mayor Allison's mind. I was suspect in her eyes. She'd told me many times since that first trip we took to South Chicago that I should understand I had opinions but she had facts.

So I was hoping to get some of the affluent Republicans in town to talk to her. Tomi was definitely open to their words. We tried to get that to happen but she wasn't hearing any of it.

There wasn't much more for me to say to her. We no longer had a friendly relationship. It was clear she was going to barrel through with this plan.

That's why I ran against her in the 1987 Democratic primary for mayor.

I worked very hard on that campaign. I tried to get my message out about the incinerator. I was told Tomi had the support of the city council. That certainly helped her. Some of them told me, "You're our dear friend but you're wrong about the incinerator. The EPA says it's the only thing we can do."

Which was wrong. None of them had done the kind of research I had. That's really what it boiled down to. I understood the consent decree was complicated and boring but it was really important and somebody had to play the role I did.

I almost won that primary. I lost by 75 votes out of 5065 cast.

Frank McCloskey had promised me he would stay out of the primary fight but he didn't. At the very end, he jumped in the fray with an endorsement of Tomi. That was probably worth 70 votes right there.

Eight years later, Frank told me it was a big mistake over a steak dinner in Washington, DC.

The general election turned out to be a very heated race. Tim Ellis, a moderate Republican, ran against Tomi in November. He came within a handful of votes of beating her.

Losing the primary didn't mean I would shut up about the incinerator. A bunch of people, maybe a hundred, went down to the Dillman Road sewage treatment plant near where the incinerator was to be built. I was with them; I was still curious about this prevailing wind idea.

The people blew up black balloons with little notes attached reading, "If this has landed in your backyard, please call us."

It was not a windy day so it seemed that if there was a prevailing wind, it would be wafting from that site right in the direction of town.

We released those balloons and over the next few days got a lot of phone calls from people who found balloons in their Bloomington gardens.

\*\*\*

*Much had happened in a bit more than two years since Charlotte was given her copy of the consent decree. Federal District Court Judge Samuel (Hugh) Dillin in Indianapolis approved the document in August, 1985. Three months later, Westinghouse announced it would store thousands of yards of PCB-contaminated soil in concrete containers of South Walnut Street until the incinerator was finished. The EPA then notified the city it would be held liable for all cleanup costs if it didn't allow Westinghouse to build the incinerator. The company opened a PCB-cleanup office, open to the public, in January, 1986.*

*That March, the City of Bloomington sued the Monsanto Company for $387 million in damages for supplying Westinghouse with PCBs (Monsanto manufactured the product containing PCBs that Westinghouse used in its capacitors). In the fall, the city's utilities department issued a progress report saying Westinghouse's work in digging up and storing PCB-tainted soil would be complete by 1989. The report also predicted the incinerator would be up and running by 1991. It would take, the report said, some 15 years after the incinerator began operating for all the PCB-contaminated materials in and around Bloomington to be completely destroyed by fire.*

*In January 1987, Westinghouse submitted its required hazardous emission reports and risk assessments for its permit application to operate an incinerator.*

*From an official vantage point, it looked as though the anti-incinerator forces—and Charlotte—had lost.*

*The story, though, still was a long way from being played out.*

\*\*\*

By the spring 1988 it seemed the tide had turned. I began to realize the plan was destined to fail. The incinerator was not going to work. I think Westinghouse was coming to the same conclusion at the time.

One of the nails in the coffin was a report issued by the EPA in April 1988. It was titled "Evaluation of Scientific Issues Related to Municipal Waste Combustion." It laid out the many severe problems that burning trash in a big incinerator would create, primarily, the environmental threat posed by its emissions.

And Westinghouse, by then, was not in a financial position to go off and build this multi-million-dollar experiment. At some point, the top people in the company must have sat down and said, "Wait a minute; we don't even know if this is going to work!"

\*\*\*

*In the last two decades of the 20th Century the Westinghouse Company underwent huge changes. In the 1980s, it sold off many of its parts to raise cash. The Bloomington operation was sold to a Swiss multi-national, ASEA Brown Boveri (The ABB Group) in 1889.*

*What remained of Westinghouse bought the CBS Corporation in 1995. Two years later, the Westinghouse name, in existence since 1886, ceased to exist as the company adopted to CBS brand. That entity was bought out by Viacom in 1999, ending the Westinghouse lineage.*

\*\*\*

My thought was the whole incinerator idea was dying of its own weight. By the spring of 1988 I was really confident it wouldn't be built. It was dead. I never worried that we would have it after that. I'd done my job.

I was exhausted.

Not only that, I was being seriously recruited to work for the United Way. The board wanted me to be the executive director; they wanted me to raise money, an area the organization had been lacking in for several years.

They told me if I came to work for the United Way, I would have to refrain from speaking publicly about the incinerator and the consent decree. I wouldn't be able to do anything, politically. These were welcome stipulations.

I resigned as commissioner in May 1988.

***

*As late as 1992, the by-then-renamed* Herald-Times *reported that The ABB Group expected the incinerator to be completed in 1998. That year came and went without an incinerator. The company demolished the old Westinghouse capacitor factory in August, 2006.*

*By the year 2019, an estimated two million pounds of PCBs had been released in and around Bloomington. Old capacitors and liquid PCBs still are being turned in at the Monroe County Hazardous Waste Center. These materials get sent to a processing center in Phoenix, Arizona.*

*City officials here say PCBs will remain in the area's groundwater for decades to come.*

*Westinghouse and ABB over the years have spent at least $250 million on clean up operations. Contaminated soil from underneath the old capacitor factory was dug up and stored in a $2 million facility on South Walnut Street. The tainted soil was then transported by truck to a hazardous waste dump in Coffeyville, Kansas. That temporary storage facility is now empty but remains off limits to the public and, presumably, is still a health hazard.*

# 18

# Bandwagon

*The kids were away at college. Charlotte had led the effort to renovate and build a couple of key county structures. The incinerator question still loomed over Bloomington and Monroe County. And another election was on the horizon*

***

Now we've done the courthouse. We've dedicated the new justice building with an endless 45-minute rant of a speech by Indiana Supreme Court Chief Justice Richard M. Givan. We'd started working on the old post office on 7th St, which the Postal Service had given to the county with the proviso that it be dedicated to health services. And then there was the totally all-consuming incinerator dispute.

I was busy trying to figure out ways to stop the incinerator. By this time, even the newspaper, by and large, was tired of it.

I was busy and I was tired. I was working at the store, too. Marilyn was tired, too. We'd both been doing our public service work and running the store for more than a decade.

I remember coming home one night and saying to Paul, "I'm really tired."

"You know," Paul said, "you don't have to continue."

I thought about that. I could see that so much of my work already had begun paying off.

The idea of the incinerator kept hanging over our heads.

Marilyn's latest term in the Indiana General Assembly came to an end in 1986. But she stayed in Indianapolis where she had taken a job as the head of a mental health association and then she became assistant to the dean of the IU school of medicine. So she still had to commute between Indianapolis and Bloomington.

Meanwhile, Marilyn was about to get married to her second husband, Dick Good. They were going to move to Indianapolis and she really wanted out of our business.

I thought about buying her out but I realized I couldn't handle it, both financially and in terms of the time and effort I'd have to put in, running the store on my own. It would be too much work. I just was not ready to do that.

We put the store up for sale. I handled the task. Eventually, I found a potential buyer, Bob Swanson, in the fall of 1988. His father was a professor at Ball State University who'd written a textbook on typing or something. It turned out to be a goldmine for him and his family. He made lots and lots of money on it. So his son Bob had a big chunk of that money and he thought owning a kitchen goods store would be kind of fun.

I felt so bad about it. It was three days before I called Marilyn and told her, "We've got a buyer."

It was like giving a baby away. It really was hard. I loved the store. It represented a lot of what we were.

Bob Swanson didn't really know much about the products or the business. He turned out to be much more interested in wine than food but he had the good sense to make Lynn Schwartzberg his manager. She saved the store.

While all this was going on, the United Way board was coming after me.

The executive director position at United Way came open in the spring of 1988. Harmon Baldwin, who'd been the superintendent of instruction in both Terre Haute and Bloomington and was a revered person, talked to me about applying for the position. Harmon was president of the United Way board. He knew I wasn't going to run for a third term as commissioner; I'd already announced it.

I thought about it for a while. It meant leaving the commissioner's office before I was finished with my term.

I was kind of surprised by the board's interest but I knew I was a good candidate for the job. I'd made a few enemies around town and Mayor Allison didn't like me but most people were friendly with me. I knew how to ask for money and I had a bunch of ideas. The United Way at the time needed both talents in its new executive director.

The job appealed to me. It seemed like a haven after years of the political fight. The job wouldn't be political; I didn't mind that at all.

The United Way had never gone over the million-dollar mark in fundraising for the year. It was dying a slow death in Monroe County. The board had decided that I would be the one to revive it. Harmon really courted me.

I accepted the position. I agreed to do no political work while I served as executive director. I wasn't to have any political profile at all because I'd have to work with everybody in the community.

I resigned as Monroe County Commissioner in May, 1988. It was not a bad decision.

I jumped into my new job at the United Way and tried to turn the organization around.

Ellen Ehrlich was the wife of the president of Indiana University, Tom Ehrlich. They were still pretty new to town; Tom had been named president in the summer of 1987. Ellen was very energetic and she wanted to learn the community, to become a part of it. I'd heard that she had no fear of asking people for money. I got the idea that we could give her the opportunity to become part of the community if we asked her to be our fundraising chair. She jumped at the chance and took the chair about a month after I took the job.

It was the right decision. Ellen was very organized and dynamic. We worked well together.

The United Way in Monroe County hadn't been building a sense of community around itself. People weren't very interested in the organization when I took over.

I went to a training session developed by the fundraiser for the Lafayette chapter of the United Way. It was called the Vanguard Program. This man had selected 75 people in Lafayette who were capable of giving a thousand dollars apiece. I thought, "Let's do that!" I adopted the idea in Bloomington.

I looked at our donation records and found that nobody had made big contributions. The biggest gift I could find was $500. I told the board, "That's ridiculous. We should be getting thousand-dollar gifts! There are plenty of people in town who can do it. We can make a list of them!"

Ellen and I put together a list of ten people who'd never given to the United Way and we would ask them to give a thousand dollars apiece. It was a start.

We took turns visiting them, recruiting them. We'd give them a short sales speech and we appealed to their vanity: "If you do this, lots of other people will do it too." They were very impressed to be asked by the wife of the president of the university.

I came up with an idea for a brochure that was totally different. It was about people. We had pictures of people and very specific stories, personal stories, for each agency that our chapter supported.

I got the Indiana University student body involved, the Panhellenic and the Inter-fraternity councils. And then we had very active mini-campaigns aimed at local corporations and businesses. It was a much fuller fundraising campaign than the local United Way had had for years.

Everybody who worked for and with the United Way jumped on the bandwagon. We all really just whooped it up.

We were starting to turn Monroe County's United Way around.

In the summer of 1989, Paul and I took a vacation by car, a great American road trip. It lasted about four weeks.

We drove from Bloomington to Milwaukee for a big United Way conference there. Then we went west across Minnesota and South Dakota, through the Badlands and past Rapid City. We went into

Wyoming and stayed at a rustic lodge at the Buffalo Bill Cody museum and then on to Yellowstone National Park.

We drove from Yellowstone to Missoula, Montana to visit Paul's niece who was married to a Blackfoot. After that, we spent a week in Seattle where Nathan happened to be doing a summer internship as a clerk for Perkins Coie, the largest law firm in that city. Among other things, it handled the Boeing Company account.

Then we went down the Pacific coast, California State Highway 1, a wonderful drive, to Los Angeles where Rebecca had a summer internship at a big firm, at that time called Hufstedler Miller Kaus & Beardsley. We spent a week with her.

We were going to come back to Bloomington via Route 66—what was left of it—through Arizona and Gallup, New Mexico and Oklahoma and Missouri.

On the way down the Pacific Coast Highway, we had stopped in to visit our old University of Michigan friend Whitney Buck and his wife, Susan, in Arcata in far northern California. As soon as we got there, Susan told us my mother had called and left a message. My mother knew what our itinerary would be. She was living in Bloomington by that time, in the Meadowood retirement community.

I called her. She said, "Charlotte, the state police came here, looking for you."

"What did I do wrong?"

"No," she said, "You're not in trouble. They had some information they wanted to give you. I'm not sure I understand what it was all about. They said something about the governor and Indiana State University."

"That's wonderful," I said.

She said, "I don't know what that means."

"I'll explain it."

Some faculty members at ISU had contacted me about a month before. They asked me if I'd be willing to have my name put in nomination to become a university trustee. Apparently, Governor Evan Bayh had chosen me to serve on the board of trustees.

I would be the only Democrat and the only woman on the board at the time. It was the beginning of a 16-year-long involvement between me and Indiana State University.

\*\*\*

*Charlotte added the ISU trusteeship to her already impressive résumé. This on top of her work revitalizing Monroe County's Untied Way chapter*

\*\*\*

My time at United Way was not an unmixed story. There was a downside.

Before I started, United Way had been involved in a big fight with local labor unions. Years before that, the labor unions had been very helpful to the organization. Across the country there was always a labor representative on the staff of a local United Way. But our outgoing executive director hadn't done too well in nourishing the relationship between the Monroe County United Way and local labor.

I knew the labor people from as far back as my time running for city council in 1971. After I took the job we gradually worked out an agreement with the local labor council. We let the council pick a new labor representative and we hired him.

He would be on our paid staff and he would interact with the labor unions, trying to raise money. At first everything seemed to be good. The new man and I got along fine for a while.

The problem was his role hadn't been fully spelled out. He kind of went his own way. There was tension. It became a very uncomfortable situation for me.

It got to the point that I realized the man and I couldn't work together anymore. I went to the board and asked for assistance. They gave me a list of procedures to follow to document his performance. A board member told me, "You worked so hard to get this labor thing fixed. Now we don't want to endanger that new relationship by getting rid of this man."

I made case to them, I followed the procedures, and I fired the man. The board of directors came back to me and said, "You can't do that."

The board chose to keep him on.

At that point, I thought, "I have to go." It was June, 1990 when I resigned from the United Way.

The upshot was I was with the Monroe County United Way for two full annual fundraising campaigns, getting ready for a third one.

The job had become unpleasant. The board didn't support me. They were saying, essentially, "We love you, Charlotte, but you can't do this thing." They were willing to let me go.

It was all very painful. I found a therapist to help me through it. I was very distressed. I don't think I handled that situation very well.

# 19

## Halfhearted

Then I went to work for a while for the Indiana Women's Political Action Committee. It was a group of women trying to underwrite campaigns for pro-choice candidates. I raised money, a thousand dollars at a time, from women around the state.

It wasn't very long before the director of the regional Planned Parenthood came to me and said, "I want you to come work for me." This was about September 1990.

I became the Community Development Coordinator. I was to raise funds and travel around southern Indiana, helping build up groups of advocates for Planned Parenthood.

I went to Madison. I went to Rising Sun. I went to Aurora. I went to Versailles. I went to Salem. I went to Paoli. I went to Bedford. I went to Evansville, North Vernon, Columbus, Terre Haute, Greencastle. I developed little advisory groups; they would identify local people who could donate money and they would become advocates for each town's Planned Parenthood clinic.

And the clinics were doing well! They served a huge purpose in these small towns. We had clinics in nearly every town. Planned Parenthood was the place to go for women's health care—and men's health care, too! Clients got basic health care as well as STD testing.

Not all the state legislators in those districts were big fans of Planned Parenthood but they saw the benefit those clinics brought to their constituents: good nurse-managed facilities, clean, professional, and free for the most part.

In 1995, while I was still working there, the southern Indiana regional office was merged with the Indianapolis office. The man in charge in Indianapolis then closed down most of the small town clinics in the southern half of the state and centralized operations. Suddenly, many clinics just were not there anymore. There was no place for many people to go.

\*\*\*

*As of 2020, there are five Planned Parenthood clinics south of Indianapolis. They are in Bloomington, Evansville, Columbus, New Albany, and Seymour. That's two locations on the Ohio River and three clumped closely together in south central Indiana, leaving hundreds of thousands of people many miles away from the nearest Planned Parenthood clinic.*

\*\*\*

Once those clinics were closed, things shifted. There were many, many unintended consequences. I think the opioid epidemic is one of them.

A lot of us who worked for Planned Parenthood quit in response to that shift. I found it unacceptable and objected strenuously. I left in October 1995.

\*\*\*

*Fall, 1994. After 11 years in office Mayor Tomi Allison announces she won't run in the next year's municipal election. The announcement leaves the Democratic primary race wide open. Lawyer John Fernandez begins considering a run and some Bloomingtonians begin whispering in Charlotte's ear.*

\*\*\*

I hadn't thought about running again until people told me they'd support me. Mark Kruzan did. So did Frank McCloskey and some businesspeople. The people who owned Sunrise card company, Michael Fitzgerald and Jeff Wilcey, and their friend, real estate developer Michael Pollock, thought I'd be a good mayor. They were willing to raise money for me. They really wanted me to run but I was hesitant.

Then, around the New Year, John Fernandez declared and all those people threw their lot in with him. They had given up on me by then. They thought he'd be okay as mayor and they donated to his campaign.

***

*Charlotte Zietlow wasn't the only woman in Bloomington who was a force of nature. Charismatic and determined, Toby Strout was the executive director of Middle Way House. She had shepherded the nonprofit through its transition from a halfway house for people with substance abuse disorders to a safe harbor for women who'd experienced domestic abuse.*

***

Toby Strout still wanted me to run. She didn't think John Fernandez had the right values. She urged me to consider declaring.

John Fernandez and I didn't share values—social services, for one. He wasn't much of a people person. I don't think he was interested in Bloomington very much; he was interested in something more than Bloomington. He had run for Indiana Secretary of State. Later, he would work for an Indiana real estate investment firm, expanding its national reach, and he worked for a high-powered law firm, advising cities on economic development. He eventually went to Washington when President Clinton named him Assistant Secretary of Commerce under Norman Mineta. Bloomington was a rung up the ladder for him.

The idea of running did interest me but it didn't overwhelm me. I just couldn't decide. I eventually got talked into it. I declared in January, 1995. It was late.

I waited too long; that was a mistake.

***

*The Democratic primary would be held, as usual, in May. Fernandez and Charlotte criss-crossed the city throughout the rest of the winter and into spring, trying to scare up votes. Then Charlotte shot herself in the foot.*

***

I had a good chance of winning but I was halfhearted. I did something foolish. Paul and I went to Italy for a week in March when I should have been home campaigning.

Mark Kruzan and Frank McCloskey were behind Fernandez now. I could have felt kind of betrayed, but it was my fault. Fernandez really wanted it. Still, I only lost by 31 votes! People came up to me later and said, "Oh, if only I'd voted that day!" I hadn't worked hard enough to get them out to the polls.

I don't hold Mark and Frank responsible for my loss. And I didn't feel bad about losing. I still don't feel bad about it.

# 20

# Impossible

*Charlotte would be employed by one final organization, Middle Way House, before she retired in 2010. Yet, even as she steered one non-profit or raised funds for another, she worked as a trustee for Indiana State University. Work is the key word. All too often members of boards of trustees, often being highly successful people whose lives were otherwise completely subsumed by their businesses, give whatever energy and attention they have to spare to their boards. Charlotte, in keeping with her well-established work ethic, invested herself fully in her responsibilities to ISU. The board would meet some ten times a year, on weekends so that trustees who had their own business responsibilities could get away to Terre Haute.*

*The seemingly disparate worlds of politics and academia in reality aren't so different after all. Whether an elected public official or an appointed university overseer, Charlotte tilted against hidebound, stubborn, biased, and even venial characters. She accepted Governor Evan Bayh's nomination to serve on Indiana State University's board of trustees. The skills and talents she'd honed as a public servant came in handy when the board grappled with issues of importance to the university.*

\*\*\*

The trustees got packets in the mail several days before the meeting outlining its agenda. I always read my packets and I was pretty sure the others didn't.

We would meet the day before the regular meeting, on a Friday, just to get oriented and to go over the agenda. Sort of a pre-meeting. The regular meeting would be scheduled for Saturday.

In the spring of 1992, the ISU president Richard Landini spoke to us at the pre-meeting, as he usually did. He said, "I'm going to be asking you at the meeting tomorrow to give us permission to raze the education school building."

That building housed the ISU Lab School. ISU was started in 1865 as a Normal school, where they trained teachers. The school of education was a heart and center of Indiana State. It was the history of the school.

I said, "What? Why would you do that?"

Tearing down the education building was not listed in the agenda packet we'd been sent. It was a surprise. What I didn't know was Landini wanted to set in motion a plan to eliminate the Lab School entirely.

\*\*\*

*By 1992, the ratio of education school students to the rest of the student body had dropped dramatically over the decades. In earlier years, ISU education school students had actually outnumbered all other students. By this time, ISU's future teachers had become a minority of the overall student body, albeit still a large one.*

\*\*\*

Landini said, "It's just a useless building. We don't need it anymore. And we need that space."

To get that new space, the university would have to destroy old space. Indiana had a law that said if a state university wanted to build new buildings, it had to get rid of an equal number of square feet of old buildings. Each state university had a cap on the total square footage built up on its campus

"What information do we have on this?" I said. "This sounds like a very serious decision that requires a lot of information. Do we have a packet of information on this?"

"No, we don't."

"How can we possibly act on it?" I said. "To tear down a building that we know nothing about? I've never even been in that building! I wouldn't even consider voting yes on that."

Many government buildings like post offices, federal buildings, and others were put up during the Great Depression, partly as a way to put people to work. Others, like our education building, would be financed by federal dollars. The buildings of that era were historically significant, with Art Deco architectural features and "New Deal art," like Post Office murals.

I said, "I'd really like to see the building before we even talk about it."

"We-e-e-ell," Landini said. "We could do that but we should get it on the agenda now so we can start working on it next spring."

Through all this, the other trustees just sat there. They never questioned the president. Whatever he wanted, they rubber-stamped.

But, again, I was the problem child because I kept asking questions. Early on I had even been rebuked for asking questions! The vice president of the board of trustees wrote me a note that read, "We realize you're quite new to the board but you should understand, we do not ask questions. That's not what we do at our meetings."

The implication was clear: Stop asking questions right now!

Nevertheless, I raised this question. It just seemed stupid to me. We shouldn't even have been talking about it until we knew a little bit more. There was one trustee, a lawyer from Indianapolis whose wife had come with him to Terre Haute for the weekend of the meeting. I talked to her about it after the pre-meeting.

"We can't let this happen!" I said. "I don't know what that building's like but I've heard it's very nice. I don't think we can just tear it down. They haven't even told us what's going to happen to the Lab School. This is so premature." The teachers at the Lab School didn't even know what was going on. The wife agreed with me.

"We've got to do something to stop this," I said.

She said, "What do we do?"

I said, "Let's just protest!"

We went to the stationery store nearby and bought some poster board and some markers and made placards reading, *Do Not Tear Down the Lab School!* and *The Lab School Is Too Good to Tear Down!* We walked around campus with these signs!

It was commencement weekend so there were a lot of people milling about. Many of them asked us questions about the plan. We started a lot of dialogue.

I ran into Landini the next morning before the regular meeting. "Charlotte," he said, "we have to have the trustees' OK so we can go forward. This is just the beginning of the process.

"And that's why I'm protesting now!" I said.

We'd put the whole thing out in the open. Suddenly, all the teachers from the Lab School were clamoring and the campus just went berserk because nobody had known about the plan to tear down the education building. People came up to me and said, "That's a really good building. You should see it."

So we went through the building. It had all these incredible terra cotta architectural pieces built into the interior walls and socialist-type murals from the '30s. A really interesting building. It had a big auditorium. Landini said, "Look at this; it's so dark in here."

I said, "Yes, it's so dark. We can put more lights in here."

We really created a big hubbub. It started a big fight about what was going to happen with the Lab School. No one had talked to any of the teachers there. The education school faculty said to me, time and again, "This is not way we should be making decisions."

So we really created a huge ruckus.

***

*As promised, Landini brought up the plan to tear down the education building at the board of trustees regular meeting the next day. The board is comprised of nine members: seven appointed by the governor (with the current governor's party in the majority) and two trustees elected by the alumni.*

\*\*\*

We had stirred up a storm and it had time to gestate in these two other trustees' minds, the other two Democrats. So they actually voted against it. We had a split vote. Unheard of! Landini didn't like having a non-unanimous vote. It made him very uncomfortable.

And the bottom line was nothing happened. It killed the project.

The building is still standing. It was refurbished. It's a beautiful building. It had an inner courtyard and they made it into a covered atrium. In fact, in 2018 when Indiana State honored me for my service, the ceremony was in that building. It's now called University Hall of the Bayh College of Education.

\*\*\*

*Charlotte's was not a complete victory. Months after Landini's plan to tear the building down was dropped, the university announced it was closing the Lab School. It seemed an inevitability. High school classes had been terminated in 1978. Elementary classes at the Lab School continued for another 14 years.*

\*\*\*

We saved the structure but we lost the school. They had to work with the Vigo County School Corporation to absorb the students. We were taking jobs away from people, too.

Lab School was put out of business a few months after the building fight. They got rid of the teachers; they just dissolved the school.

I talked to the people from the Lab School, the teachers and the principal and so forth. I was the only trustee who would talk to any of them. They actually came out to Bloomington to meet with me.

There was a big hubbub about that so that we had to move our regular board meeting into a much larger space. We usually met on the 11th floor of a high-rise building where we would be out of sight and out of mind to everyone else. But after the announcement came that the Lab School was to be closed, we had to go out into the main campus, to the Dede Auditorium in the Student Union auditorium, for our meeting.

There were 200 hundred and some people who came to that meeting, protesting the closing of the Lab School.

The education school faculty was there to state its opposition. The president of the board would not let them talk. He allowed only one representative from the faculty to talk but she didn't represent the majority of them. The rest of the faculty was raucous.

I raised my hand to make a motion that we set up a meeting with the faculty in a separate place and time so we could go into this in greater detail.

I could not get a second for my motion. I've never seen so many people looking at their feet! All the other trustees avoided looking at me.

One of the trustees, a Democrat, called me that evening and apologized for not seconding my motion. He said he just felt uncomfortable but he knew he should have done it. He apologized to me for being such a coward, basically.

I said, "Well I would say that's okay but it's not. It's our job to make these decisions and to listen to people. We not there just to be bumps on a log." I was pretty mad.

And I had the feeling, "Okay, I'm being really bad again." *You child, who do you think you are? Oh well, you're from Bloomington. What else can we expect from you?*

That was really a hard moment for me.

The faculty generally was on my side, and a lot of alums. At one point, almost all superintendents of schools in the state of Indiana had gone through the Indiana State education school. They'd gotten their Masters or Doctors degrees there. It had a big reputation. So we were really betraying the alumni who had taught at the Lab School, who learned how to teach there, and learned how to run schools there.

When I left the board of trustees in 2005 the faculty gave me a farewell party. As far as I know I was the only trustee that had ever been so honored.

***

*In keeping with her "bad girl" history, Charlotte again ran afoul of the authorities at Indiana State University. Some six months after the education building set-to, university president Richard Landini announced he was leaving. Replacing him easily became as contentious an issue.*

\*\*\*

I was at a conference in Florida along with several other trustees. It was sponsored by the Association of Governing Boards of Universities and Colleges. It had conferences once or twice a year where people discussed running these schools.

Generally, the ISU trustees were not so involved with being trustees that they would go to these things. The people at these conferences would be talking about things the ISU trustees weren't interested in, like academic freedom.

While I was down there in Miami, I got a phone call saying Landini was going to retire. When I came back to Indiana I found out Landini and the president of the board of trustees had taken it upon themselves to appoint a search committee for a new president.

The board president, by the way, was Bob Green, a big Evansville Republican who owned a bunch of hotels in southwest Indiana.

The faculty was all up in arms over Landini and Green's search committee. Years before I joined the board there had been a real tussle between the faculty and the ISU president over how the university would go about choosing a new president. The faculty and the American Association of University Professors had certain principles and ISU had violated those principles. It became a lawsuit.

The parties had worked their way through the courts and ended up with a consent decree, legally binding, that laid out the process by which a presidential search committee would be selected. The university president and the president of the board of trustees were not supposed to create it on their own. This was wrong.

People were very upset because this was a clear violation of the consent decree. The trustees all got copies of the consent decree and the faculty's complaint. It was all pretty obvious and straightforward.

So, what were we going to do? We had a meeting of the board of trustees. Some of them said, "Well, we've got a search committee. We're not going to undo that! We're not going to go backward."

I said, "We've got to undo it! It's very, very clear to me. Just read this!" I held a copy of the consent decree in my hand. "We have violated it!"

One of the trustees was Rex Breeden, a real estate man from Columbus who was a big donor to the university. He'd been a past president of the board. He said, "Well Charlotte, if you don't like the way we're doing things, you can quit the board!"

"Well Rex," I said, "I won't be doing that. I've been appointed by the governor for a purpose and I'm going to be here to carry that out. And I think we're in trouble if we continue along this path."

They rest of trustees just ignored the faculty's complaint. The board chose not to do anything about it. The next thing we knew, the faculty hired a lawyer and was suing the board of trustees for violating the consent decree.

The case went to court in Terre Haute. We, the trustees, were all notified about it. We were all parties to the suit. We had the obligation to go speak our piece in court. But in fact, I was the only one who got in my car and drove to Terre Haute for this trial. The only one! There were members of the board from Terre Haute but they didn't get in their cars and go downtown!

I went into the court with the faculty. They went over here to sit on one side of the courtroom and I went over there to sit on my side.

The judge said, "I'm not going to deal with this. This should be settled between you two parties so I'm sending you home."

I went back to the university. The faculty lawyers and representatives were there. The ISU lawyer, Ed Pease, was there. Ed later became a member of Congress and then joined the board of trustees. And then he became president of the board, strangely enough.

We were the ones who were going to come up with a resolution to this dispute! And since none of the other trustees had bothered to show up, I was the one who had the say in it.

We just walked our way through it all. Everybody agreed: There was a clear cut map; it was called the consent decree. We ended up retaining some of the members of that first search committee and then expanding it, according to the way it was supposed to be done.

Landini and the president of the board had not even drawn up a profile for candidates. When you go and search for somebody to hire, you want to define what you're looking for. Rex Breeden later said, "That doesn't matter! We'll know him when we see him!"

Without question it would be *him*.

I was not a member of the new search committee but I attended the committee's meetings in my role as trustee. I traveled with the committee around the country and even did some of the interviewing.

We came up with this one person who looked pretty good. He was the president of California State University-Stanislaus. His name was John Moore.

My good friend Whitney Buck happened to be teaching at the California State University campus in Humbolt at the time. I called Whitney and said, "What do you know about this guy?"

Whitney said, "Oh, he's great. He's a real friend of unions and he loves faculty and treats the staff really well."

I said, "Okay. Good." I was satisfied.

Rex Breeden then met John Moore and said, "He's our man! Look at him: he's tall and he's broad-chested and he wears blue suits." John Moore looked like what Rex Breeden thought a university president should look like.

So that's who we hired.

It turned out John Moore was a flaming liberal! When he came and we installed him in the job, he spoke very strongly of the rights of the staff and the faculty and the need for good benefits and so forth.

The irony was Rex Breeden and other trustees never would have picked him if they'd known what they were getting.

*\*\**

*As all this was going on in Terre Haute, Charlotte still had responsibilities in Bloomington. She continued in her position as executive director of the local Planned Parenthood operation but she'd soon shed that title.*

*\*\**

Even before the Planned Parenthood consolidation became a reality and I left the organization, Toby Strout began a relentless campaign to recruit me to work for Middle Way House.

In the summer of 1995 Toby had been awarded a three-year federal grant to pay for a new position, economic development coordinator.

There wasn't much of a job description other than its title. Toby had decided she wanted me in that job.

While I was still at Planned Parenthood, Toby asked me to help find somebody for the job. I made several suggestions. Then she said, "No. I want you."

I said, "I have a job!"

She came back and said she wanted me three times that summer. "I want you to do it," she said.

I still had a job to do, but Planned Parenthood was considering something I found unacceptable. Under a proposed consolidation, the South Central region was to be swallowed up by the Indianapolis office. A large part of the consolidation including closing many of the little clinics in remote, rural areas of the state. Many of people on staff were crestfallen and planning to leave the organization. I objected strenuously to the plan. Soon, I started listening closely to Toby's pitch.

I asked her, "So, what's an economic development coordinator?"

It did not have to do with fundraising, she explained. It had to do with creating jobs for Middle Way House clients. "We want you to start two businesses a year," Toby said.

"Is there any money attached to it? Will there be a budget?"

"No," Toby said. "You'll have to figure that out for yourself. You'll have to figure out the businesses. You'll have to figure out the funding to develop the businesses. You'll have to figure out all the details of those businesses."

And, she added, I'd have to take a $15,000 a year cut in pay from what I made with Planned Parenthood.

She asked: "How does that sound?"

"That sounds impossible," I said. "I think I'll do it."

So I did.

I quit Planned Parenthood and took the job with Middle Way House in October, 1995.

With Planned Parenthood, I had been making the most money ever in my life. I think I was earning $45,000 a year. I was to get $28,000 from Middle Way House. I took a big cut in pay with no real direction whatsoever as to what I was supposed to do. I had to make it all up, whole cloth. It was a big, ridiculous challenge.

And I did it.

My first idea was that maybe there would be people at Middle Way House who would want to start their own businesses.

In the Fall of 1995, I went to a micro-business conference set up by the state in Indianapolis. Two women spoke at the conference. They had set up a micro-loan program for low-income people in an area that was being redeveloped. Governor Frank O'Bannon was pushing to set up programs like these around the state. I took the bait.

For the next year, I planned a class in how to start up a small business. It would be aimed primarily at women but it wasn't restricted to women-owned businesses. Then they could apply for start-up loans through local banks who'd agreed to participate in the program. The successful end result of the class for any of the people taking it would be a real business, a going concern.

It was to be a collaborative effort. We would work with the state's small business development local office headed by David Miller. We also worked with the City of Bloomington's Randy Lloyd, who was the economic development director under Mayor Fernandez. We worked with the commercial loan officer at Bank One, Bill Munse, who coordinated a loan program with other banks.

We would all take different approaches to helping people figure out how to start a small business, a micro business, and to develop it. The banks agreed to loans up to $25,000 to each person with a viable business idea. Middle Way House would run the program and the banks would handle the loans.

We started the class in early 1997, February or so.

*** 

*Some 900 people, mostly women but a lot of men as well, took the class for the nearly 20 years of its existence. Some of the businesses that emerged from the class include:*

*Latest Glaze, started by Mary Jo and Bill Benedict. They provided bisques, pottery ware that had been fired once. Customers would decorate them with paints and then glaze them before a final firing.*

*Joni McGary, started Lucky Guy Bakery, making single-wrapped brownies.*

*Angel B's Galleria of Cakes, a fancy patisserie, on Patterson Drive at Madison Street.*

*Dmitri Vietze started Rock Paper Scissors, a public relations and communications firm that specializes in technology and music clients.*

*John Bethel had already started his title insurance business, but attended the class.*

*The class ran until 2014.*

*** 

When Sunrise Publications, the local greeting card company, was sold to Hallmark, they left behind lot of creative people who didn't know what to do, so many of them came to our class to see about starting their own businesses.

There were lots of people in town who, one way and another, had gone through the course and either created their own businesses or went to work for somebody using the skills and knowledge they got from us.

Lots and lots and lots of people went through the class. A lot of people went through it and then decided not to start their own businesses. Many came to me after the course and said, "So that's what it's like! I don't want to do that." That was good. That was a success, too. We saved them from themselves. We saved them a lot of time and money.

A plumber came to my house once on Thanksgiving. We couldn't find any other plumber. He was in our basement and he said, "You don't recognize me, do you?"

I said, "No, I'm sorry, I don't."

"I was in your class," he said. "I wanted to start my own plumbing business but I decided I really wasn't up to running my own business so I went to work for some other guys. But I did that because of what you taught me. And you sure helped me understand how business works."

I was at a party some time ago at Susan Gubar's and Don Grey's. This man who runs a farm that produces local food came up to me. I got to talking to him. He said, "You know, we wouldn't have our farm if it weren't for you, Charlotte. We went through your class."

Now I needed to create a business that would hire Middle Way House clients. So many of the women who were Middle Way House clients were lacking in skills and confidence. We wanted to create jobs that would give them money while they could learn skills. I worked hard to figure out what business might work.

Toby had wanted us to start a green cleaning service. I went to Las Vegas—the only time I've been to Las Vegas—to attend a dry cleaning conference. Most of the exhibits dealt with the old traditional chemicals, trichloralethylene and tetrachloroethylene as cleaning solutions, poisonous stuff, stuff that kills you. A movement had already started in this country to use non-toxic chemicals to clean clothes—some people called it "soap"—in machines that are very gentle.

I went around the country to do green cleaning research. There were some green cleaners in Chicago. I went to San Francisco and visited a bunch of them. I gathered a lot of information. It required a fair amount of capital investment to start one.

It seemed to me, as well, if people took their clothes to a dry cleaner, they wanted them to come back the same size. So quality control would be difficult. Dry cleaning had to be done by people who knew what they were doing.

Then I investigated the possibility of starting a coffee wagon. I wanted to look for businesses that had relatively low capital investment, had a short learning curve, and could generate money for the people who were running them. I was interested in creating jobs and helping women become economically self-sufficient. I thought coffee was really good idea but, with a coffee wagon, we wouldn't have been able to hire enough people to make it worthwhile.

I went to a business expo in town. As a display, I built a house out of cardboard that looked like the Middle Way House. It had tiles that people could write on, suggesting business ideas. It generated a lot of interest and I got some good ideas from it.

Sometime after the expo, Melinda Seader, who was in charge of recycling for the city at the time, said we needed to start a mobile document shredding service.

"I have no idea what that is," I said. I had never heard of a document shredding business before.

"This is a no-brainer," she said. "All you need is a truck with a lift gate, an industrial-sized shredder, a baler, a pallet jack, and a warehouse."

She said she had a baler that she would give me. She talked me into it. So I had to learn all about the document shredding business.

So I did a little circuit run around shredding services. I went out to visit one in Milwaukee. Then I visited a company in Delmont, Pennsylvania, just outside of Pittsburgh, that manufactured the big shredding machines. As far as I could tell, the company, Allegheny Shredders —it's still in business—seemed to have the best shredders I could find. I called them and they said come on out and we'll help you. One woman named Evelyn, a sales rep for the company, took me under her wing and taught me all there was to know about the business. She took me all around the Pittsburgh area and showed me different shredding companies. I spent two days with shredders in Pennsylvania.

When I got back home to Bloomington, I applied for and got a grant from the Indiana Department of Environmental Management. With that we were able to buy a used, 16-foot box van with a lift gate and a big shredder from the Allegheny company. Then I called the graphic arts people at the university and said "I need name for a business and a logo." Together, we came up with the name Confidential Document Destruction. We rented half a warehouse on Yost Avenue.

We got business cards and we started up our business.

We got everything mobilized and then I had to go out and persuade the doctors' offices and the banks and the accountants that they shouldn't throw their confidential papers in the wastebasket.

I drummed up a bunch of business. I learned how to drive the truck and how to run the shredder.

I started by hiring six people. What I didn't know at the time—but would learn in short order—was that many of our people at Middle Way House had substance abuse issues, primarily alcohol. As such, they would be problematic employees in the outside world. But they weren't stupid and our new business turned out to be really good for them.

The operation was very simple. You got in the truck. You drove out to the customer. You bring the documents out to the truck. You turn the shredder on and run the documents through it.

You drive back to the warehouse and unload the shreds and bale them. When you get 40 bales, you call the paper company to come get them.

At every stage, there was some level of satisfaction of completing a job. There was an immediate gratification. And our new hires did well with that.

Their personal lives were kind of messy, though. That didn't help us much but we kept going. I was tough but compassionate.

We had one woman who was a really good worker but she had a terrible history. She came out of an extremely abusive situation—she'd nearly got killed. She had a part-time job cleaning toilets at the GE plant on Curry Pike and when she was finished doing that, she would walk a couple of miles all the way down to our warehouse on Yost Avenue. That's how much she wanted to be with us.

I went out of town for a couple of weeks and when I came back I found she had lost her driver's license. She'd gotten a DUI. She was sure I'd fire her. She was devastated.

I had a long talk with her. I said, "You're a good worker but you shouldn't have done what you did." I asked her about attending AA meetings or getting some type of appropriate help.

"My understanding of the situation is if you're clean for three months, you can get your license reinstated. I'm going to give you a chance. But don't do it again," I said.

She worked for Confidential Document Destruction for four years. Then, with that now on her record, she was able to get a job with benefits at Indiana University. She was able to buy herself a home. Her life isn't perfect but she's doing well now.

There was a young Filipino woman, a mail-order bride. Her American husband abused her badly. The sheriff from another county brought her to Middle Way House. She'd never had a job in her life so she was happy to get a job with us.

Even though she had a serious heart condition, she told me she really wanted to work with us. She turned out to be a good worker. She went on to get a scholarship to Indiana University and earn her bachelor's degree. She met a young man here in town and they are living happily together.

Eventually, Toby said, "This seems to be going pretty well. Now you have to start another business."

Many women who came to Middle Way House came from abusive situations and had little self-confidence. A young woman named Debra Morrow was one such person. She went from chin on the chest to shoulders held high. She's now the executive director of Middle Way House.

She worked for the third company I started, FoodWork. I'd been thinking about applying for a loan to purchase kitchen equipment and finding a good location for a catering service for day care centers. This business got underway right at the turn of the century.

Then I was invited to take a tour of the facilities of The Villages, a not-for-profit child and family services agency. The Villages works with foster children. It had started a day care center in a facility on Smith Pike that had a wonderful, fully-equipped industrial kitchen.

I asked, "What are you doing with this kitchen?"

"We haven't figured that out yet."

I said, "I'm going to make you a proposal." We'd start a catering service that would make meals for children in the day care center, healthful and delicious food, breakfast, snacks and lunch. The Villages had the kitchen, the equipment, and the need. We had the people.

We would rent the kitchen and prepare food for the day care center kids on contract. We would cook breakfast, lunch, and snacks. The Villages would pay us for the meals through a grant it had got from the United States Department of Agriculture.

And so we started our new business.

I hired a cook from Venezuela. She was here learning English as a second language at Indiana University. She was great. She ran the kitchen for four months. Then two things happened: Hugo Chavez took over in Venezuela and 9/11 happened here. Together, those two events put her visa in jeopardy; she was basically deported. She'd been a really good cook and we made good food from scratch for those kids.

We hired more people to cook and clean up even if they didn't know how to cook. We taught them how to cook. We started the women at $9.00 an hour, Debra Morrow included. We went through a lot of women in that kitchen who would go on to do many different jobs, thanks to what they'd learned with us. FoodWork was much more impactful in terms of its participants' future employment than Confidential Document Destruction was.

We expanded, getting contracts to make meals for other institutions, Operation Headstart, the Bloomington Developmental Learning Center, and the Area 10 Agency on Aging. Eventually, we had five contracts and we were doing a thousand meals a day. Then we started making take-out dinners. People could order them over the phone and then come pick up the three-course meals at five o'clock, after work.

We were making some money for Middle Way House and providing jobs for 15 people.

I started Food Works at the end of 2001 and we worked at it until 2005 or '06. At that time, Toby said, "Okay, you've got that going. Now we're going to try to get the Coca Cola building and we're going to build a new shelter and we're going to build a new day care center, and we're going to build apartments for our clients and you're going to raise $5 million."

Toby was a force of nature.

I said, "Toby, I told you when I came here, I didn't want to raise money. That's not why I took the job with you."

"I know," she said. "But you're going to do it." Toby was right. That's what I did. All those things were done.

***

*2010: Charlotte retired from the work-a-day world. Still, she remained active in politics, serving as a member of the Democratic Women's Caucus and as Democratic precinct chair. She also kept seats on the boards of a variety of civic and cultural organizations. Her phone con-*

*tinued to ring night and day and local political hopefuls—especially women—never ceased coming to her for her blessing when they contemplated running for office.*

# 21

# Persistent

I've lived many, many lives. They just happened. One thing I've learned is planning one's life probably isn't a consistently successful idea. Life just happens.

My life has been more like a constant series of lives, one melding into the other, depending on happenstance and intention. One doesn't know what one is here for in the world.

I was shy as a child. I used to go with my father to visit other churches and hospitals in his role as a Lutheran minister. I would hide behind his gown. During one visit to a mission festival drumming up support to send Lutherans to China and the Philippines where they could save the "heathens," I asked, "What does that mean?"

The elders around me said, "The people of China and the Philippines must have our religion in order to go to heaven."

I didn't understand that. I don't understand it to this day. Why would that be?

Even as a child, I wasn't stupid. I knew a Jewish family lived next door to us in Milwaukee. "Okay," I replied, "what about our Jewish neighbors?" They don't know about all this Lutheran stuff. Why should they be punished forever through no fault of their own? It just wasn't fair.

No one ever adequately explained that to me.

Still, when I was small, one of the things that impressed me was every morning in my parochial grade school my teacher would write on the board, "Do unto others as you would have them do unto you."

That left an indelible impression on me. I took it as an order and have obeyed it ever since, as much as I could.

It has been the compelling principle of my life: You have to do the best you can for other people. And each time in my life that I have thought, "What good can I do for other people?" has gotten me into all sorts of situations leading from one thing to the other.

Paul helped me understand the value of helping and caring for other people. Social justice was Paul's religion, and it became mine. That's why I married him. I was very lucky; Paul was the absolutely right choice for me. We were just in love until the day he died.

At the same time, my life is guided by a principle I adopted in high school—Don't be bored! I decided to constantly keep doing things that would be interesting and challenging. From that point on, I told myself, "Don't get bored. Take on challenges. Keep going."

My resiliency I learned as a young girl, when my family experienced the hardships of the Great Depression and World War II. I knew we didn't have much money. My parents were anxious about that. They didn't talk about it but I could pick it up. Somehow we survived. We always had a decent house and, when I was very little, the neighboring farmers brought us food, so we never starved or went hungry.

Looking back, I realize that somewhere along the way I became stubborn—or persistent, to put it nicely. A voice from deep inside me says, "If you start something, you must finish it, no matter what it is." That has carried me throughout my life.

There are characteristics basic to my nature. I don't stop until I'm finished. I keep going. I don't know if that was born in me but over time it developed. It became a habit.

Trying to make the world a better place has been a primary theme throughout my life. It sounds hokey, but there it is.

The most important thing was to do things that really and truly enhanced people's lives. I guess I did that; I often forget that I've done it but every now and then I'm reminded of it.

I've had my hand in a lot of good things that happened in this community over the last fifty years. There aren't many that I wasn't involved in. The retired editor of the *Herald-Times*, Bob Zaltsberg, and Malcolm Abrams, publisher of *Bloom* magazine, both tease me about that.

"Charlotte," Bob says, "you're always doing something!"

As I say, I'm often reminded of things, and often I'm surprised. This project has resurfaced many reminders, including a newspaper clipping from 2012 with the headline, "Justice Has A New Name."

It ran the day after Monroe County's justice building was re-dedicated in my name in March, 2012. People really thought I had made a difference in enhancing the justice system!

That spring, I remembered, Francie Hill had called, she wanted to take me out to lunch. The Republican circuit court judge, Frances had founded our local Court Appointed Special Advocates (CASA) office and had dedicated her professional life to justice for children. At lunch, Francie gave me a book of pictures of the courthouse and the re-dedication of the justice center. She said, "You are fearless."

I said, "Fearless? Really?" That just amazed me.

But I think, actually, I am fearless. I do things that everybody says, "No, no. That won't work."

The fact of the matter is I have reacted on several occasions in a way that I'll say were fearless. There was the meeting in the governor's office on the proposal to build an above-ground sewer pipe down the middle of Clear Creek. Then there was the time when I was invited to resign the Indiana State University board of trustees by men of some stature after I told them we were choosing a new president the wrong way. They were not happy to hear that but it was true! And we ended up getting a good president for the university.

And I'm surprised again when I read about the election in 1971. I think about how I went out there and worked hard and delivered a clear message. I just did it, even though I was dismissed as the "PhD housewife."

People tell me I inspired them and I think, I don't know what that means. But what I've done obviously means something to them. I guess it's because I do persevere. I do try to do things. I try to get other people involved. And I make sure that the people of this community have a chance.

And when I look back, I think, "What if I hadn't been here?"

We'd have a big, polluting incinerator. We wouldn't have our beautiful courthouse.

I like to use the phrase, "Nothing doesn't matter." All the isolated little things that happened to me added up to my total life. Everything matters.

The bottom line is there are principles that are very ingrained in me, that keep me going every day. When I think I see something that is not right, I just say so and try to turn it in the right direction.

That has led me down some difficult paths. Sometimes I've had to say to people that I've loved and respected, "No, we can't do that. That doesn't make any sense at all." I've generated some enemies, I believe, along the way. Although in the long run I was proven right.

I've also had wonderful allies along the way, including people I've never expected to be allies.

I identify with the turtle in a greeting card that I saw years ago. The turtle is walking down the sidewalk alongside a brick wall. In the second panel, the brick is beginning to fall out of the wall. In the next panel, the brick comes down and hits the turtle on the head. And in the fourth panel, the turtle keeps going, leaving the brick behind. I kind of feel that's the story of my life.

I've gone through a number of bricks falling on my head and I kept going anyway. Some good things happened and some things deterred me from going further, but here I am. I have lived through all these lives with some major successes and with wonderful support from many people. And I have never been bored, that I can remember.

I've lived some good lives.

*Charlotte Zietlow*

# 22

# Acknowledgements

Isaac Newton once remarked, "If I have seen further, it is by stand-ing on the shoulders of giants." His point? That all advancements, all successes—even his revolutionary innovations in thought—were de-pendent on the work of many people, not just the ones who got credit for them.

I'm no Newton but, like him, I realize I could only be successful be-cause so many other people had done so much work before me. In so many ways the following people and institutions either laid the groundwork for my success here, helped me in some way, or inspired me.

At the top of the list, Karen Roszkowski, my wife, has never wa-vered in her support of me. We've made a great team, something I never thought I'd be able to accomplish with another person for the long haul until she came along.

I've spent hours, days, *years*, in coffeehouses, researching, transcrib-ing, and writing. Bob Costello of Soma Coffee and Jane Kupersmith and Jeff Grant of Hopscotch Coffee have been kind and indulgent in allowing me to take up room in their establishments far beyond the time it takes to finish a mug of coffee and eat a bagel with cream cheese.

Margaret Taylor, proprietor of the Book Corner, and Patty Wong Swie San, manager, have helped me in innumerable ways, starting with giving me the opportunity to become part of this community. From my perch at the checkout counter of the book store, I got to know the people here and they me. And I got to be surrounded by books and people who love them. What better life can there be?

I started working at community radio WFHB, Firehouse Broadcasting, just a few short months after arriving in this town. Chad Carrothers, the founder of the station's news department and news director at the time, put me to work immediately covering Bloomington and Indiana. We were heading into an election year and I got a virtual Ph.D. in Hoosier politics. Since Chad left the station, a succession of equally helpful news directors have shown confidence in me. They include Alycin Bektesh, Joe Crawford, Wes Martin, and Kade Young. Fellow reporters Ryan Dawes and Shayne Laughter bucked me up and showed me the ropes. General managers Will Murphy, Cleveland Deitz III, and Jar Turner also have placed their trust in me.

Ron Eid, publisher of *Limestone Post*, gave me an outlet to do what I do best—get to know who's who and write about them. Peter LoPilato, publisher of the *Ryder* magazine allowed me the same opportunity as well.

Malcolm Abrams, publisher of *Bloom* magazine saw fit to run couple of profiles on me in his publication, notably a sweet piece written by David Brent Johnson.

My good friend, former city council member and one-time head of the city's utilities department, Pat Murphy, has guided me through the thicket of Bloomington politics and done his best to advise me when to speak and when to keep my mouth shut, an invaluable talent in this growing town that retains a few of its small-town ways.

Maryann Pelic of Bunger & Robertson has provided legal counsel for this project. She and her husband Tom Thickstun, are good neighbors and good friends.

Charlotte's daughter, Rebecca Zietlow, her son, Nathan Zietlow, and her sister, Harriet Statz, have helped us remember the few things that have slipped Charlotte's mind.

When I wasn't in coffeehouses or in my home office, I was hunkered down in libraries across southern Indiana. My favorites are the libraries of Monroe, Brown, Columbus, Washington, Lawrence, DuBois, Floyd, Jackson, Johnson, and Jefferson counties as well as that of Indianapolis/Marion County.

The office of the Monroe County Clerk opened its books and records for me.

Tomi & Jim Allison's book, *The Accidental Mayor*, recounting her term as Bloomington's chief executive, was a great help in laying out a timeline of events in this city during the 1980s and '90s.

Investigative journalist Steven Higgs, former reporter for the *Bloomington Herald-Telephone*, one-time publisher of the *Bloomington Alternative*, and now a lecturer at Indiana University's Media School, was gracious and patient enough to review my chapter on the proposed PCB incinerator.

Again, on a personal level, I learned the arts of writing, editing, fact-checking, digging, and persevering by working with and/or for International Events Group, The *Chicago Reader* (with special thanks to Pat Clinton, Pat Arden, Allison True, and Michael Miner), and the *Chicago Tribune*.

I've been inspired and guided by a wide variety of mentors, teachers, icons, and passersby, some of them, sadly, not with us anymore. They include: Charna Halpern and Del Close of iO; Greg Campbell of the City Colleges of Chicago; Molly Daniels of the University of Chicago; Pat Jordan, author of *A False Spring*; Jim Bouton, author of *Ball Four*; Mary Karr, author of *The Liars Club*; oral historian and author Studs Terkel; Mike Royko of the *Chicago Daily News*, *Sun-Times* and *Tribune*; Irv Kupcinet of the *Chicago Sun-Times*, WMAQ, Ch. 5, and WTTW, Ch. 11.

Finally, editor Emily Esola, a lecturer in the Indiana University English Department, tightened our manuscript up and stood on her head to help me retain the essence of Charlotte's voice. Emily did her work even as she struggled to keep up with teaching class during the COVID-19 crisis. She was a gem.

*Michael G. Glab*